This book applies recent theoretica
development of Castilian and Latir
Middle Ages onwards, through pro
mixing both within the Iberian Peni
The author contends that it was this ...g which
caused Castilian to evolve more rapidly than other varieties of
Hispano-Romance, and which rendered Spanish particularly
subject to levelling of its linguistic irregularities and to
simplification of its structures. These two processes continued as
the language extended into and across the Americas.

These processes are viewed in the context not only of the
Hispano-Romance continuum (which includes Galician,
Portuguese and Catalan), but also of the New World varieties of
Spanish. The book emphasizes the subtlety and seamlessness of
language variation, both geographical and social, and the
impossibility of defining strict boundaries between varieties. Its
conclusions will be relevant both to Hispanists and to historical
sociolinguists more generally.

Ralph Penny is Professor of Romance Philology at Queen Mary and
Westfield College, University of London, where until recently he
was Head of the School of Modern Languages. He is the author
of four previous books, including *A History of the Spanish
Language* (1991) and *Gramática histórica del español* (1993). In
addition, he has edited or co-edited four further books, and has
published articles in many learned journals.

Variation and change in Spanish

Ralph Penny

CAMBRIDGE
UNIVERSITY PRESS

PUBLISHED BY THE PRESS SYNDICATE OF THE UNIVERSITY OF CAMBRIDGE
The Pitt Building, Trumpington Street, Cambridge, United Kingdom

CAMBRIDGE UNIVERSITY PRESS
The Edinburgh Building, Cambridge CB2 2RU, UK
40 West 20th Street, New York NY 10011–4211, USA
477 Williamstown Road, Port Melbourne, VIC 3207, Australia
Ruiz de Alarcón 13, 28014 Madrid, Spain
Dock House, The Waterfront, Cape Town 8001, South Africa

http://www.cambridge.org

First published 2000
First paperback edition 2004

Typeface Monotype Dante & Adobe Futura   *System* QuarkXpress™ [S E]

A catalogue record for this book is available from the British Library

ISBN 0 521 78045 4 hardback
ISBN 0 521 60450 8 paperback

Transferred to digital printing 2004

Contents

Preface

The main aim of this book is to apply certain theoretical insights into linguistic variation and change (insights often derived from studies of English and other Germanic languages) to the Spanish-speaking world, a project I first sketched some years ago (Penny 1987). Although I do not claim, on this occasion, to advance variationist theory, it is my hope that the data deployed here will test, and for the most part support, such theoretical approaches to language.

The data used are most frequently Castilian data, but since I am at pains to emphasize that Castilian emerges from a dialect continuum which embraces the whole Peninsula (and indeed extends beyond it), it is inevitable that all varieties of Romance spoken in the Peninsula (therefore including Galician, Portuguese, and Catalan) will at times be the subject of discussion. Similarly, since dialect mixing is a constant theme of the book, it is inevitable that American Spanish (the product of such mixing) will come under close scrutiny.

Two broad themes are pursued. The first is that of the seamlessness of language variation: the fact that language presents itself to us in the form of orderly but undivided heterogeneity. This is to say that variation is almost infinitely subtle, and occurs along all parameters (geographical and social), so that it is usually inappropriate to seek to establish boundaries between varieties, whether we are dealing with geographically ordered varieties, or with socially determined varieties, or with linguistic registers or styles. Each variety merges imperceptibly with those that are adjacent to it, using the term *adjacent* to refer to varieties which are either socially or geographically contiguous.

It is not the present aim to provide the reader with an exhaustive description of geographical variation in Spanish (in the manner of manuals of dialectology such as Zamora Vicente (1967)), although detailed accounts of the distribution of many of the salient features of Spanish, as used throughout the world, will be found here. Still less can the book claim to describe in detail the correlation between the linguistic and sociological features of the Spanish-speaking communities (a project which is currently impossible, given the paucity of data available), although once again the reader will find examples here of significant cases of socially determined variation. What this book does seek to do is to present to the reader the broad patterns displayed by geographical and social variation in Spanish (with the implication that such patterns are the same for Spanish as for other languages).

The second broad theme of the book is more particular to Spanish and is historical in kind. Because of its peculiar ancestry, being the outcome of repeated dialect mixing, we shall claim that Castilian has evolved at a more rapid pace than the varieties of Romance which developed in other parts of the Peninsula. For similar reasons, we shall see that Spanish was particularly subject to levelling of its linguistic irregularities and to simplification of its structures, processes which continued in force as the language was extended into and across the Americas.

The ideas found in certain sections of this book were presented as papers given to a variety of research seminars: the Staff–Student Research Seminar of the Department of Hispanic Studies, the Research Seminar of the Centre for Language Studies (both at Queen Mary and Westfield College, University of London), the annual meetings of the Association of Hispanists of Great Britain and Ireland, and at the Romance Linguistics Research Seminar at the University of Oxford. I am grateful to the participants in those seminars for their observations, which have often found their way into these pages.

I am especially grateful to the two referees who acted for Cambridge University Press, both of whom made numerous suggestions for improvement, most of which I have adopted, and to my friend and colleague Professor Ian Macpherson, who read the whole manuscript and pruned it of numerous infelicities and errors. Those that remain are very definitely my own.

Part of the research for this book was carried out with the assistance of a grant from the Arts and Humanities Research Board, an award which I gratefully acknowledge.

RALPH PENNY

Abbreviations and symbols

Ar.	Arabic	Leon.	Leonese
Arag.	Aragonese	Moz.	Mozarabic
Cat.	Catalan	MSp.	Modern Spanish
Fr.	French	OSp.	Old or medieval Spanish
Gal.	Galician	Ptg.	Portuguese
It.	Italian	Rom.	Romanian
JSp.	Judeo-Spanish	Sp.	Spanish
Lat.	Latin		

*	Reconstructed form or meaning (whose existence is claimed)
**	Form or meaning whose existence is denied
x > y	x becomes y in the course of time
x < y	x is the descendant (reflex) of y
x · y	y is created on the basis of x (e.g., through derivation)
x~y	x coexists with y with equivalent function
Ø	Null segment (e.g., [h] > [Ø] = '[h] ceases to be pronounced')
á, é, í, etc.	Vowel carrying stress accent
ā, ī, ō, etc.	In Latin words (which appear in small capitals), a long vowel; any vowel not so marked in a Latin word is short.
[xxxx]	Phonetic transcription
/xxxx/	Phonemic transcription
<xxxx>	Letters of the alphabet, graphemes
{xxxx}	Morphemes
#	Word boundary

The symbols used are those of the International Phonetic Association, with the following modification: [ǰ] is used for the voiced mid-palatal fricative (e.g., standard *maẏo*), to distinguish it from the (frictionless) glide [j] (as in *tiẹrra*).

	Bilabial		Labio-dental		Inter-dental		Dental	
CONSONANTS								
Plosive	p	b					t	d
Fricative	ɸ	β	f	v	θ	ð	s̪	z̪
Affricate							tˢ	dᶻ
Lateral						ḷ		ḻ
Vibrant								
Flap								
Nasal	m		ɱ		n̪		n̪	
GLIDES								
Opening	ʍ	w						
Closing		ɥ̞						
VOWELS								
High								
Mid-high								
Mid-low								
Low								

₀ denotes voicelessness.

Table of phonetic symbols used

Alveolar		Pre-palatal		Mid-palatal		Velar		Glottal	
						k	g		
s	z	ʃ	ʒ	ç	ǰ	x	ɣ	h	ɦ
		tʃ	dʒ						
l				ʎ					
r									
ɾ									
n				ɲ		ŋ			

| | | | | j | | (ʍ) | (w) | |
| ɹ | | | | i̯ | | (y̯) | | |

		Front	**Central**	**Back**	
		i		u	
		e		o	
		ɛ	ɐ	ɔ	
		æ	a	ɑ	

1 Introduction: language variation

1.1 Synchronic variation

All languages that we can observe today show variation; what is more, they vary in identical ways, namely geographically and socially. These two parameters, along which variation occurs, are in principle independent of each other, although we shall see that there are ways in which they (and others to be discussed later) are interlinked. We shall consider each in turn.

1.1.1 Geographical or diatopical variation

It is a universal characteristic of human language that speakers of the 'same' language who live in different parts of a continuous territory do not speak in the same way.[1] Careful observation shows that such variation is usually smooth and gradual: the speech of each locality differs in some feature or features from the speech of each neighbouring locality, but without seriously impairing mutual comprehension.[2] Successive small differences accumulate as one crosses an area, and in an extensive territory this accumulation of differences may result in total mutual incomprehensibility between the speech belonging to distant parts of the territory being examined.

We shall see in Section **4.1.2** that the northern part of the Spanish Peninsula displays this kind of variation; that is, we can observe there what is known as a *dialect continuum*. A village-by-village journey from the west coast of Galicia to the Costa Brava reveals at each stage only small linguistic differences between a particular village and its neighbours on either side, these differences being few where communications are good between the villages concerned and more numerous where communications are poorer. Provided one skirts the Basque Country (where one faces forms of speech unrelated to those which surround it), there is no point on the journey where mutual comprehension between speakers from neighbouring villages is threatened, even though speakers will often be aware, sometimes acutely, that their neighbours speak a little differently from them. The greater the distance travelled, the greater the total number of differences between the speech of one's present location and that of one's starting point, and such accumulation of differences causes a correspondingly increased degree of mutual incomprehension, to the extent that the speech of a Galician fisherman will be barely understood, if at all, by a fisherman on the coast of Catalonia.[3]

In fact, dialect continua are not only unaffected by internal administrative boundaries (such as those which divide Galicia or Catalonia from the rest of Spain), but also pay no heed either to national frontiers. The northern Peninsular dialect continuum is part of a broader Romance continuum which extends in unbroken fashion over all the European territory where descendants of Latin are spoken (with the exception of now-isolated varieties of Romance such as Rumantsch in Switzerland and the various kinds of Romanian used in Romania and other parts of the Balkans). At the level of everyday rural speech, the Pyrenees do not form a frontier; the varieties spoken on the northern and southern flanks of the central Pyrenees have long been known to be similar and, to a substantial degree, to be mutually intelligible (Elcock 1938). Similarly, in the eastern Pyrenees, there is close continuity between the speech used on Spanish territory and that used in neighbouring parts of France; we are here discussing the way in which Catalan straddles the political frontier.

It will be appreciated from this discussion that geographical variation is a two-dimensional phenomenon. Although our main example (a journey across the northern Peninsula) presents linguistic variation in one dimension only, the fact is that variation is observable in whatever direction or combination of directions one moves across a territory.

1.1.2   Social variation

It is also evident, from even casual observation, that in any one place not all people speak alike, even if they were all born there. Differences of speech are correlated with one or more social factors which apply to the speaker concerned. These factors include age, sex, race, class background, education, occupation, and income. To take an example, Spanish participles in *-ado(s)* (and some other, similarly structured, words) reveal a range of pronunciations; the final segment of words

like *cansado, pescado* may be pronounced in one or other of the following ways: [-áðo], [-áᵈo], [-áo], [-áu̯]. But the appearance of one or other
of these variants is controlled (at least in part) by the sociological characteristics of the speaker. Thus, the variant [-áu̯] is much more frequent
in working-class speech than in that of the middle classes; similarly, in
certain studies of this phenomenon (Williams 1983b, 1987: 71), women
of all classes are seen to be substantially more resistant to total deletion
of the consonant than are men.[4]

It follows from this brief account of social variation that such variation is multi-dimensional; there are many parameters which define
the social 'space' within which the speaker is located, and his or her
speech varies, in different ways, in accordance with each of these parameters.

We shall see shortly (**2.5**), however, that even a single individual
does not use just a single variant from the range of those available in the
community. Rather, each individual commands at least part of the
range and selects a particular variant according to the circumstances
(formal, informal, relaxed, etc.) in which he or she is speaking. And even
in the same speech environment, a speaker may alternate between two
or more variants.

1.2 Diachronic or historical variation

All languages for which we have information (e.g., written records or, in
the last hundred years, recordings) which is spread over a period of time
show more or less rapid change. The traditional view of such linguistic
change was that one variant succeeded another in the community concerned, so that one could establish a chain of events in which each form
was replaced by its successor. Such a chain is typically expressed thus:
Latin LĀTUS > Hispano-Romance [ládo] > medieval Spanish [láðo] >
modern Spanish [láᵈo] or [láo]. As a summary of what has happened
over time to particular linguistic features, particularly in highly codified
languages, such a statement is not unreasonable.[5] But closer examination of recent language development has revealed that, at any moment
of time, a feature which is undergoing change is represented (in the
community and in the speech of individuals) by two or more competing
variants. Change takes the form of the addition of further informal
variants and the loss over time of the most formal variants.[6] Linguistic
change can therefore be pictured as the replacement of one state of

	[láto]	[ládo]	[láðo]	[láᵝo]	[láo]	[láu̯]
Stage 1	[láto]	[ládo]				
Stage 2	[láto]	[ládo]	[láðo]			
Stage 3		[ládo]	[láðo]	[láᵝo]		
Stage 4			[láðo]	[láᵝo]	[láo]	
Stage 5			[láðo]	[láᵝo]	[láo]	[láu̯]
* Stage 6				[láᵝo]	[láo]	[láu̯]
* Stage 7					[láo]	[láu̯]

Table 1.1   Model of diachronic variation

	[nído]	[níðo]	[níᵝo]	[nío]
Stage 1	[nído]	[níðo]		
Stage 2	[nído]	[níðo]	[níᵝo]	
Stage 3		[níðo]	[níᵝo]	[nío]
Stage 4		[níðo]	[níᵝo]	
Stage 5		[níðo]		

Table 1.2   Regressive development

variation by another. To take the previous example, we can restate the change which leads from LĀTUS to *lado* in the (deliberately oversimplified) way shown in Table **1.1**, in which Stage 5 represents the present and Stages 6 and 7 have not yet been reached, but are tentatively predictable.

Note that it is not claimed here that change exclusively progresses through the addition of newer variants and the loss of older ones. There may be blind alleys or reversals. That is to say that variants which are added at a certain stage to the range of existing variants may be subsequently lost while older variants remain. This kind of process can be seen in the history of words like *nido*, and others whose intervocalic consonant descends from Latin -D- (see Table **1.2**).

Many words offering intervocalic -D- in Latin show the smoother development in which the variants with some internal fricative are dropped after Stage 3, leaving the variant with no internal consonant to descend into the modern language (e.g., SEDĒRE > *ser*). Other words, however, followed the pattern outlined for *nido*, frequently appearing without /d/ in the Middle Ages (CRŪDU > *crudo* > *crúo*, VADU > *vado* > *vao*), and then appearing to go into reverse, leaving behind only *nido, crudo, vado,* etc. Such reversals are impossible to conceive, I suggest, outside a variationist framework.

It will be evident from this discussion of diachronic variation that such variation is not independent of geographical and social variation, in the way that geographical and social variation are independent of one another. In particular, diachronic variation results from social variation (see note 6) and is inconceivable without it.

It also needs to be clarified that, since change proceeds item by item, each change occupying a different segment of time in a particular community, while the same change will occupy different segments of time in different communities, all notions of periodization are misplaced in language history. Although we are far from understanding all the factors which hasten or restrain linguistic change (but see **3.3**), it seems fairly certain that at some places and times change is more rapid than at other places and times; that is to say that in the history of a particular variety there will be changing rates of innovation. However, the way in which linguistic innovations succeed one another, without exactly coinciding, implies that there can be no linguistic basis for dividing one period of that history from another. It may be a convenience, in the interests of relating language history to political and cultural history, to refer separately to, say, Old Spanish, Golden-Age Spanish, or Modern Spanish, but such periodization can have no linguistic motivation. Linguistic development is as seamless as all other cases of linguistic variation (Penny 1998).

1.3 Variables and variants

All aspects of language (sounds, phonemes, morphemes, syntactic structures, lexemes, meanings, etc.) are subject to variation according to these parameters. A linguistic feature which displays variation according to one or other parameter is called a variable and is indicated by a symbol between parentheses. For example, the phoneme /x/ of Spanish, the *jota*, varies geographically in its articulation, being pronounced in some places as the velar fricative [x], in others as the glottal fricative [h], and in yet others with sounds intermediate between [x] and [h], or as the palatal fricative [ç]. We can therefore say that the variable (x) (or (h)) is realized (in different, specific places) as [x], [h], [hˣ], [ç], etc.

1.4　Co-variation

The parameters of linguistic variation are independent, but a feature which shows variation according to one of these parameters (say, the geographical dimension) may show similar or identical variation along another (say, a social or diachronic dimension). Thus, the feature known as *yeísmo* (see **4.1.7.2.2**, **4.2.1**, **5.1.2.1**, **6.3.3(2)**) can be described as showing variation along all three.[7] For some speakers, a meaningful contrast is available between the phonemes /ʎ/ and /ǰ/ (*pollo* 'chicken' vs *poyo* 'stone bench'), while for others these phonemes have merged, and a single articulation is used for both sets of words (frequently [ǰ], but also [dǰ], [ʒ], etc.). Variation between distinction of these phonemes and their merger is, firstly, geographical: in rural areas of the northern half of Spain, in the Andean area of America, etc., distinction is found, whereas in the larger part of the Spanish-speaking world merger is the norm. However, the same variation can be observed along sociolinguistic parameters: older, middle-class, urban speakers from the north of Spain use distinction between /ʎ/ and /ǰ/, while younger speakers from the same cities, whatever their class background, allow the phonemes to merge. Likewise, the same variability can be seen over time: several centuries ago, all speakers of Spanish no doubt distinguished words with /ʎ/ from those with /ǰ/ (e.g., *pollo* from *poyo*), while at some stage in the future all speakers of Spanish will no doubt have allowed the two sets of words to merge.

The implication of this three-fold variation is that over time *yeísmo* has progressed geographically (occupying more and more territory), and socially (affecting the speech of more and more members of society in any given locality).

1.5　Register

No speaker uses the resources of his or her language in exactly the same way on all occasions; according to the social circumstances in which the act of communication occurs, the speaker may choose different variants of a particular variable. More precisely, register variation appears to be as multidimensional as social variation. Halliday (1978: 33) distinguishes three parameters of register variation: 'field' (within which, variation is determined by the purpose and subject matter of the communication), 'mode' (which controls variations due to the channel, written or spoken, of the communication), and 'tone' (according to which, variation is determined by the person to whom the communication is addressed). Thus, in choosing particular features of language with which to communicate, the speaker/writer places himself or herself at a particular position in a complex social matrix.

Of course, the range of variants between which a speaker/writer chooses in any act of communication may be similar or identical to the range of variants strung along any of the parameters already discussed (the geographical, the social, and the historical). Thus, to take the case of *yeísmo* (discussed in **1.4** as an example of geographical, social and historical variation), the speaker who in formal circumstances (delivering a lecture, say, or speaking to people he or she is seeking to impress) distinguishes the medial phonemes of *malla* and *maya* may pronounce these two words identically one to another when speaking informally (that is, in relaxed circumstances, with friends, etc.). Similarly, the different variants discussed in **1.1.2** in connection with words like *pescado* (currently [-áðo], [-áᵈo], [-áo] and [-áu̯]) also correspond with different points in the communicative matrix: speakers who command all four variants will use the first only in formal or fully monitored speech, the second when a moderate degree of formality is felt to be required, and the last two only in unmonitored, relaxed speech.

It is this kind of register variation which gives rise to *hypercorrect* forms. For example, since the word *bacalao* shares some of the range of variants also shown by *pescado* (namely [bakaláo] like [peskáo], [bakaláu̯] like [peskáu̯]), the similarity may be extended to the full range. Thus, in communicative circumstances which require care or formality, such as speaking to a stranger, the pronunciation [bakaláðo] may be used, matching formal [pescáðo]. Since hypercorrect forms are most usually produced by the illiterate, who by definition cannot be guided in their pronunciation by the standard written forms of words, they are usually heavily stigmatized.[8]

1.6 Variation in the past

Since it is the case that all languages observable today or in the recent past show all the kinds of variation discussed here, we are entitled to conclude that such variation must be true of all languages that have ever been spoken, in all places, at all times. This principle cannot be tested, since linguistic evidence from the past (except the very recent past) comes only in written form, and such written evidence is incapable of showing more than a small fraction of the range of variation we assume to have existed. In particular, each piece of written evidence will typically reflect the formal register (because written) of a particular user of the language concerned, a user who must, of course, reflect the variants in use only at one place, in one social milieu, at one moment. Comparison of different pieces of historical evidence can amplify the range of variation observable, but can never come close to establishing the full range of variation which must have existed at each moment in the past.[9]

2 *Dialect, language, variety*: definitions and relationships

A common perception, among those who are not linguists, is that there is some difference in kind between a 'language' and a 'dialect'. The question is often posed in the following form: 'Is *x* a language or a dialect?', where *x* is some such label as 'Valencian', or 'Asturian'. And it is a question which the linguist, as linguist, cannot answer, first because of the insuperable difficulty of defining the concepts *language* and *dialect* (see **2.1** and **2.2**), but secondly because any difference between these concepts resides not in the subject matter of linguistic description, but in the social appreciation accorded to particular codes of communication. The historical linguist will make it clear that every code to which the label 'language' is attached (e.g., 'the Spanish language', 'the English language', 'the French language', 'the Latin language') has its origins in what would usually be called a 'dialect', loosely defined in terms of geography (as the speech of a particular locality or area) and in terms of social class (as the speech of a particular social group, usually the dominant, educated, classes). Thus, the French language has its origins in the speech of upper-class Paris, specifically of the Court.[1] If 'dialects' can gradually become 'languages', it follows that there cannot be any difference of kind between these concepts, but only differences of degree.

But degrees of what? A full answer to this question would duplicate the discussion in Chapter **7**, but it is perhaps in order here to anticipate the conclusion reached there. What the non-linguist means by a 'language' is most usually what is otherwise called a 'standard language', that is, a dialect which has undergone the various processes which together constitute standardization (selection, codification, elaboration of function, acceptance; see Haugen 1972; Hudson 1996: 32–4), all or most of which are inconceivable in the absence of writing. A 'language', then, differs from a 'dialect' only in the degree to which it has been subjected to each of these processes (although the process of selection should perhaps be disregarded here, since it is not a matter of

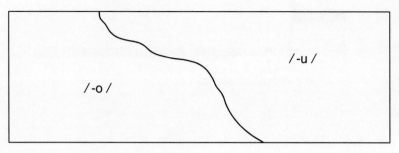

Figure 2.1   Territory divided by a single isogloss

degree). A 'language' will be more highly codified (it will possess such things as an agreed orthography, and prescriptive grammars and dictionaries), it will have an expanded vocabulary and more elaborate syntax (to allow the discussion of topics which are simply not handled by speech), and it will enjoy higher social prestige (because of its association with high-prestige activities, such as education, and with high-prestige sectors of society, such as the educated and the wealthy).

Although it is possible to define a *standard language* (along the lines of what is said in the previous paragraph), it will now be seen that there are insuperable problems in defining the concepts of *dialect* and *language* (as in *the Spanish language*, etc.). For further discussion of these concepts, see Alvar (1961).

2.1 *Dialects*

We have already seen (in **1.1.1**) that geographical dialects (that is, 'dialects' in the sense most frequently used by non-linguists) have no definable boundaries. Examination of data from linguistic atlases, such as the *Atlas lingüístico de la Península Ibérica* (*ALPI* 1962), reveals that each item (such as a word, a meaning, a sound, or an element of grammar) occupies an area which is usually continuous and almost always differs from the area occupied by any other item. To take a theoretical example, the territory represented by the box in Figure **2.1** is divided into an area where a large class of masculine singular nouns ends in /-o/, and a second area where the corresponding class of nouns ends in /-u/. The dividing line between these two areas is called an

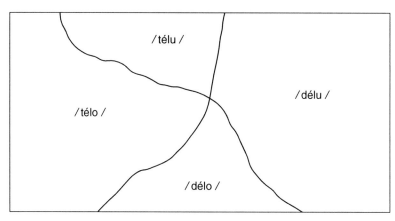

Figure 2.2 Territory divided by two isoglosses

isogloss (see **3.2.1**). Let us now imagine that the same territory is divided into localities whose speakers use the word *telo/u* while people from the remaining localities say *delo/u* to express the same concept. Since it is overwhelmingly improbable that the line separating localities showing /-o/ from those with /-u/ will exactly coincide with the line separating localities where *telo/u* is used from those where *delo/u* is used, the consequence is that our territory is divided, on the basis of only two items, into four 'dialects', as in Figure **2.2**. The mapping of each further item used in the territory will double the number of identifiable 'dialects' used there, and given that the language of any locality consists of at least several thousands of items, it follows that the number of 'dialects' identifiable in a real territory of any extent is infinite. Therefore, unless we restrict the meaning of *dialect* to 'the speech of a specific locality' (which, in turn, we shall see is unsatisfactory), we are forced to reject the notion of a *dialect* as a discrete or separately delimitable entity. To put the matter only slightly more strongly, there is no such thing as a dialect. It will be possible to talk about, say, the 'dialects of Castile', in the sense of the totality of the speech varieties used within Castile, but without any implication that there exist separate identifiable dialects within Castile, or that the dialects of Castile do not merge imperceptibly with those of surrounding areas, such as Aragon, Leon, or Andalusia.

The term *dialect* has sometimes been used to distinguish types of speech which are differentiated by social factors. In this sense, the term *dialect* (sometimes *social dialect*) alternates with *sociolect*, typically to distinguish the speech of one social class, or one age group, etc., from another. But as in the case of the geographical dimension, the various social dimensions provide us with no basis for demarcating one social dialect from another. On the contrary, the speech of one social group merges imperceptibly with others, just as the speech of any age group fades into that of younger and older people. This observation does not deny that there are correlations, often strong, between the distribution of linguistic items and such social features as age, social class, etc. But the transitions between the speech of 'adjacent' social groups are smooth and not abrupt. In the social sense too, the term *dialect* corresponds to no objective reality.

2.2 *Languages*

Our problem lies not so much in defining language in general (which we might define as 'the universal symbolic activity by which humans convey meanings from the mind of one person to that of another'), as with defining what is meant by '*a* language', or, for example, 'the Spanish language'. The problem is essentially one of delimitation: what are the temporal and geographical limits of, for example, Spanish?

2.2.1   Do languages have temporal limits?

Since linguistic change proceeds item by item (at one moment a feature of pronunciation, at another moment an item of grammar, then the addition or loss of a word, etc., but in no particular order), it follows that there can be no moment in the past at which any language can be said to have begun.[2] At any specific moment, the speech in use in a given community differs only in minor ways from the speech used a generation earlier.[3] To take the specific case of Spanish, there is no point, objectively arrived at, at which it can be said that Latin gives way to Spanish; at the level of spoken communication, there is no break in the continuity (with the usual minor modifications in each generation) which leads back from the present day to what we would call 'Latin' two thousand years ago (or indeed to the Italic, Indo-European and earlier ancestors of Latin). So why do we give the name 'Spanish' to recent stages of this continuous development and apply the label 'Latin' to earlier stages? There are two answers to this question.

Firstly, and more trivially, there is a need to distinguish what are now regarded as distinct descendants of the same ancestor. It is well known that in the Middle Ages, the spoken descendants of Latin (and eventually also the written forms of these spoken descendants) were referred to collectively by nominalized reflexes of the Latin adverb ROMĀNICE (lit. 'in the Roman manner'), e.g., Sp. *romance* ('any oral descendant of Latin'), usually by contrast to the then most prestigious (and exclusively written) form of language, namely *latín*.[4] Since people in the Middle Ages were evidently as aware as we are of geographical variation, it was often desirable to specify which kind of *romance* was under discussion. This was achieved by adding an adjective referring essentially to political entities (and by implication to geography), thus: *romance castellano, romance leonés, romance aragonés*, etc. And since, in phrases like [to speak] *en romance castellano*, the word *romance* was redundant, the phrase being perfectly unambiguous without it, it was eventually dropped, with the result that the politico-geographical adjective (*castellano*, etc.) became the name of a form of language.[5]

The second (and more important) reason why a separate name was required for some varieties of Romance springs from the fact that these varieties underwent standardization. As we shall see (Section **7.1.2**), standardization is a process which is inseparable from writing (purely oral varieties never undergo standardization), and the identification of a written code sharpens speakers' awareness of the newly codified variety as a separate entity requiring a separate name.[6] So although Castilian is a variety of Romance which (like all other such varieties) results from an unbroken series of earlier varieties stretching indefinitely into the past, the fact that at a certain point it achieved written status and underwent increasing standardization forced upon its users, and others, the need for a name by which to identify it and differentiate it from other written linguistic codes (Latin, Catalan, French, etc.).

2.2.2 Are languages delimitable?

If we mean by this question 'Do official languages have spatial limits?', then the answer is obviously yes, since languages can only be made official by political entities, such as nation-states, and their officiality is usually co-terminous with that entity. Thus the official language of the Spanish state stretches exactly to the Pyrenean frontier and there abuts abruptly on the official language of the neighbouring state. But this kind of sharp linguistic boundary, at which a piece of writing produced on one side of a frontier consists of a set of items which is different from the set of items which characterize a piece of writing produced a few hundred metres away on the other side of the frontier, provides a very unsatisfactory basis for the delimitation of languages. Coincidence between national frontiers and boundaries which separate official languages is anyway relatively rare (and perhaps only occurs at all in the Europe of the last two centuries). So what other basis is there for delimiting one language from the rest?

One criterion that is sometimes used is that of *mutual intelligibility*; if one speaker does not understand another, then they speak different languages. But the problem with this criterion is that mutual intelligibility is a question of degree rather than being an all-or-nothing matter. Speakers of Spanish will understand a good deal of what a speaker of Catalan says, yet on the basis of the criteria outlined at p. 9 above to define a standard, both Spanish and Catalan would qualify. Similarly in the case of Spanish and Portuguese: speakers of Spanish understand at least some of what is said in Portuguese, and the Portuguese speakers will understand a good deal more of what is said in Spanish (which goes to demonstrate that mutual intelligibility can be asymmetrical: an absurd conclusion would be that this shows that Portuguese is more different from Spanish than Spanish is from Portuguese!).

There is also the matter of experience. Different speakers of Spanish will have different experience of, say, Portuguese, and will therefore understand spoken (and written) Portuguese in different measures. So that mutual comprehension, or its lack, is a quite unsatisfactory means of marking off putatively distinct languages.

What often underlies the layman's view that language A and language B are separate entities is the fact that these two 'languages' have distinct orthographic systems, especially since a common lay view is that a particular variety can only be accorded the status of 'language' if it is a variety which appears in written form.[7] However, since it is perfectly possible for distinct orthographical systems to be applied successively to the same variety, or even simultaneously as in the case of Serbian and Croatian, it is clear that the orthographical principle cannot serve as a satisfactory criterion for delimiting one 'language' from another.

In the end, we are forced to a similar conclusion to the one we were forced to reach in the case of 'dialects': there is no purely linguistic means of delimiting one 'language' from another, since closely related 'languages' form part of a continuum and any dividing line which cuts through this continuum is drawn not for linguistic reasons but for political reasons.[8]

2.3 Relationship between *dialects* and *languages*

If dialects cannot be delimited in space and languages cannot be delimited in time or space, what are we to make of such commonly used formulations as 'X is a dialect of language Y'? What underlies such statements as 'Andalusian is a dialect of Castilian' is a significant historical misapprehension, namely that over time 'languages' are fragmented into 'dialects'.

The reason underlying this misapprehension is a failure, albeit an understandable failure, to compare like with like. It stems from the fact that our direct knowledge of past linguistic states comes to us through writing, and writing almost exclusively preserves standard languages.[9] By their nature, standard languages are the result of processes (see Chapter 7) which have reduced variation to as near zero as possible, so that the picture we receive of past language-states is one of linguistic uniformity. However, our examination of current language-states reveals a picture of variation along a host of parameters. It is therefore tempting to conclude that an earlier state of uniformity has been 'degraded' or 'debased' into a state of variation.[10] Thus, for example, the perceived uniformity of Latin is judged to have broken down into a large number of medieval Romance dialects, and in a situation where (written) Latin continued to be the standard, such dialects could be considered to be dialects 'of Latin'. Likewise, in the case of the Spanish of America, it is often thought that the present language variation results from the 'debasement' of some supposed earlier state of uniformity, although in this case such a supposition is less frequent, because we have written evidence of the variation within the Spanish that was carried to America from the sixteenth century onwards.

However, such a view of increasing fragmentation over time is clearly erroneous. If it is agreed, as argued here (**1.6**), that variation of all types (geographical, social, etc.) has always existed in human language, at all times and in all places, then it follows that linguistic development takes the form of change from one state of variation to another state of variation, even though one can argue over the different degrees or ranges of variation which apply in successive stages of a particular development. A further consequence is that it is illogical to label

any variety A as a 'dialect of language X', or any set of varieties, B, C, D
. . ., as 'dialects of language Y', if (as is usually the case) the unspoken
assumption is that there is a historical relation between A and X or
between B, C, D . . . and Y, such that (in some sense) A springs from X,
or B, C, D . . . are developments (often 'debasements') of Y.

This view is to stand history on its head. If we take standard languages such as our X or Y, each has its origin in a specific local / social
variety, which has been selected (for non-linguistic reasons) from a host
of other competing varieties (see **7.1.1**). So each 'language' can be said
to descend from a 'dialect', rather than the reverse. It is therefore meaningless to say that the spoken varieties used in, say, Soria or La Mancha
are 'dialects of Spanish', since this implies a false historical relationship
between each of these varieties and Spanish (i.e., the standard language
which has its origins in the dialect of Burgos, later transferred (with
modifications) to Toledo at the time of the Reconquest and later still
becoming codified into the standard language of Castile and subsequently of the Spanish state).

It is equally meaningless to enquire whether a particular variety,
say one used in the Pyrenees, is a 'dialect of Spanish' or a 'dialect of
Catalan', since such formulations imply historical descent from either
Spanish or Catalan, which is nonsense. A particular Pyrenean variety
will have a certain number of items in common with standard Catalan,
and a certain number in common with standard Spanish (as well as a
number in common with both, and a few in common with neither), so
that all one can do is to attempt to measure the degrees of affinity
between the variety in question and each of the two prototypes labelled
'Spanish' and 'Catalan'. However, this is not an easy task (and is perhaps
impossible) since not all the thousands of items of which any variety
consists can be taken into account, and there is no agreed basis upon
which to give different weight to different classes of items (say, sounds
over vocabulary, or items of syntax over items of word meaning).

We have so far found no justification for formulations of the type
'variety A is a dialect of language X', but it might be thought that such
justification could be found in cultural history. Might we claim that
such statements are meaningful by reformulating them in the following way: 'variety A is a dialect of language X where A is spoken in a territory in which X is the standard language'? Clearly we would have to
add the rider that A and X must be historically related, otherwise our
formulation would claim that, say, Basque or Quechua were dialects of
Spanish, a claim no one would wish to make. But even after making

this restriction, our formulation still gives unacceptable results, since it entails that we classify any variety spoken in, say, Galicia or Catalonia as dialects of Spanish, again a proposition to which few would subscribe.

So 'dialects of Spanish', we must conclude, are spoken in an area which is smaller than that within which Spanish is the standard language (or, at least, smaller than the area within which Spanish is one of the standards). But how much smaller? What about varieties spoken in, say, Zamora or Saragossa? Here it is crucial to remember that in almost all contexts the label 'Spanish' is interchangeable with 'Castilian'; so that to claim that the varieties used in Zamora or Saragossa are dialects of Spanish is also to claim that they are dialects of Castilian. Is this an acceptable statement? Dialectologists and language historians would deny that it is; the speech of Zamora represents the local development of those forms of Latin introduced into the northwestern part of the Spanish Peninsula some 2,000 years ago, a development which was at first quite independent of those other developments which led from the Latin of north-central Spain to the dialects of Old Castile (including the dialect of Burgos, which was to become 'Castilian' *par excellence*). Later, it is true, and especially from the thirteenth century onwards, the speech of Zamora underwent progressive castilianization, that is, the introduction, item by item, of Castilian features spread from central Castile in wave-like manner (see **3.2**). This process is ongoing and still incomplete, so that the rural speech of Zamora (and of other areas outside Castile) preserves many pre-Castilian features (González Ferrero 1986). It is therefore quite unsatisfactory to claim that the varieties used today outside Castile are 'dialects of Castilian'.[11]

Even within Old Castile, it remains unsatisfactory to assert that the varieties in use, say, in Palencia are 'dialects *of* Castilian'. They might be called 'Castilian dialects', but only in the sense that they are varieties spoken in Castile, i.e., using 'Castilian' in a purely geographical sense. In principle, the history and status of the speech of Castile, *vis-à-vis* the standard, is no different from the history and status of varieties used elsewhere in Spain; each locality in Old Castile has a linguistic history which is a little different from that of the cultural and political centre, Burgos, whose variety of speech influenced that of its neighbours, item by item, as the speech of Burgos increasingly became the model to be imitated elsewhere, owing to the prestige of those who spoke in the Burgalese manner, a prestige which (as we shall see in **7.1.1**) was due entirely to cultural, political and economic factors and not at all to any inherent qualities of that variety. It is true that the influence of the speech of Burgos on that of the rest of Old Castile is deeper than its influence on the speech of areas outside Castile, but this is due only to the obvious fact that localities within Castile were in closer contact with the prestige centre than were localities in Leon or farther afield. So the speech of, say, Soria retains fewer of the features it must have had, prior to the establishment of Burgos as a prestige centre, than is the case with the speech of, say, Zamora. But the relationship between the varieties used in Soria and the standard, on the one hand, is of the same kind as the relationship between the varieties used in Zamora and the standard, on the other. Only the degree of approximation to the standard is different, and in neither case is it appropriate to speak of them as 'dialects of Castilian'.

The formulation 'variety A is a dialect of language X' therefore has no validity. The phrase 'dialect of X' should be limited to cases where X is a geographical term and not a language name, as in the 'dialects of Castile', which should be taken to mean 'that range of speech varieties used within the borders of Castile'. This formulation carries no implication that there will be any coincidence between any isogloss (see **3.2.1**) and any part of the Castilian border; it is axiomatic that the Castilian border (like all other politico-administrative boundaries) arbitrarily bisects the dialect continuum.[12]

2.4   *Varieties* and *idiolects*

The definition of the term *variety* is no easy task, since, as we have seen in Sections **1.1.1** and **1.1.2**, there is no linguistic basis upon which one geographical dialect can be delimited from others, nor are social dialects discrete entities which can be distinguished one from another. Variation in speech extends gradually and smoothly through both geographical and social space, and does not present boundaries between varieties, only more or less rapid transitions along the geographical and social parameters. Even if one limits consideration to a single locality (a town or a village, say), it is evident that each individual living there locates himself or herself at a different point in the social matrix and therefore makes use of a slightly different set of linguistic items from that controlled by any other individual; that is, every individual uses his or her own *idiolect*.

In fact, we have seen (in Section **1.5**) that the linguistic universe is even more amorphous than this, because each individual deploys a different set of linguistic items in each different speech situation, depending on the degree of formality which is felt to be required.

So how is the term *variety* to be used? It is used here to denote any set of linguistic items used in a specified set of social circumstances. These circumstances may be broadly or narrowly defined, so that all of the following, and many more, can be regarded as *varieties*: the English language, the Spanish language, American Spanish, Mexican Spanish, middle-class Spanish, the Spanish of the oldest generation, Valencian, Andalusian Spanish, the Spanish of auctioneers, the idiolect of a partic-ular individual, standard Spanish.

2.5   Relationship between varieties

From the previous discussion it will be seen that each linguistic variety consists of a set of items which differs minimally from each 'neigh-bouring' variety. That is, each 'neighbouring' variety will be similar to the variety in question, but will differ from it in one or more items. Here 'neighbouring' is taken to mean not just 'geographically adja-cent' (i.e. adjacent along the diatopical parameter), but adjacent along any of the parameters which are correlated with linguistic variation, including the many social parameters (age, socio-economic status, education, etc.) as well as the parameter of registers.[13]

Each variety can be visualized as occupying a segment (however large or small) of the multidimensional 'area' constituted by the total-ity of the parameters or 'dimensions' which govern linguistic behav-iour (two spatial dimensions, many social dimensions, together with the dimension of register). The segment may be small (for example, the set of items used by an individual in a given register), or large (say, the set of items used by all educated members of the Spanish-speaking world, or indeed the set of items shared by all speakers of Spanish). Each variety, except perhaps the last, shades almost imperceptibly into all neighbouring varieties.

It should not be thought, from the claims being made here, that the gradient of variation along any parameter is of necessity uniformly steep; the rate of variation may be steeper in one section of the para-meter than in another. It is easiest to appreciate this point in the context of geographical variation, but the same principle can probably be applied to all parameters: equal distances do not imply equal degrees of variation (degrees of variation being measured by the number of items

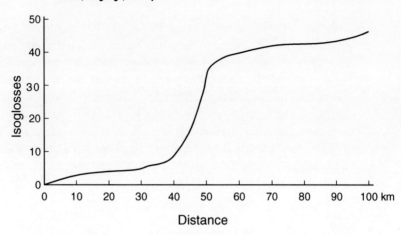

Figure 2.3　Variation gradients

that are not shared by adjacent varieties). The speech of any two points
in space may be separated by more linguistic differences than those
which separate another two points which are the same distance apart
as the first pair. Looked at in terms of isoglosses (see **3.2.1**), which are
the graphical representations of linguistic differences between places,
it is not true to say that isoglosses are distributed with equal density in
all parts of a territory. On the contrary, in some parts of the territory
the isoglosses will be closer together (the gradient of variation will be
steeper), while in other parts the isoglosses will be spread more
sparsely, although in both cases it will be rare for two isoglosses to coincide exactly. This irregularity of gradient can be illustrated by the chart
in Figure **2.3**, in which the vertical axis represents numbers of
differences and the horizontal axis represents distance in space. And
what is true of the spatial parameters of variation seems likely to be
true also of the social parameters, although 'distance' here is a more
problematical concept and social parameters have no agreed calibra-
tion.[14] That is, there may be more differences between the speech of
two given individuals than between another two (elsewhere on the
scale), even though the members of each pair are separated by the
same social 'distance'.

2.5.1　The tree model of relationships between varieties

The model of the genealogical tree continues to be a frequent way of
expressing the relationship between linguistic varieties, and will be

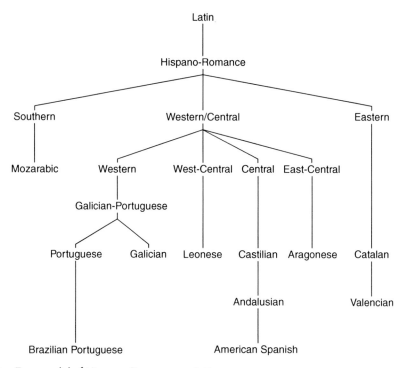

Figure 2.4   Tree model of Hispano-Romance varieties

discussed here in relation to diatopically related varieties, since there is no question (and there never has been) of using the genealogical tree to model the relationship between socially related varieties. The tree model has its origins in historical linguistics, where, since the early nineteenth century, it has been used to express the degree of historical relatedness between varieties (usually 'languages').[15]

  A tree model employed to express the relationships between certain geographically distinguished varieties used in the Peninsula might have the appearance of Figure **2.4**. But the organization of such a tree is open to infinite discussion, argument, and potential re-adjustment, since a tree is capable of expressing only one spatial dimension (given that the vertical axis of such diagrams represents the passing of time), while linguistic varieties are located in two-dimensional space.[16] For example, anywhere that one places Mozarabic will be open to objection; the Mozarabic dialects developed in wide areas of the southern Peninsula and share a number of features with Leonese and Aragonese (and to a lesser extent with Galician–Portuguese and Catalan), features which are not shared by Castilian (see Section **4.1.1**). On the other hand, although it is possible to place Galician–Portuguese, Leonese, Castilian, Aragonese and Catalan in an appropriate left-to-right array, reflecting their west-to-east distribution, the branches on which they are located in this diagram suggest degrees of relatedness which are open to challenge. Let us take a single case: Is Aragonese more similar to Castilian than it is to Catalan? This question immediately raises another: What variety of Aragonese and what variety of Catalan? And assuming that that question can be answered (a large assumption), how is one to measure the degree of difference between Aragonese and Castilian on the one hand and between Aragonese and Catalan on the other?[17] It would be theoretically possible (although actually impracticable) to list all the items over which each pair of varieties differed. But if we discovered that there were more items of difference between Aragonese and Castilian than between Aragonese and Catalan (or vice versa), would that solve the matter? Or would we wish to give greater weight to certain items than to others, since certain features strike us as more 'salient' or 'important' than others? In the absence of any principled way of assigning different weight or importance to particular features, such an enterprise is doomed to failure. And yet such a judgement of relative degrees of relatedness is inherent in the tree model. What is reflected in any given tree is a particular scholar's hunch or 'feel' for the various degrees of relatedness between varieties.

Not only is the tree model inadequate to express the relationships between diatopically related varieties, but it may seriously distort the diachronic and synchronic study of language. Some would argue that this model works well within Indo-European linguistics, where the varieties under consideration (all written and therefore partially or fully standardized) are usually well separated in space and time and where the intervening varieties have all vanished without trace, removing any possibility of viewing the Indo-European family as a continuum. However, where the object of study is a series of now-existing varieties or a range of closely related varieties from the past, the tree model is open to a number of grave objections.

2.5.1.1   Although the origins of the tree model lie in genealogy, it was its adoption by Darwinian biology that fixed this pattern so strongly in the consciousness of linguists.[18] Its use in linguistics therefore presupposes that speech varieties are like biological organisms: in placing speech varieties on the branches of a tree, we act as if we were biologists ordering species by their degree of resemblance. This is a false analogy; biological species are sharply differentiated, because, for speciation to take place, the varieties between the surviving species have to be suppressed (because these are the varieties which are in unsuccessful competition with the variety which carries the mutation which confers advantage). But human language has nothing comparable with genetic mutation. Competition between dialects is not based on structural advantage but on non-linguistic factors like the socio-economic and cultural status of the users of those dialects. And dialects which are intermediate (geographically) between successful varieties do not usually disappear; they persist as rural or working-class varieties.

This should not be taken to imply that intermediate varieties remain unchanged; they are as subject to internally and externally motivated change as any other variety. But they continue to form a continuous chain between successful varieties. It is only through exclusive concentration on successful varieties (usually standard languages) that use of the tree model, with its denial of continuity between varieties, can be justified. What is more, awareness of this contradiction at the heart of geographical and historical linguistics is not new; it has been clear at least since the advent of linguistic geography in the last decade of the nineteenth century. But the image of the tree has exercised such a powerful pull that linguists working in this field are constantly in danger of operating simultaneously with self-contradictory models.

2.5.1.2   There is a second and more powerful reason for rejecting the tree as a model of linguistic relationships. The existence of branches presupposes the existence of a trunk, and this implies that the linguistic varieties which are located on the branches of the tree have a common, unitary origin, that they spring from a single original variety, once again as if linguistic varieties were akin to biological species. But such a pattern of development is evidently not what happens in linguistic history. To take an example, the Romance languages, like the members of any family, are the product of a language-state which must have offered all the variation (geographical and social) observable in every language we can examine in detail (see **1.1**). The range of variation may be greater now than 2,000 years ago, but it is becoming ever clearer that language history consists of the change from one state of variation to another state of variation, so that any insistence on the biological/genealogical model, with its single species/individual branching into distinct species/individuals, totally distorts linguistic reality.

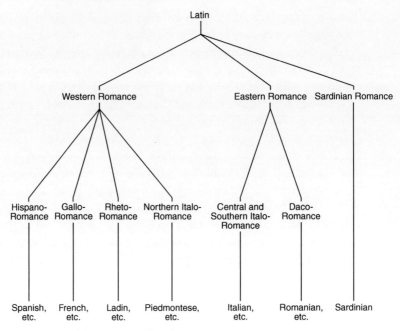

Figure 2.5   Tree model of the Romance family

A key example of this misconception can be found in traditional (but frequently repeated) classifications of the Romance language family. A common view of this family establishes a tree with three branches: a western branch, an eastern branch and a Sardinian branch, each with further branching, a simplified version of which appears in Figure 2.5. In accordance with highly respected and influential classifications, beginning with that proposed by Wartburg (1952), the division between Eastern Romance and Western Romance runs across the top of the Italian peninsula (the famous La Spezia–Rimini line). This division is based on distribution of only two features: first, the voicing of voiceless intervocalic consonants in Western Romance (but not in Eastern Romance), and second, the loss of final /-s/ in Eastern Romance (but not in Western Romance). However, if we examine the fate of the Latin voiceless intervocalics, we can see that the argument for an early bifurcation of the Latin tree into an eastern and a western branch (or its trifurcation, if one includes Sardinian Romance) is hard to sustain. One can find as least five reasons to dispute such a division:

1   Pompeiian graffiti show numbers of cases of *g* for expected *c*, and of *d* for *t* (Väänänen 1959, 1968: 102). It scarcely needs saying that

Pompeii is well south of the La Spezia–Rimini line. There is also more widespread evidence of early voicing of intervocalic plosives in the eastern Latin-speaking world (Cravens 1991).

2   The Tuscan dialects of central Italy, from one of which standard Italian principally descends, and which geographically belong to the eastern Romance branch, show frequent cases of voicing of the Latin intervocalics (*riva* < RĪPA, *grado* < GRATU, *ago* < ACU, etc.).[19]

3   Sardinian dialects, which are generally considered among the most conservative varieties of Romance, and therefore might be expected to agree in their treatment of intervocalic consonants with the Eastern Romance varieties, nevertheless show frequent voicing, at least in the south: Logudorese [neβóðe] < NEPOTE, [seɣáre] < SECĀRE, etc. (Lausberg 1965: 351).

4   Central Pyrenean dialects, despite belonging to the western branch, show frequent lack of voicing in the traditional lexis (e.g., *apella* < APICULA, *ito* < ITU) (Elcock 1938).

5   The Mozarabic descendants of Latin, spoken in Islamic Spain, most usually show retention of these voiceless consonants (a phenomenon which cannot be ascribed to orthographical conservatism, since the texts concerned are written in Arabic script).[20]

What these facts demonstrate is that we find both voicing and preservation of the Latin intervocalic consonants on both sides of the putative dividing line which, it is claimed, separates Eastern from Western Romance. And it is this dividing line which justifies the early bifurcation of the Romance tree.[21] Although these facts are well attested in standard reference books, there is a strong reluctance on the part of Romanists to abandon the tree model and the notion of an early bifurcation of the Romance tree.[22]

A potential approach to the problem of the treatment of voiceless intervocalics would be to examine the possibility of social variation in Latin between voiced and voiceless realizations of the phonemes concerned, so that what was spread from Rome to the provinces was not a set of unvarying phonemes, nor even the spread of one variant in one direction and other variants in other directions, but a variable rule whose voiced and voiceless variants were correlated with social and stylistic factors.[23] At all events, it is unacceptably simplistic to believe that a single innovation took place to the north of the La Spezia–Rimini line, which then spread to all or most of 'Western Romance', while this innovation did not penetrate south and east of the line.[24]

2.5.1.3   A third reason for rejecting the tree is that it imposes a distinction, which is often indefensible, between inherited and borrowed forms. Linguistic histories make a rigid distinction between features which are due to internal development (or to simple conservation of any earlier state of affairs) and features which have been borrowed through contact with other varieties. If the two varieties are distant in time or space, such a distinction is sound. But where the two varieties form part of the same continuum, the distinction may distort reality. To take an example, we can see that historical grammars of Spanish describe the reduction of Latin AU to /o/ (AUDIRE > oír) as a characteristic feature of the language, while the suffix -ete/-eta is labelled as foreign, borrowed from Catalan/Occitan/French. But the presence of these two features in Spanish could arguably be better explained as being due to the same process: the spread of an innovation from east to west across part of the Romance linguistic continuum. The reduction of AU certainly seems to have reached the area of Castile by diffusion (probably word by word) from the east (and to have petered out without fully affecting Portuguese). This is probably also the way in which -ete reached Castilian. Obviously there are differences of chronology: the phonological process is earlier (beginning before the break-up of the Empire) but not becoming regular in Castile until well into the Middle Ages, while the spread of the suffix is later.[25] There are also differences in the source areas of the innovations, since the reduction of AU did not affect Occitan although the suffix -et was common there from early times. However, despite these differences of chronology and geography, the process of spread is arguably the same in each case.

Why then are these two innovations in Castilian classified so differently? The answer can only be that the notion of geographical diffusion is incompatible with the tree model. The reduction of AU to /o/ can be placed before the bifurcation which separated the Castilian branch from other branches, and so can be regarded as an inherited feature;[26] but the arrival of -ete is later than this supposed bifurcation and it can therefore only have arrived by jumping from branch to branch, a process more usually labelled borrowing.

2.5.1.4   A fourth reason for abandoning the tree model lies in the need it imposes on scholars to weight linguistic features differentially. In order to decide where the nodes of the family tree should be, it is necessary to give more importance to some features than others. For example, in order to justify a classification which places Galician–Portuguese on a branch separate from that of the central Peninsular varieties, very few features are available, and maximum attention is given to the non-diphthongization of Latin ĕ and ŏ (by contrast with their diphthongization in the centre). If such attention is not to be regarded as arbitrary, then some objective justification for the prominence of this feature must be found. However, there seems to be none; some attempts have been made to provide such justification, based on the naturalness or unnaturalness of innovations, but this approach has not met with success. Therefore, since trees depend crucially on giving prominence to certain features over others, the absence of a rationale for this selection must fatally weaken the value of the tree model.[27]

2.5.1.5 The tree model can therefore be seen to be an inadequate model of relationships between linguistic varieties. But is the matter more serious than one of inadequacy? Can the tree model be considered to be responsible for dangerously distorting reality? In the case of Peninsular Romance, at least, it can, for the following reasons.

First, it imposes a tripartite division of Peninsular varieties (into Galician–Portuguese, Castilian and Catalan) in which Leonese and Aragonese are in some sense subordinated to Castilian. For example, Corominas and Pascual (1980–91) use examples drawn from texts written in Leon or Aragon to illustrate the earliest attestation of Castilian words. The only motivation for such a procedure is the three-pronged view of Hispano-Romance: if a form does not belong to the Galician–Portuguese or the Catalan branch, it is assigned to Spanish, i.e. Castilian.[28] It goes without saying that the three-branch pattern does not express the distribution of varieties in northern Spain. We have repeatedly stressed that in this region we observe an east–west dialect continuum in which, as in the rest of the Romance-speaking world (and indeed elsewhere), all dialects are transitional and there are no dialect boundaries (see **4.1.2**).

Second, it follows that the division of this continuum into three branches, or into any number of branches, falsifies our picture and leads to such false concepts as the following: 'Galician is spoken in the extreme west of Asturias' or 'Catalan is spoken in the eastern fringe of Huesca', when all that can be meant is that the isogloss separating diphthongization from non-diphthongization of Latin ĕ and ŏ passes down a little to the east of the political boundary between Galicia and Asturias, or a little west of the boundary between Huesca and Lleida/Lérida.[29]

It is true that the organization of varieties in the southern two-thirds of the Peninsula is different; here we do find three discrete blocks of varieties, with sharp boundaries between Portuguese and Castilian and between Castilian and Catalan. But this pattern is exceptional in Romance (and elsewhere), and (as we shall see in **4.1.7**) is due to very special circumstances which arose as southern Peninsular territories were resettled following their reconquest from Islamic Spain.

In conclusion, the tree model has a limited use in expressing the relationship between standard languages which have emerged in a particular family, or between varieties which have been arbitrarily selected from a continuum. But this model is inadequate to express the subtle overlapping of features that occurs at the level of normal speech. At this level, relationships are of the gradual kind. We perhaps find it difficult to deal with relationships that are based on gradation, but language is nevertheless gradated along a number of parameters. We find it easier to use models which impose boundaries (like the colours we arbitrarily distinguish within the spectrum of visible light). This subdividing process can sometimes help, but in diachronic and synchronic language studies it more often distorts.

2.5.2   Geographical discontinuity

We have earlier emphasized that geographical variation of speech normally takes the form of a continuum of varieties which merge almost imperceptibly one with another. However, it remains true that under special circumstances we can observe lines at which sharp transition between very different varieties takes place, that is, where on either side of a geographical line there are large numbers of differences of linguistic items. There would appear to be, in principle, only two sets of circumstances under which such sharp linguistic transitions occur.

First, the wave-like spread of features from a specific prestige centre may be arrested at a political frontier, beyond which the prestige centre can offer no attraction, because those living beyond that frontier are subject to linguistic pressures coming from a different direction (see **3.1**). That is, those on either side of a frontier may accommodate their speech only to that of those living on their own side of the line, at the expense of contacts and the consequent accommodation with the speech of those living across the frontier (see **3.3**). Such circumstances have arisen in recent centuries at frontiers between European states, but may have been rare or non-existent in earlier

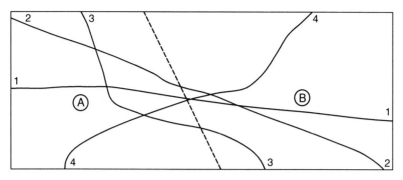

Figure 2.6 Prestige centres and isoglosses (time 1)

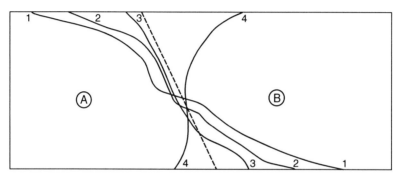

Figure 2.7 Prestige centres and isoglosses (time 2)

times, when frontiers represented no barrier to personal contacts and when prestige centres were less powerful.[30]

This process of hardening of the transition between varieties, which in an extreme case can have the effect of splitting a dialect continuum, can be envisaged as the simultaneous convergence of isoglosses (see **3.2.1**), radiated from competing prestige centres, upon an intervening political frontier. A theoretical case can be presented in Figures **2.6** and **2.7**, in which A and B are prestige centres separated by a frontier (dotted line), and where the solid lines are isoglosses moving away from points A and B. Figure **2.6** represents a time shortly after the appearance of A and B as prestige centres, at which stage isoglosses can be expected to be randomly spaced. Figure **2.7** represents the same territory, at a later time, after the isoglosses have moved towards the frontier, in some cases coming to coincide with it. Theoretically, given stability of prestige centres and frontiers for a sufficient length of time, such a process could lead (without movement of people) to a pattern in which all the isoglosses separating points A and B (that is, each and every item of difference between the speech of A and that of B) coincided exactly with the frontier, creating an abrupt linguistic boundary. However, such stability seems rare or non-existent in the real world, where we observe some bunching of isoglosses at long-established frontiers (like that between Spain and France) but always some gradualness of transition as one moves from one country to the next.

The second way in which sharp linguistic boundaries arise is less theoretical and can be easily exemplified in the real world. This process is carried out by the movement and resettlement of groups of people in new territories, where the existing population (of course) speaks differently from the incoming group. If the movement involves sufficient people and is on a broad enough front, the result will be a sharp boundary between the speech of the old and new populations; naturally, depending on the distances involved in the population movement concerned, the difference of speech across the boundary may range from partially impeded communication to total mutual incomprehension. What is described here has of course happened repeatedly in the history of mankind and is responsible for creating major (as well as minor) language frontiers, some as striking as that between the Germanic languages and the Romance family or between Hungarian and Slavic/Germanic/Romance languages in Europe. Since the process envisaged in Figures **2.6** and **2.7** above is so slow-acting as to be effectively negligible, it is worth emphasizing that movement of population is the only real agency by which sharp linguistic boundaries are created.

Movement of population is the only explanation for the fact that the southern two-thirds of the Iberian Peninsula is divided sharply into three linguistic blocs (see **4.1.3**). In this case, the resettlement of population in new territories was the consequence of the Christian reconquest of Islamic Spain, during which each state expanded into territory defined by agreement (amicable or otherwise) with its neighbour or neighbours. The result of these movements has been the creation of linguistic boundaries which are considerably sharper than those seen in the Pyrenees.

2.5.3 Diasystems

The notion of the *diasystem* is for some just a descriptive device for expressing the relationship between adjacent varieties, while for others it is a model of the way speakers perceive such relationships.[31] The notion was introduced by Uriel Weinreich (1954), in an attempt to bring together what were then seen as irreconcilably different approaches to linguistic description, namely classical structuralism and traditional dialectology. Although it is an adventurous idea, many scholars have found it problematical to apply (see Chambers and Trudgill 1980: 41–5, McDavid 1961), and it has not found universal favour.

As a descriptive device, and in cases of straightforward correspondences between one variety and another, some success can be claimed for the diasystematic approach. To take an example of this approach, the speech of Castile (and other central and northern Peninsular areas) displays the following range of phonemes in part of its phonemic inventory:

$/\theta/$ vs $/s/$ vs $/x/$ (e.g., *caza* 'hunt' vs *casa* 'house' vs *caja* 'box')

while the corresponding part of the phonemic inventory used by speakers in much of Andalusia (as well as the Canaries and America) offers only two phonemes:

$/s/$ vs $/x/$ (e.g., *caza* 'hunt' and *casa* 'house' vs *caja* 'box').[32]

To use the notation suggested by Weinreich, we can go on to say that these contrasting phonologies make up a single diasystem which expresses their partial similarity and their partial dissimilarity:

$$\text{C(astilian), A(ndalusian)} \;\;//\;\; \dfrac{\text{C}/\theta/ \approx /s/}{\text{A}/s/} \approx /x/ \;\;//$$

However, although Weinreich's scheme can handle differences of phonemic inventory (as in the case just examined, where varieties used in Castile have one more phoneme than varieties used in most of Andalusia), there are apparently insuperable difficulties in making it cope with differences of distribution and of incidence.

To take first the problem of distribution, it is probably impossible to reduce to a single diasystem those varieties of Spanish (e.g., those of Old Castile, Mexico, Peru) which allow the phoneme $/s/$ to occupy both syllable-initial position and syllable-final position (e.g., $/k\acute{a}sa/$ *casa* 'house' and $/\acute{a}sta/$ *hasta* 'until') from those (e.g., in eastern Andalusia) which allow this phoneme only at the beginning of syllables (e.g., $/k\acute{a}sa/$ *casa* 'house' and $/\acute{a}ta/$ *hasta* 'until').[33]

The handling of differences of phonemic incidence is also problematical. For example, all Andalusian varieties have a phoneme $/x/$,

WESTERN ANDALUSIA	EASTERN ANDALUSIA
/xámbre/ *hambre* 'hunger'	/ámbre/ *hambre* 'hunger'
/axogár/ *ahogar* 'to suffocate'	/aogár/ *ahogar* 'to suffocate'
/xuégo/ *juego* 'game'	/xuégo/ *juego* 'game'
/káxa/ *caja* 'box'	/káxa/ *caja* 'box'

Table 2.1   Incidence of /x/ in Andalusian dialects

but the words which contain this phoneme in rural western Andalusian varieties do not all contain it in eastern dialects (Table **2.1**).[34] It can be seen from the data in Table **2.1** that, without the aid of non-phonological information such as spelling or historical knowledge, it is impossible to distinguish between the class of lexical items which contain /x/ in all varieties and the class of items which have /x/ in some varieties but /Ø/ in others. One has to resort simply to listing the members of each class, so that a diasystem which showed both eastern and western Andalusian dialects sharing the phoneme /x/ would fall some way short of reflecting reality.

If diasystems are to be understood as models of speakers' perceptions of language variation, as Weinreich implies, then they are surely open to even more severe challenge. The use of terms like *seseo*, *ceceo*, *yeísmo*, and *leísmo* by people other than linguists suggests that speakers are aware of differences of phonemic inventory, pronoun usage, etc., between their speech and that of others. But such consciousness would seem to be limited to a small number of very salient features, and it seems highly unlikely that awareness of variation extends to matters of distribution and incidence of features.[35]

2.5.4   Diglossia

The term *diglossia* was introduced by Charles Ferguson (1959) to refer to language situations in which two distinct varieties are used by the same community, but with very different status attached to each. In the societies originally described as diglossic (Greece, the Arabic-speaking world, etc.), the two varieties, although related, are sufficiently distinct for them to be thought of as different languages. One (referred to as the H (high) language) has high status, is highly codified, is usually a medium of literature, and is restricted to use in certain social situations, while the second language (the L (low) language) is used by everybody in the community for all everyday purposes. The term *diglossia* was later extended by some scholars to include situations in which the two languages are unrelated. A case in point is Joshua Fishman's (1971) treatment of the language situation in Paraguay, where the H language is Spanish and the L language is Guaraní.

Diglossia, then, indicates a pattern of language use in which some or all speakers have access to two different sets of linguistic items, which either overlap little (Ferguson's original definition) or not at all (the extended sense of the term). Of course, none of this excludes variation in the L language, although since the H language is normally a standard, it will offer only very limited variation.

In the Spanish-speaking world, the concept of diglossia has not only been applied to such situations as that of Paraguay, but has sometimes been further extended to cases such as that of Galicia. Although many would agree that the early extension of the term to encompass coexistence of unrelated languages was a useful one, it is far from clear that it is helpful to use the term *diglossia* to describe the coexistence of codes we see in Galicia. It is true that until recent times, the use of Castilian in Galicia matched to a large extent the definition of an H language, while many of the everyday varieties would attract the label *Galician*.[36] However, Galician and Castilian share a large number of their linguistic items, so that it can be argued that they constitute overlapping codes, with exclusively Galician items belonging to typical L uses and exclusively Castilian items reserved for H uses, but with a broad intermediate set available for both H and L environments. Various studies of language contact in Galicia describe a situation of continuum, in which traditional Galician features predominate at rural level, but gradually diminish in intensity, in favour of typical Castilian features, as one examines the speech of small towns, larger towns, and cities, and as one moves along the social scale from uneducated to educated (see Woolnough 1988, Rojo 1981). A case in point is the degree of vowel nasalization observable in Galicia. According to Porto Dapena (1976, 1977: 23) and Sampson (1999: 207), nasalization is most intense among the least educated, that is, among those who have least familiarity with Castilian, and declines in intensity in accordance with speakers' degree of integration into Castilian-speaking sectors of society. This notion of a continuum of varieties extending from fully Galician at one end to fully Castilian at the other is supported by the apparent fact that many speakers in Galicia are unable to label the variety they use except by some such term as *galego chapurreado*, labels which appear to indicate that the variety concerned is not fully or properly Galician (that is, presumably, that it contains many Castilian items).

Such a continuum, assuming it can be objectively verified, has been substantially altered by the re-emergence of Galician as a written language and as a spoken medium for certain educated classes, a development which began in the nineteenth century and has gathered pace in the post-Franco period. The existence of a codified version (or versions) of Galician means that items previously identified as belonging to the L varieties have come to be used as part of an alternative H code.[37]

The notion of diglossia is perhaps even less appropriate in the case of Catalonia, Valencia and the Balearic Islands. Certainly, it is arguable that the overlap between the set of items making up standard Castilian and the set constituting everyday Catalan is smaller than the overlap between Castilian and Galician items; nevertheless, it is far from true that Catalan varieties fulfil exclusively L functions; a highly codified variety of Catalan, used in writing and at least some high-prestige social circumstances, ensures that Catalan competes with Castilian in these areas for H functions.

It is perhaps only in part of the Basque Country that classic conditions of diglossia can be said to exist. Between such unrelated languages as Castilian and Basque there is, of course, little overlap of features.[38] And in those areas where Basque is used alongside Castilian, the fact that levels of literacy in Basque are so low among those who speak it ensures that Basque is used especially in L roles, while Castilian fulfils almost all H roles. But even in the Basque Country, this diglossic relationship cannot be said to be stable, for two quite opposite reasons; one the one hand, constant effort is made to introduce certain varieties of Basque into H roles (the media, education, etc.), while, on the other, the proportion of inhabitants of the Basque Country who make use of Basque (rather than some variety of Castilian) in the majority of domains for H functions is in steady decline.[39]

2.5.5 The neolinguistic model

A further way of expressing relationships between varieties was formulated in the early part of the twentieth century under the rubric of *neolinguistics* or *spatial linguistics*. This approach is particularly associated with the work of Matteo Bàrtoli (see, for example, Bàrtoli 1945) and attempts to lay down the principles which govern the temporal and spatial relationships between varieties, especially between Romance languages. The neolinguistic approach is founded upon a codification (some would say a rigidification) of the findings of linguistic geography, combined with neogrammarian principles, and most of the tenets of this school have been dismissed by subsequent generations of linguists.[40] However, one of the central ideas of neolinguistics is still frequently appealed to, and is especially relevant to the Peninsular varieties of Romance, namely the notion that peripheral zones preserve archaic features. This notion is based upon that of linguistic waves (see **3.2**), by which innovations spread outwards from some prestige centre, but without necessarily reaching all parts of a given territory, in such a way that distant areas may be unaffected and retain an older feature. In studying the Romance lexis, this approach has a good deal of validity and a large number of cases have been unearthed in which a lexical item, thought to have once been used throughout the Latin-speaking world, has persisted in use only in peripheral areas (for example, in the central and western Peninsula, in the Alps, in southern Italy, in Dacia (approximately, modern Romania)), while speakers in more central areas (in this case, central and northern Italy, and Gaul) have replaced the term concerned with a neologism. The results of this geographical approach to the Romance lexis can conveniently be seen in the maps contained in Rohlfs (1960), where with some frequency it is possible to demonstrate that a given, older, lexical type (say FERVERE 'to boil') is found in the centre and west of the Peninsula and in Dacia (Sp. *hervir*, Ptg. *ferver*, Rom. *a fierbe*), while 'central' areas display descendants of a later replacement (in this case BULLĪRE, originally 'to bubble': Fr. *bouillir*, It. *bollire*, etc.).[41]

However, it has to be said that, while lexical data provide some limited support for the notion that territorial marginality is allied with archaism, a balanced view leads to a contrary conclusion.[42] Marginal areas, which by definition are distant from, and only loosely communicated with, prestige centres, can often be seen to develop and perpetuate innovations which the centre is powerless to obliterate. The Peninsular varieties of Romance are an excellent case in point. Spanish and Portuguese are often categorized as 'archaic' forms of Romance, on the basis of such lexical data as those reviewed here (see note 41). It is true that both have their origins in areas (Galicia, Cantabria) which are marginal both within the Peninsula and, even more so, within Romance-speaking Europe. But, looked at from any point of view but that of lexis, one has to say that both Spanish and Portuguese, each in its own way, is a rather eccentric form of Romance.[43] And the most innovatory Romance varieties of all (those which gave rise to standard French) certainly belong to the margins of the Romance area, to its northwestern periphery. Marginality should not therefore be equated with conservatism. Quite the reverse: the marginality of the Latin varieties which underlie Castilian is one of the factors associated with its speakers' openness to radical change.

2.5.6   Other models

Our need to visualize complex relationships is intense, so that the desire for visual models (such as the genealogical tree) to help us understand the complexities of the distribution of linguistic features is acute. But no simple model is adequate. The spectrum of visible light is a possible model for geographical variation, or for any single one of the many social parameters along which linguistic variation occurs, since it consists of an infinitely gradated range of wave-lengths which is arbitrarily segmented by the human eye into the 'seven' colours of the rainbow. However, the rainbow is essentially a one-dimensional model, and language variation is multidimensional. When we come to consider the standard languages of the Peninsula and their relationship with non-standard varieties (**7.3**), we shall use the model of the roof or cupola, eloquently expounded by Vàrvaro (1991); the roof represents a standard language and covers a discrete area beneath which non-standard varieties are spread in their interlocking fashion. In modern Europe, contiguous roofs typically abut sharply upon each other, while at ground level the most unpretentious varieties usually pay no attention to the joins between roofs but interlock seamlessly across frontiers. Such a model is complex (and therefore lacks the immediate appeal of simple models). But language is multidimensional and is distorted by any one-dimensional or two-dimensional model.

3   Mechanisms of change

Language history is predicated upon the notion that most linguistic change is regular; what this implies is that all the words, phrases, or other units which are candidates for a particular change are in fact affected by it in a given speech community. Although there are great difficulties in defining what is a speech community, and although, as we shall see when we look at lexical diffusion (Section **3.5**), changes do not affect all eligible items at once and some words may not be affected at all, nevertheless it remains true that many if not most changes operate in a remarkably regular way, with all eligible units being affected, in a given place, in a measurable period of time. It may seem paradoxical that this regularity is particularly observable when there are many items eligible for change. For example, we can be fairly sure that in all the words inherited by Spanish through oral transmission from Latin and which in Latin contained an intervocalic [t] (e.g., ACŪTUS 'sharp', CANTĀTUS 'sung') there occurred the same process of voicing and fricatization which produced [ð] in Spanish (*agudo, cantado*). By contrast, it is when there are few words which display the feature which is subject to change that we find the greatest irregularity. Thus, there is only a small group of words which in Latin presented the combination NG followed by a front vowel and which have been inherited by Spanish (e.g., TANGERE 'to touch', GINGĪVA 'gum', QUĪNGENTĪ 'five hundred'), yet this small group provides evidence of three different developments: [ɲ] (*tañer*), [nθ] (*encía*), [n] (*quinientos*).[1] We shall be offering a possible explanation for this kind of fragmented development in Section **3.1.6**, but we should not lose sight of the fact that every linguistic change, however regular or irregular, presupposes a lengthy chain of imitations of one speaker by another. This chapter is concerned with this kind of imitation, the process by which change spreads through social groups, and how the composition of such groups can affect who imitates whom.

In the second half of the twentieth century, linguists reached unanimity that not only change but also variation is inherent in human language. While it has long been clear that change leads to variation, it is becoming gradually more clear that language change is dependent upon (some would say caused by) linguistic variation. This is not the place to enter into the continuing and fascinating debate about the ultimate causes of linguistic change; this debate can be followed in, for example, Aitchison (1991), Kiparsky (1988), Lass (1980), or Milroy (1992), each writing from a different perspective. However, there is one major distinction which needs to be made at this point, for the sake of clarifying all the later discussion in this chapter; this is the vital distinction between, on the one hand, the cause and establishment of some change in a particular social group, and, on the other hand, the spread of such a change through the community.

We shall be concerned here with the second of these two phenomena, the spread of change through geographical and social space. In doing so, we shall need to keep an important principle in mind, namely that almost all changes are spread through face-to-face conversation between individuals, as a result of which one individual adapts some aspect of his or her speech to that of the other, and then, at least sometimes, passes on the newly acquired item to another individual.[2] Until the introduction of mass media, such as radio and television, it is axiomatic that *all* linguistic changes were spread in this face-to-face manner, but even in the global electronic village, it is far from clear that these media are responsible for spreading much change. They may be responsible for introducing new concepts to listeners and viewers, together with the appropriate new terminology, and they may even occasionally cause hearers to replace some existing item with a more fashionable item (for example, of vocabulary or pronunciation), although even this is open to dispute, on the grounds that the media may only reinforce items which a speaker has heard in face-to-face conversation. But it is far from being evident that the media have any more profound effect on the way people speak, and until more work is done in this area, we are safe to assume that the vast majority of changes are spread through person-to-person interaction.

3.1 Dialect contact

Uriel Weinreich (1953) began an important series of studies into the mutual effects exercised upon one another by languages which are in contact, namely in bilingual communities, and helped to define the kinds of adaptation processes which are to be expected in such situations. More recently, such study has been extended to include situations in which the varieties in contact are not mutually unintelligible languages but dialects which offer complete or substantial mutual intelligibility to their respective speakers. An important example of this work is that of Peter Trudgill (1986), which establishes that the main effect of contact between speakers of such mutually intelligible dialects is short-term *accommodation*, which may become long-term adjustment.

3.1.1   Accommodation

It is becoming increasingly clear that all speakers of all languages are subject to some degree of accommodation. That is, every speaker adjusts his or her speech (by selection of certain items rather than others) to the speech of the person or persons he or she is talking with. It is a common experience that some individuals adjust their speech in this way more than others do, but we probably all make some short-term adjustments of this kind during conversation. Accommodation of speech becomes more obvious when an individual goes to live in another part of the same country or to another country where the same language is spoken; again there are different degrees of speech-adjustment on the part of such speakers, some retaining almost all the features of their native variety, others apparently adjusting completely to their new speech environment, and most falling between these extremes. In the last decade, it has been recognized that contact between speakers of mutually intelligible varieties may lead to broader effects; features which are adopted as a result of adjustment in face-to-face interaction between individuals who speak different varieties may come to be used even between individuals neither of whom once used that feature. An example relevant to Spanish would be that of a couple who emigrate from central Spain to Spanish America. At first such speakers of Spanish would observe the contrast /θ/ vs /s/ (that is, they would remain non-*seseante* speakers, distinguishing *caza* from *casa*) whether speaking to one another or to others, but then can be expected to adopt a *seseante* pronunciation in at least some words when talking to local people. The crucial next step comes when the Spanish couple begin using *seseante* pronunciation between themselves, probably first in the case of words they have only come across in their new environment, but later possibly also in words they have always used. Although this process is not an inevitable one, and some individuals are much more open to it than others, it seems likely that this is the mechanism by which change is propagated from individual to individual, even in contact situations where there is something closer to numerical balance between the groups who use contrasting features. In this way, a feature which begins as a temporary adjustment in face-to-face interaction may eventually come to be adopted by an entire speech community.

Almost all the systematic work on which accommodation theory is based has been carried out in the Germanic-speaking world, most frequently as a result of observation of contact between mutually intelligible varieties of English, for example in new towns. Trudgill (1986: 1–82), exploiting earlier work by Giles (1973), uses English and Scandinavian data to identify the factors which accelerate or restrain linguistic adaptation in conditions of face-to-face contact. Most of the data are phonetic and phonological, but the conclusions drawn are probably not restricted to these domains. They are that particularly salient items are the ones most readily adapted to, and that salience can be measured in terms of a number of factors, which include the following: contribution to phonological contrast, relationship to orthography, degree of phonetic difference, and different incidence of shared phonemes. In turn, such findings help us to understand why certain features, rather than others, are more readily transmitted through geographical and social space.

Permanent adjustment resulting from dialect contact is particularly relevant to Spanish, since from at least the tenth century there has been constant mixing, in the Peninsula and in America, of speakers of mutually comprehensible varieties of Hispano-Romance, followed (one presumes) by the emergence of new dialects. Throughout the period of the Reconquest of Islamic Spain, during the colonization of America, and during the resettlement of Sephardic Jews in the Balkans and other areas, new communities were constantly being formed, consisting of speakers drawn from different dialectal backgrounds. We can therefore expect that the same kinds of linguistic processes observable today in newly established communities, such as new towns, will also have occurred in medieval Castile, in Andalusia, in colonial America, and in the cities to which the Spanish Jews emigrated.

When speakers of different varieties come into long-term contact, the normal result is, at first, fairly chaotic dialect mixture in which a large number of variant features are in competition. This range of variants may include some which were not present in any of the varieties which contribute to the mixture; such forms are referred to as cases of *interdialect* (**3.1.2**). The range of variation is then gradually reduced, leading to the creation of a new dialect, one which differs in some degree from all those that entered into the mixture. The precise mechanisms by which dialect mixture leads to the formation of a new dialect have been identified as: *levelling* of linguistic differences (**3.1.3**), *simplification* of linguistic systems (**3.1.4**), *hypercorrection* (see also **1.5**), and *hyperdialectalism* (**3.1.5**).[3] Even after the formation of the new dialect, a process sometimes called *koinéization*, some competing variants (originally from separate varieties) may survive.[4] Where this is the case, such variants are frequently subject to *reallocation*, that is to say that what were once geographically determined variants may be redistributed in such a way that they become social or stylistic variants. We shall examine reallocation in Section **3.1.6**.

3.1.2   Interdialect

As we have just seen, interdialectalisms are variants which arise under conditions of dialect contact and which do not belong to any of the varieties which have contributed to the mixture. Most frequently such variants are intermediate between the variants in competition. Although most of the studies which have revealed interdialectalism (see Trudgill 1986) are based on phonological data, where the notion of *intermediate* is usually interpreted to mean 'physiologically intermediate', there seems to be no reason in principle to limit interdialectalism to the phonological domain, and therefore it seems we should expect dialect mixing to produce, say, morphological or syntactical variants which are novel and intermediate between those that existed before the mixture came into being. Such interdialectal forms are, it would seem, by no means always eliminated through subsequent processes of levelling, and may survive as stable variants of the emerging speech variety. In Section **4.1.2.3**, we shall consider a possible case of syntactical interdialectalism, one which arguably gives rise to the present system of third-person atonic pronoun reference in Old Castile and Madrid.

It is especially difficult to sustain a claim that a given development in the past was due to interdialectalism resulting from dialect contact, since such a claim amounts to attempting to prove a negative, namely that the feature in question did *not* occur in any of the varieties which contributed to the mixture being studied. We may strongly suspect that an innovation arose in this way, but we lack the data to demonstrate that the feature was not already present, but unrecorded, in the speech of one or more of the groups coming into contact. We shall therefore limit our discussion of interdialectalism in the history of Spanish to the case outlined above.

3.1.3   Levelling: early modern Spanish

Studies of modern dialect mixing (e.g., Trudgill 1986: 98–102) reveal that in the generations which follow the establishment of a new community (or dramatic expansion of an existing community through massive influx of speakers of related dialects) there takes place a process of increasing *focusing*. That is, the range of variants is reduced, through levelling and simplification (**3.1.4**). It would seem that, in the first generation after dialect mixing, such levelling occurs only in face-to-face conversation with speakers of other dialects, usually by avoidance of those features which represent the most marked or noticeable differences between the dialects in contact. However, later generations may not make any use of such marked variants, in which case those particular cases of levelling become established as part of the speech of the whole community.

It can be argued that cases of levelling are very frequent in the history of Spanish. Both the phonology and the morphology of the modern language are notably simpler than those of most other varieties of Romance, and perhaps offer fewer contrasts than any other variety at all. This relative simplicity has been caused by the repeated dialect mixing which has occurred among central Hispano-Romance varieties, from the beginning of the Christian Reconquest of the Peninsula onwards. We shall examine here a number of cases of linguistic levelling observable in the history of late medieval and early modern Spanish, and attempt to reinterpret them in the light of the theoretical insights produced by modern studies of dialect contact.

3.1.3.1   The Old Spanish sibilants

The history of the reduction of the six medieval Spanish sibilants to only three in central and northern Spain, and to two elsewhere, has been intensively studied.[5] The facts of the case can be stated succinctly: during the sixteenth century, prestigious varieties of Spanish give evidence of a series of mergers affecting the sibilant sub-system, which (leaving aside /tʃ/, which underwent no change) consisted of the six units shown in Table **3.1**, illustrated with typical words shown in their

	VOICELESS	VOICED
Pre-palatal fricative	/ʃ/ *caxa* 'box'	/ʒ/ *muger* 'woman'
Apico-alveolar fricative[a]	/s/ *passo* 'step'	/z/ *casa* 'house'
Dental fricative[b]	/ş/ *caça* 'hunt'	/z̧/ *dezir* 'say'

[a] These phonemes were of the retroflex type, like the surviving /s/ of the central and northern Peninsula.

[b] These dental (laminal) fricatives resulted from earlier affricates.

Table 3.1   Late-medieval sibilants in Spanish

usual contemporary orthography. By contrast, it is known that in Old Castile and adjacent areas (Alonso 1962a), already in the Middle Ages, certain varieties had allowed the voiced phonemes to merge with the voiceless, with voiceless result. The reasons offered for this merger do not concern us here, but include Basque substratum effects, and levelling rooted in morphology (Penny 1993).

Following its establishment as the capital of Spain in 1561, Madrid grew dramatically, and its population, previously that of a small to medium-sized town, mushroomed in a few decades. Madrid was the 'new town' of sixteenth-century Spain, and the immigrants who contributed to its expanded population would have been drawn predominantly from the north, since the north of the Peninsula had always been, and continued to be until recent times, the main source of surplus population. Many of these new settlers in Madrid, it can be speculated, brought with them varieties of Castilian in which the voiced and voiceless sibilants had merged, with voiceless results, while the existing population and any immigrants from further south would be users of the traditional system. Knowing what is now known about the effects of dialect mixing in twentieth-century new towns, it is not hard to imagine that the linguistic effects of the demographic expansion of Madrid included levelling of the two main sibilant sub-systems that were brought into competition there. No doubt levelling was preceded by a fairly chaotic flux of competing forms, in which words like *muger, casa, dezir* were pronounced by some with a voiced and by others with a voiceless intervocalic consonant, and in which speakers adjusted their pronunciation only in face-to-face interaction with users of the other phonological pattern. But, by the second or third generation at most, preference for the voiceless pronunciation became general, for the

	VOICELESS	
Pre-palatal fricative	/ʃ/ *caxa* 'box'	*muger* 'woman'
Apico-alveolar fricative	/s/ *passo* 'step'	*casa* 'house'
Dental fricative	/ş/ *caça* 'hunt'	*dezir* 'say'

Table 3.2   Late sixteenth-century sibilants in Spanish

following reasons. First, there may well have been more speakers who used only voiceless sibilants than speakers who contrasted voiceless with voiced, since the new population seems to have been drawn predominantly from the north, and many areas of the northern Peninsula had by this time probably abandoned voiced sibilants. Although we cannot hope to reconstruct the demography of sixteenth-century Madrid, and although numerical superiority of speakers of one variety over others is not the crucial deciding factor in the results of dialect contact, we cannot ignore the possibility that voiced sibilants in late sixteenth-century Madrid constituted the *marked* variant, one which was salient because of its oddity. Secondly and perhaps more importantly, all speakers used voiceless sibilants, but only some had previously used voiced sibilants, so that the all-voiceless solution was phonologically simpler (see **3.1.4**). Finally, the number of minimal pairs which were sustained by the contrast of each voiced sibilant with its voiceless counterpart seems to have been extremely small, so that the adoption of the voiceless-only variant scarcely impeded communication, if at all.[6]

It is presumably in this way that a feature of pronunciation which had previously characterized low-prestige varieties of Castilian, principally from the rural north, came to gain ground in the capital. For many decades, the prestige norm, still for many people enshrined in the speech of Toledo, continued to maintain the earlier phonemic contrasts. However, careful scrutiny of the data, by Amado Alonso (1967b, 1969) and others, has shown that the new pronunciation found its way fairly rapidly into elegant usage in the capital and elsewhere and established itself as the norm, probably by the end of the sixteenth century (Table **3.2**). A later (or overlapping) change to this system, in which the pre-palatal phoneme was velarized to /x/ or /h/ and (in central and northern Spain) the dental was interdentalized to /θ/, gave the result shown in Table **3.3**, in which the illustrative words are shown in their modern spelling.

	VOICELESS	
Velar fricative	/x/ *caja* 'box'	*mujer* 'woman'
Apico-alveolar fricative	/s/ *paso* 'step'	*casa* 'house'
Interdental fricative	/θ/ *caza* 'hunt'	*decir* 'say'

Table 3.3   Modern Spanish sibilants

LATIN	OLD SPANISH
FĪLĀRE	*filar* = /hilár/ 'to spin'
FABULĀRE	*fablar* = /haβlár/ 'to speak'
FŪMU	*fumo* = /húmo/ 'smoke'

Table 3.4   Development to Old Spanish of words displaying F-

3.1.3.2   Old Spanish /h/

By the late Middle Ages, it is likely that everywhere in Castile the glottal phoneme /h/ had displaced earlier labiodental /f/ in words whose Latin ancestors displayed initial F-, and that this /h/ had progressed into that part of Andalusia so far reconquered and was progressing into Murcia. This development is exemplified in Table **3.4**, showing the usual medieval graph *f* to represent /h/. This success of what is agreed to be a northern feature was no doubt due, in large part, to the resettlement of southern areas by speakers from northern Old Castile (the main area where this change originated), or to the resolution of variation in southern Spain between /h/ (brought by speakers from northern Old Castile) and /f/ (brought by others or continued by speakers of Southern Hispano-Romance (i.e., Mozarabic; see **4.1.1**)) in favour of the Old Castilian variant /h/. Contemporary with this north–south spread of /h/, there was lateral spread of the phoneme into Leonese and Aragonese territories, not apparently mediated by movement of population and dialect mixing, but by the more frequent mechanism of person-by-person imitation of a feature radiating out from Old Castile (see **3.2** and **3.5**).[7]

The development which interests us here is the subsequent success of /h/-dropping, a phenomenon which may have more ancient origins but which gains significant attention in the middle of the sixteenth century, when interested observers contrast the speech of Old Castile, where /h/ is lost, from that of the prestige centre, Toledo, where /h/ is retained. It appears that, very rapidly, in the second half of the sixteenth century, /h/-dropping became acceptable. Why should this feature, associated with what was by this time a culturally peripheral area, have prospered? After all, to take a comparable case from another European language, standard British English shows no sign of adopting /h/-dropping, despite the fact that the large majority of non-standard varieties show loss of earlier /h/.

The answer again appears to lie in the results of dialect mixture in sixteenth-century Madrid. As we have seen (3.1.3.1), the dramatic demographic expansion of the new capital after 1561 brings an influx of northerners into Madrid, and many of the new arrivals would have come from /h/-dropping areas. They thus introduced into urban Spanish what had up till then been a disregarded provincialism. But introduction does not guarantee success, since /h/-dropping must have competed with /h/-retention in the dialect mixture created by the expansion of Madrid. But what we know about the normal patterns of development which follow dialect mixing helps us to explain the success of /h/-dropping.

Although we cannot establish what was the demographic balance between /h/-droppers and /h/-retainers, relative numbers are not, we recall, the most important factor in determining the outcome of competition between variants. Levelling can take place even in favour of a minority variant, although in this case it is possible that /h/-droppers were in the majority. More important is the fact that levelling usually disfavours marked variants (Trudgill 1986: 126), and use of /h/ was clearly a highly noticeable feature. Equally relevant, levelling can be expected to favour linguistically simpler variants, and it is evident that /h/-dropping varieties are phonologically simpler than their competitors. /h/-retaining varieties need to keep separate two classes of words (shown in Table 3.5 with their modern spellings), which can be conflated by /h/-droppers.[8] Of course, the /h/-less solution would be unlikely to gain ground in the community if it were to impede communication. But this is scarcely the case; once again, there are few if any cases where homonymic clash is brought about by /h/-dropping.[9]

3.1.3.3   The merger of Old Spanish /b/ and /β/

A similar argument can be deployed in the case of the merger of the two Old Spanish voiced labial consonants as has been used in the case

Words with /h/	Words without /h/
hilar 'to spin'	*igual* 'equal'
hijo 'son'	*historia* 'story'
hiel 'bile'	*hielo* 'ice'
henchir 'to fill'	*empezar* 'to begin'
herido 'wounded'	*helar* 'to freeze'
hablar 'to speak'	*ala* 'wing'
hacha 'axe'	*hábito* 'habit'
hoja 'leaf'	*oler* 'to smell'
hongo 'mushroom'	*hombre* 'man'
humo 'smoke'	*uno* 'one'
huir 'to flee'	*humilde* 'humble'

Table 3.5 Words with and without /h/ in conservative sixteenth-century varieties of Castilian

of the sibilants and in the case of /h/-dropping, although here we lack some of the abundance of chronological and geographical data which have been unearthed in connection with the previously discussed changes.[10]

On the basis of data drawn from rhyming verse, it can be established that until the fifteenth century in Spain, the two letters *b* and *v* indicated distinct phonemes; the first was most probably a voiced bilabial plosive, while the second was a voiced fricative. To judge by the absence today of voiced labiodentals across the whole north of the Peninsula, and in Gascony, it seems likely that the voiced fricative phoneme was a bilabial in many, if not all, northern areas, while the southern half of the Peninsula was probably occupied by a labiodental variant, linking the surviving areas of /v/ which are to be found in Southern Catalan and in Central and Southern Portuguese. If this distribution of variants is the correct one, we can summarize it in Table **3.6**. In all parts of the Peninsula, then, the distinctive feature which separated the two phonemes under discussion was that of manner of articulation (plosive vs fricative). However, in those areas where this was the only distinctive feature, namely in the north, the two phonemes were

	PLOSIVE	FRICATIVE
Northern Peninsula	/b/ *cabe* 'it fits'	/β/ *cave* 'he digs (subj.)'
Southern Peninsula	/b/ *cabe* 'it fits'	/v/ *cave* 'he digs (subj.)'

Table 3.6   Voiced labial phonemes in medieval Spain

Northern Peninsula	/b/ *cabe* 'it fits' = *cave* 'he digs (subj.)'
Southern Peninsula	/b/ *cabe* 'it fits' ≠ /v/ *cave* 'he digs (subj.)'

Table 3.7   Voiced labial phonemes in late medieval Spain

increasingly neutralized, leading to total merger, with allophonic variation between [b] and [β], by about the fifteenth century (Penny 1976; see
Table **3.7**). The fact that the northern solution has triumphed in all areas
to which Castilian was extended (including the whole of America), with
the sole exception of some Judeo-Spanish varieties (see **6.3.2(3)**), suggests that the competition in southern Spain between the traditional
system (/b/ vs /v/) and the newly introduced system (/b/ alone) led to
rapid levelling in favour of the northern type.[11] The reason why levelling took place in favour of the northern system rather than the southern is no doubt the same as that we have seen in the case of
sibilant-merger and /h/-dropping: the northern system was simpler,
and its adoption posed little or no threat to communication, since the
number of minimal pairs sustained by the /b/-/v/ contrast (or the
earlier northern contrast between /b/ and /β/) was very small.

3.1.4   Simplification: the result of the territorial expansion of Castilian

The simplification which takes place in the wake of dialect mixing is
closely related to levelling, since levelling usually favours the simpler or
the simplest of the competing variants. What is notable about
simplification, however, is that it may occur even if the simpler variant
belongs to a variety or varieties used by a minority of speakers in the
new community (Trudgill 1986: 102–7). What is claimed in this chapter
is that the variety which we know as standard Spanish has emerged

from a series of dialect mixtures, and has undergone repeated new-dialect formation or *koinéization*, beginning at least as early as the ninth century (see **3.3** for further development of this idea). In that century we see the beginnings of the Castilian reconquest of central Spain, in the resettlement of the Burgos area, a process which brought in speakers of a number of Romance varieties from regions such as Cantabria, immediately to the north. The next major step was the advance into New Castile and the recovery of Toledo in the late eleventh century, whereupon a new series of dialect contacts took place, involving not only varieties which had earlier emerged in Old Castile (including perhaps the most prestigious, that of Burgos) but Leonese and Mozarabic varieties, together with some from more distant parts of the Peninsula, and even beyond. The *koiné* which emerged from that mixture was to form the basis of the thirteenth-century Alfonsine standard (see Chapter **7**), but the process of mixing was repeated at each major stage of the Reconquest, most notably next in Seville, reconquered in the mid-thirteenth century and the destination of an enormous influx of people from all over the Peninsula, a migration which resulted in a further process of dialect mixture and the focusing or *koinéization* which produced the distinctively Andalusian varieties of Spanish. Later migrations (to the Canaries, to Granada after 1492, to the Balkans, and to the Americas) all gave rise to new contact situations, with at least some of the expected linguistic outcomes, namely levelling and simplification. However, these later dialect mixtures took place in a period when the prestige of the Castilian standard was increasing, so that the solutions adopted in each new community were not always those predictable by sociolinguistic theory, but were (at least in part) determined by adherence to the prestige norm (see **7.1**).[12]

If we contrast the phonological and morphological structures of Castilian with those of Peninsular varieties which have not emerged from successive stages of dialect contact, we note that such 'unmixed' varieties show markedly greater complexity. A case in point is provided by the varieties spoken in Asturias and Cantabria, regions of northern Spain which, until the nineteenth century, received little or no immigration; on the contrary, they were a continual source of emigration. The traditional speech varieties used in these regions, which do not result from dialect mixing, are more complex than those of Castilian, in at least the following ways (see García Arias 1988): most Asturian and Cantabrian varieties show a system of five unstressed final vowels, by contrast with the three of Castilian; the metaphonic raising of stressed vowels, in anticipation of a high final, with all the morphological and semantic information this phenomenon usually carries, is present in many Asturian and Cantabrian varieties, but is entirely absent from Castilian; the morphological expression of 'countability' (the use of separate formatives to represent countable referents, from those used to represent uncountable or mass concepts) is common throughout Asturias and neighbouring areas, but has no counterpart in Castilian (Penny 1970b). Since a considerable proportion, but not all, of those who settled Burgos after its reconquest in 884 came from Cantabria, it can be assumed that the features just considered belonged initially to their speech but were lost in favour of simpler alternants, as a result of the first episode of dialect mixing in the history of Spanish.

The implication, from the standpoint of sociolinguistic theory, of the view that Spanish results from repeated phases of dialect mixing, is that Castilian has undergone more simplification (and levelling) processes than other Romance varieties. It has frequently been noted that the phonology of Spanish is simpler, and its morphology more regular, than those of the other standard Romance varieties; and these characterizations of structural simplicity also hold true if one compares Spanish with the large majority of non-standard Romance varieties.

3.1.4.1   The merger of the perfect auxiliaries

Old Spanish, like most other Romance varieties, inherited from spoken Latin a double series of verbal auxiliaries, used with past participles to provide a series of paradigms including present perfect, pluperfect, future perfect, etc. (Penny 1991a: 141–4). On the one hand was the descendant of the Latin verb HABEO, at first in Latin used only with the participle of a transitive verb in such constructions as HABEO CĒNAM PARĀTAM (lit. 'I have the meal (and it is) prepared'). In such constructions HABEO retained its full lexical value ('I possess, I have with me'), and required an overt direct object (here CĒNAM), to which the participle was appended as a modifier, agreeing with it in case, gender and number.[13] Already in spoken varieties of Latin, it is reasonably clear that HABEO began to lose its full lexical value, that is, it was weakened in sense in such a way that the notion of possession was attenuated, perhaps via that of metaphorical possession, until it became essentially a grammatical particle indicating the tense and aspect of the total construction, as well as the person and number of the grammatical subject.[14] However, in the medieval period, the Spanish perfect (*he cantado*, etc.) retains a number of the features which had belonged to this construction in Latin: it was appropriate, in essence, for transitive verbs only, and the participle, at least sometimes, continued to agree in gender and number with the direct object.

By contrast with the *he cantado* perfect, many non-transitive verbs in medieval Spanish offered the type *son venidos* 'they have come'. This structure almost certainly descends from the perfect paradigm of Latin deponent verbs, in which the past participle (which agrees in gender and number with the grammatical subject) is accompanied by the auxiliary SUM 'I am' (e.g., NATUS SUM 'I was born', whence Old Spanish *so nado* 'I have been born').[15] This pattern was evidently extended in spoken Latin to include the perfect (and other tenses) of many intransitive verbs, such as verbs expressing movement, existence, etc., as well as to reflexive and reciprocal constructions involving transitives.

All Romance languages show some blurring of the categories of verbs requiring each of the auxiliaries descended respectively from HABEO and SUM.[16] For example, the subjectless verbs which indicate weather conditions everywhere unexpectedly allow HABEO as the auxiliary, sometimes beside SUM (e.g., Old and Modern Spanish *ha llovido* 'it has rained', Italian *è* or *ha nevicato* 'it has snowed'). However, Spanish is in advance of other Romance varieties in the simplification of this part of its grammar, by allowing the total obliteration of the SUM perfect by the HABEO perfect during the Middle Ages.[17] There is no evidence, for example, that Spanish verbs expressing existence ever had a SUM perfect (we always find *he sido, han estado, ha quedado*, etc.), by contrast with most other Romance languages (e.g., Italian, Catalan). Reflexive and reciprocal expressions once had SUM perfects, but these were soon replaced by the alternative type, and by the early sixteenth century it was only verbs expressing some types of motion (*ir, venir, salir*, etc., but not *andar, viajar*, etc.) which occasionally allowed the SUM perfect (*son idos, (ella) es venida*, beside *han ido, ha venido*), and this possibility then rapidly disappeared and simplification of the two types to one was complete.[18]

3.1.4.2 The Old Spanish strong preterites

A further example, and a dramatic one, of the simplification to which Castilian has been subjected during the Middle Ages is provided by the history of the strong preterites (those which carried the word stress on the stem in the first and second persons singular). Medieval texts give evidence of a broad array of such preterites, belonging to all three verb-classes, although it is probable that not all the forms in the following list were present simultaneously in any given Castilian variety:

-ar: **andove**/*andude*/*andide* 'I walked', *catide* 'I looked', *demandide*
       'I sought', **di** 'I gave', *entride* 'I entered', **estove**/*estude*/*estide* 'I was';
-er: *aprise* 'I learned', *atrove* 'I dared', *conuve* 'I knew', **cope** 'I fitted',
       coxe 'I cooked', *crove* 'I believed', *despise* 'I spent', **fize** 'I made',
       fui/*sove* 'I was', *mise* 'I put', *nasque* 'I was born', **ove** 'I had', *plogue*
       'I pleased', *prise* 'I took', **pude** 'I could', **puse** 'I put', **quise**
       'I wished', *remase* 'I remained', *respuse* 'I replied', **sope** 'I knew',
       tanxe 'I touched, played', **tove** 'I had, held', *troxe*/**traxe**
       'I brought', **vi**/*vide* 'I saw', *yogue* 'I lay';
-ir: *aduxe* 'I brought', *cinxe* 'I girded on', **conduxe** 'I led', *destruxe*
       'I destroyed', **dixe** 'I said', *escrise* 'I wrote', *fuxe* 'I fled', *rise*
       'I laughed', *sonrise* 'I smiled', *tinxe* 'I dyed', **vine** 'I came', *visque*
       'I lived'.

Of these forms, some were already infrequent in the earliest texts, but
the large majority had been abandoned by the end of the Middle Ages,
leaving only the forms printed in bold (which in some cases have undergone minor restructuring of their vowels and/or consonants). In a few
cases, the loss of a strong preterite was caused by the complete loss of
the verb concerned from the Spanish lexis (e.g., *despise/despender*,
remase/remanir), but more usually, the verb has survived but its strong
preterite has been replaced by a weak form (one whose word stress
always falls on the ending). Thus *entride* gave way to its competitor
entré, *escrise* was replaced by *escreví* (later *escribí*), etc. This reduction of
strong preterites marks a notable contrast between Castilian and, say,
French and Italian, where a whole variety of stem-stressed preterites
survive.[19] It is best explained by simplification of the verbal paradigms
which took place in medieval varieties of Castilian under conditions of
dialect mixing during the Reconquest.

3.1.4.3   The -*er* and -*ir* verb classes
A case of morphological simplification, whose origins are to be found
in the earliest documents from the Castilian core area (Burgos and surrounding towns), is the near-merger of the -*er* and -*ir* verb classes. Such
texts show that, already in the eleventh century, as now, there were few
differences of verbal ending between the two classes. No difference is
found between the preterites of -*er* and -*ir* verbs, unlike what is observable in other areas (Menéndez Pidal 1964: 364), where such contrasts
are found not only in the endings of the preterite paradigm but also in
those paradigms morphologically related to the preterite (the -*ra* paradigm, at first carrying pluperfect meaning, and the past subjunctive -*se*

paradigm). In Castilian, the contrasts of ending between verbs of these two classes were reduced to four: infinitive -er vs -ir, first- and second-person plural, present indicative -emos, -edes vs -imos, -ides, and plural imperative -ed(e) vs -id(e).

It is true that there were some differences in the range of vowels that could appear in the stems of the two verb classes (thus /i/ and /u/ were excluded from the *stem of -er* verbs) and that certain stem-vowel alternations (/e/~/i/ and /o/~/u/: *medir~mido, sobir~subo*) were limited to -ir verbs. But even these differences were reduced over time (through the loss of the /o/~/u/ alternation, in favour of /u/: *subir~subo*),[20] and Spanish verbal morphology is considerably simpler in this area than that of almost all other Romance varieties.[21]

3.1.5   Hyperdialectalism

Yakov Malkiel has identified a number of cases of what he terms 'excessive self-assertion' in the history of Hispano-Romance, instances in which a linguistic community selects or creates forms in order to sharpen or exaggerate the difference between its own forms of speech and those of some other community with which it compares itself. For example, he claims (1989) that in Medieval Portuguese a particular case of verbal stem allomorphy, *gradesco~gradeces,* was levelled to *agradeço~agradeces* in order to maximize the difference between that variety and Castilian, where the alternation *gradesco~grade(s)ces* (now *agradezco~agradeces*) was a characteristic and increasingly frequent pattern as it spread from the core group of verbs, whose Latin ancestors had had inceptive or 'inchoative' meaning, to other groups.

Malkiel apparently envisages this process occurring at a distance, by reaction of one community to the speech of another. If, however, we take the view that linguistic change of all types is originated through accommodation in circumstances of face-to-face interaction, then such action at a distance cannot be understood. However, in circumstances of dialect contact, it is easier to see how cases like the one cited by Malkiel can arise, provided we reinterpret them as cases of hyperdialectalism.

Hyperdialectalisms are interdialect forms (see **3.1.2** and Trudgill (1986: 68–9)) which originally do not exist in either of two varieties in contact, but which are created in one variety in order to sharpen the difference or to regularize the contrasts between it and the other. Thus, in a contact situation in medieval Portugal in which speakers recognize

CASTILIAN, ETC.	PORTUGUESE		
fago, faga	*faço, faça*		
yago, yaga	*jaço, jaça*		
gradesco, gradesca	*gradesco, gradesca*	>	*(a)gradeço, (a)gradeça*

Table 3.8   Hyperdialectalism in Portuguese

that the /tˢ/ which they frequently use at the end of the stem in the first-person singular and in all persons of the present subjunctive (e.g. *faço, faça* 'I (etc.) do', medieval *jaço, jaça* 'I (etc.) lie') corresponds to a non-sibilant (e.g., *fago, faga; yago, yaga*) in other varieties, not necessarily Castilian, which they hear from some of their interlocutors, they may be led to introduce /tˢ/ into the relevant forms of verbs whose stems previously did not end with a sibilant, in the way suggested in Table **3.8**.[22]

3.1.6   Reallocation of variants

Following a period of dialect mixing, such as repeatedly occurred in medieval Spain, we have seen that the normal pattern of development is for the great abundance of variants to be reduced through levelling and simplification. However, it is observable in modern situations of dialect contact (Trudgill 1986: 110–26) that, even after such *koinéization* has taken place, there may be a residue of competing forms. These surviving variants, which had earlier been brought together by speakers from distinct regions, are frequently reallocated, that is, they cease to be geographical variants and become associated with differences of social class, or with differences of register.

A possible case of such reallocation can be seen in the American-Spanish distribution of the phoneme /h/, as it occurs in words descended from Latin words which began with F-. No doubt in the early communities established in the Americas there were speakers who pronounced such words as *hilar* 'to spin' and *humo* 'smoke' with initial /h/, while others pronounced them /ilár/ and /úmo/. This variation had its cause in the different parts of the Peninsula from which the colonists came. We saw earlier (**3.1.3.2**) that in the sixteenth century (the period when Castilian began to be carried to America), much of Old Castile was an area of /h/-dropping, while in other areas (such as Cantabria, New Castile, Extremadura, and Andalusia) speakers retained initial /h/ in their pronunciation. But a competition of forms which had its origins in geographical variation appears to have been transmuted into a case of social-class variation. The articulation of /h/ in words like *hilar* is found today throughout Spanish-speaking America (Lapesa 1980: 574; Zamora 1967: 413–14), but is now confined to uneducated speakers, in rural and urban settings, while educated Spanish-American varieties, like their Peninsular counterparts, lack /h/ in words of this class.[23]

The process of reallocation of originally geographical variants may provide a useful approach to the understanding of certain recalcitrant facts observable in the history of Castilian (and of other languages). Provided we bear in mind that language history is not a matter of smooth linear development, by which a single variety undergoes a series of changes and emerges transformed, but is a process full of detours, hiccups, backtrackings and blind alleys, the reallocation phenomenon may help us to solve two closely related types of problem. On the one hand, in all languages we find instances in which a single item, observable at one phase, gives rise, at a later stage, to different and competing results within a single variety. On the other, there are those many instances in which we observe, in the past, the results of competing developments, coexisting in the same territory, and where one of the competitors is chosen, apparently arbitrarily, for survival, while the other is abandoned.

The first of these cases was illustrated in the first paragraph of this chapter, with an example taken from the history of Castilian (the competing outcomes of NG when followed by a front vowel, epitomized by *tañer, encía, quinientos*). A possible explanation for such a case is that the three different treatments of the Latin consonant group were once typical of distinct zones, from which separate groups of speakers were drawn, speakers who came together during the process of settlement of reconquered territory. The normal result of such contact, as we have seen, is that one of the variants comes to be adopted by the whole community (i.e. levelling takes place whereby all eligible expressions come to display the feature in question). We have also seen that the successful variant may be the one used by the majority of speakers, but may alternatively be a minority variant, provided that such a variant offers some advantage of simplicity in the newly emerging *koiné*. But what happens if there are few exponents of the feature in question? If there is just a handful of words, for example, in which the community is divided over whether to use one of two or three rival pronunciations, then it may be that no consensus emerges. The result of this may be that competing forms (e.g., *tañer* vs *tanzer*) continue to circulate.[24] What one would then predict (as usual, on the basis of modern sociolinguistic studies) is that competing variants would acquire different prestige, that is that geographical variation would be converted into social variation. Such reallocation of variants may proceed on an arbitrary basis, or there may be some hidden principles at work which have not yet been laid bare, but whichever of the competing variants comes to acquire high status, that is likely to be the form which is reflected in writing (since writing normally reflects the usage of high-status sectors of the community) and which, if a standard is in the process of formation (see **7.1**), will become part of that standard.

It is in terms of such reallocation that we should attempt to understand some of the minor quirks and apparent contradictions of linguistic history. By way of experiment only, we present a few cases, from the history of Spanish, in which reallocation may have an explanatory role.

The treatment of the /o/ of spoken Latin (ō or ŭ of Classical Latin) when stressed and followed by the sequence /nj/ (/n/ followed by a palatal glide, corresponding to the spellings NE or NI of Classical Latin) shows a double outcome. On the one hand CUNEU produces *cuño* 'die-stamp' (whence *cuña* 'wedge'), showing raising of the stressed vowel to the high position (/u/) followed by assimilation of /nj/ to /ɲ/. On the other hand, CICŌNIA 'stork', which displayed the same sequence [ónj] in spoken Latin, becomes *cigüeña*, showing transfer of the glide to the preceding syllable (*[t⁵igói̯na]) followed by both palatalization of /n/ to /ɲ/ and replacement of [ói̯] by [wé] (for which there are precedents elsewhere in the language (e.g., AUGURIU > [agói̯ro] > *agüero* 'omen'))). Although we can perhaps rule out the existence of an alternant *cueño* 'die-stamp', through avoidance of near-homonymy with the taboo item *coño* 'vagina', it is entirely possible that a form *ciguña* 'stork' existed, as a competitor of the ultimately successful *cigüeña*.[25]

In another case of competition between alternants which descended from rare word-structures, Old Spanish form *vergüeña* 'shame' (< VERĒCUNDIA), similarly structured to successful *cigüeña*, was ultimately discarded. This attested alternant was ousted by *vergüença*, the form later selected as standard (and eventually respelled *vergüenza)*, but the long coexistence of the two types, possibly differentiated by connotations of prestige, was possibly favoured by the rarity of the original sequence -UNDIA and therefore of both its Castilian descendants -*ueña* and -*uença*.[26]

In the case of the Latin SINGULŌS, both the successful *sendos* and an alternant *seños* 'one each' are found in thirteenth-century texts, but the latter thereafter disappears from the written record, no doubt because of its low prestige.

Variation between alternative outcomes of the same original segment is further illustrated by the treatment in Castilian of Latin words beginning with non-syllabic [j] grouped with a following back vowel (e.g., IŪGU 'yoke', IUNCU 'reed'). In this case, the words that fit the description are slightly more numerous than in the previous cases, but the total number is still low. Although the outcome represented by IŪGU > *yugo* is usually regarded as the typical Castilian treatment of this sequence, it is also to be borne in mind that words with meanings related to local flora are unlikely to be loans from other regions, so that we should keep open the possibility that these forms, and the few others like them, are the result of reallocation of competing forms (*yugo* vs *jugo*, *yunco* vs *junco,* etc.), brought together in the same Castilian communities through the process of medieval resettlement.

3.2 Waves

The use of the image of the wave, to represent the spread of an innovation across a territory, is far from new in linguistics. It was introduced into Indo-European philology by Johannes Schmidt (1872), to explain certain similarities between the features of different branches of the Indo-European family, and was further refined by Saussure (1960: 206–8), who likened the boundary of the area occupied by a new feature to the outermost edge of an undulating flood. It has not always been noted, however, that (*pace* Pulgram 1953) the image of the encroaching wave is quite incompatible with that of the genealogical tree (see **2.5.1**), since the wave can only spread across a dialect continuum and must be halted where one continuum abuts upon another (see **2.5.2**), that is, using the imagery of the tree, a wave cannot pass from branch to branch.[27] Attempts to reconcile these two models of linguistic relatedness, such as that of Malkiel (1983), confirm that, so long as one is dealing with a dialect continuum, the image of the spreading wave of innovation is the only appropriate one, while the image of the tree can only be used (if at all; see **2.5.1**) in cases of geographical discontinuity between what were once segments of the same continuum.

Provided that it is remembered that the reality which underlies the image of the wave is one in which innovations are spread as a result of imitation of one speaker by another in face-to-face interaction, then the wave image is a useful one, and will be used repeatedly in what follows.[28]

3.2.1   Isoglosses

The notion of the isogloss, introduced in Section **2.1**, can now be more rigorously defined as a line, drawn on a linguistic map, which delimits an area or areas occupied by a particular feature (say, a sound, or a grammatical item, or a particular word to express a given concept) and divides it from another area or areas in which a different feature is used *under the same linguistic circumstances* (a different sound, a different grammatical feature, a different word to express the same concept, a different meaning attached to the same word, etc.). In the context of wave theory, the isogloss can be envisaged as the outer edge of a ripple emanating from some point in the territory concerned. It is worth reminding ourselves that what this means in human terms is that the point from which the wave spreads is some town or city whose inhabitants have acquired higher social prestige than those living in surrounding areas, and that some feature of the speech of the high-prestige group has been imitated by those in their immediate vicinity, who have in turn passed this feature on, through imitation, to individuals living a little further from the prestige centre, and so on. The reasons for the special prestige associated with our centre of radiation lie outside the domain of linguistics, and are related to such matters as wealth, political power, enhanced educational status, etc.

The drawing of an isogloss on a map, as a result of a dialect investigation, cannot, by itself, tell us in which direction that isogloss is moving (or indeed if it is moving at all), since a map with an isogloss drawn on it is a mere snapshot taken at one moment in time, and does not tell us which of the two features it separates is the innovation and which is the older feature.[29] For example, it is possible to draw a map of the Peninsula with an isogloss which separates the area in which the diphthong [éi̯] appears in the suffix *-eiro* (Latin -ĀRIU) from a larger area

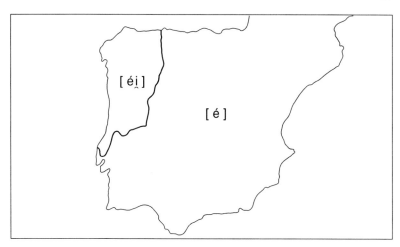

Figure 3.1   Isogloss separating [-éi̯] from [é] in -eiro, -ero, -er

in which the corresponding suffix (-ero/-er) contains the simple vowel [é] (Figure **3.1**). In order to determine in which direction this isogloss is moving, we need information from an earlier period. Such information would ideally stem from an earlier, identical inquiry, but such information is unlikely to be available, and we have to make do with partial information from written sources. Since we have pre-twelfth-century texts from northern Castile which display spellings such as -eiro (Menéndez Pidal 1964: 73–4, 483), spellings which suggest (but do not prove) that the pronunciation [éi̯] was once used where [é] now occurs, and since Southern Portuguese [é] (in forms whose standard spelling shows ei; e.g., -eiro) appears to be affecting central Portugal, it is reasonable to conclude that the isogloss in Figure **3.1** is receding towards the northwest.

There is one configuration of isoglosses which allows us, almost unambiguously, to determine the direction of movement without information from earlier periods. The map in Figure **3.2** shows a single isogloss which delimits four zones in which the plural marker {-es} appears in the case of feminine nouns and adjectives whose singular is marked by {-a} (e.g., cases 'houses', plural of casa). It is overwhelmingly likely that the three western zones are contracting, since if they were to be expanding, our conclusion would have to be that three separate centres of influence were radiating out the same feature, a possibility which is inherently unlikely. In fact, the likelihood is that these three western zones were once part of a single zone, which fragmented as it

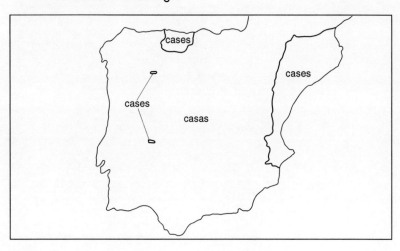

Figure 3.2   Isogloss demarcating Peninsular zones of *cases* vs *casas*

contracted, since some parts of the zone (no doubt those parts whose contacts with the outside were weakest) were more resistant than others to the incoming feature (plural in {-as}).[30]

Although it is frequently possible to establish that an isogloss is currently moving, and the direction of its movement, there are also cases in which an isogloss is seen to be static. Such cases most notably include isoglosses which have receded towards a frontier, beyond which the prestige centre which drives it has no power to attract further imitation. This was the situation envisaged in **2.5.2**, and can be illustrated by those isoglosses which have come to coincide with the French–Spanish frontier in the central Pyrenees (Guiter 1983).

Also to be included among the now static isoglosses are those whose position was determined by movement of population (see **2.5.2** and **4.1.3**). Some of the superimposed isoglosses which separate Castilian features from Portuguese features from the Douro/Duero to the mouth of the Guadiana owe their position to two similar but distinct but parallel movements of population. As the county of Portugal (from 1143 the kingdom of Portugal) expanded its territory southwards down the western coastal region of the Peninsula, people from what is now the northern third of Portugal were resettled in more and more southerly areas, within frontiers fixed by conquest or treaty. These settlers would be speakers of varieties from that segment of the Peninsular dialect continuum which belonged to the Oporto area and adjacent zones and their varieties of speech would be subject to the

processes of dialect levelling which are implicit in all cases of resettlement (see **3.1.3**). Meanwhile, or a little later, a separate resettlement
process was taking place in neighbouring territories to the east; there,
speakers of varieties belonging to a separate segment of the Peninsular
dialect continuum (perhaps principally from the Leon and Burgos
regions, but no doubt encompassing speakers from many other north-
central zones) were subject to dialect levelling as they resettled areas
adjacent to those of Portugal.[31] The result of these parallel processes
was that the isoglosses which track the differences of speech between
these two groups of settlers coincided with a political frontier, since the
western group did not settle east of the Portuguese frontier and the
inland group did not settle to the west of that frontier.

It is also implicit in this argument that, in the period since the
resettlement of these areas, contacts across the frontier have been less
frequent and important than those which linked people on either side
of the frontier with their respective prestige centres, to the west
(Lisbon) and to the east (Toledo). Otherwise, processes of accommodation between speakers on either side of the frontier would ensure
increasing similarity of speech, a result which would be demonstrated
on the map by non-coincidence between the relevant isoglosses and
the frontier. This pattern is not in fact observed.[32]

To exemplify this process of dialect-boundary creation, let us take
the case of two isoglosses which reflect the separation of Portuguese
varieties from those spoken on the eastern side of the Portuguese frontier. On the one hand, we shall consider the isogloss which separates
those (western) zones where the diphthong [óu̯] is used (in words like
pouco) from those (central and eastern) zones where corresponding
words contain [ó] (*poco*, etc.). On the other hand, we shall take the
isogloss marking the extent of those varieties which show undiphthongized [ɛ́] (in words like *pedra*) by contrast with those varieties which
show the diphthong [jé] (in *piedra*, etc.). These two isoglosses are well
separated in the north of the Peninsula, cutting through the dialect
continuum with widely different trajectories, and with the first well to
the east of the second at the north coast (see, for example, Zamora
1967, map between pp. 84 and 85). However, they converge (with one
another and with a number of other isoglosses) at a point on the
Portuguese–Spanish frontier, below the Portuguese town of Miranda
do Douro, and thereafter coincide exactly, following the frontier down
to the Atlantic at the mouth of the Guadiana, except where they jointly
diverge eastward from the frontier to encompass three enclaves on

Spanish territory, resulting from redrawing of the frontier, where the varieties spoken have a predominance of Portuguese features (including lack of diphthongs in words like *pedra*, but the diphthong [óu̯] in words like *pouco*). This near-coincidence between isoglosses and frontier (total coincidence if one takes account of frontier-shifts) is brought about in the way discussed above: whereas the settlers on the western side of the frontier spoke varieties which (probably) all lacked diphthongization in words like *pedra* and all showed [óu̯] in words like *pouco*, settlers on the east of the line came from a variety of areas, some of which were characterized by both of these features (e.g., El Bierzo, etc., with *pedra, poucu*), some by only the second (e.g., Astorga, etc., with *piedra, poucu*), and the majority probably from areas where neither feature existed (with *piedra, poco*). On the west, then, there was unanimity in this respect, while on the east dialectal variety was reduced, through normal contact processes during resettlement (see Section **3.3**), in favour of the *piedra, poco* variants.[33] Because the two resettlement processes took place under the aegis of separate kingdoms, opportunities for linguistic accommodation between speakers on one side of the frontier with those on the other were few and did not result in any adaptation with regard to these features. The isoglosses separating the two traditions have therefore continued to coincide with the frontier.

Other cases of static isoglosses are not due to movement of populations, but to the fact that both features separated by the isogloss are recessive, challenged equally by a standard feature. Thus, the isogloss which today separates, on the east, the use of an initial aspirate /h/ in words like *hierro, hilar, huso*, from the corresponding use of /f/, on the west (i.e., *fierro, filar, fusu*), runs close to the river Sella in eastern Asturias (Figure **3.3**): Menéndez Pidal (1964: 214, 219) claims that this isogloss reflects an ancient, pre-Roman ethnic boundary, one which separated the Astures (who learned and maintained the Latin labiodental fricative /f/) to the east, from the Cantabrians, a group who (like the Vascones) lacked any labiodentals in their native phonemic inventory and consequently had difficulty in imitating the Latin phoneme, replacing it with their most similar native phoneme, namely /h/.[34] Whether or not this explanation for the innovation can be sustained, it is arguably true that the /f/ vs /h/ isogloss has remained static for centuries. The explanation for this lack of movement no doubt lies in the fact that, in the class of words concerned (descended from Latin words displaying initial F-) the [f] and the [h]

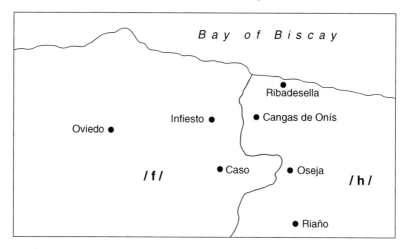

Figure 3.3   Isogloss separating /f/ and /h/ in *filar~hilar*, etc.

variants have equally low prestige, belonging now only to the speech of the uneducated rural population. Neither variant is liable to be imitated by those who do not already use it, which is to say that there is no longer any power to drive the isogloss in any direction, a power which has been lacking for centuries. What is happening, by contrast, is that the standard variant, namely [Ø] (i.e., absence of initial consonant), is steadily encroaching upon both [f] and [h] as the urban/educated pronunciation is increasingly adopted by rural speakers.[35] Once this process is complete, that is, once every rural word of the type /filár/ or /hilár/ has been replaced by the standard type /ilár/ *hilar*, the /f/ vs /h/ isogloss will be obliterated without having moved for centuries.

3.3   Social networks and speed of change

Having considered the way in which linguistic innovations travel through geographical space, or may be impeded from so doing, we turn our attention to the factors which govern the propagation of innovations through social space, that is, how a feature which originates in one part of the social matrix may spread through other parts of the matrix, or be inhibited from doing so. It should be remembered that the basic mechanisms in both cases are identical: innovations are passed from one individual to another through the accommodation processes which occur in face-to-face contacts. Occasionally, a feature which has been adopted temporarily under such conditions may become part of the normal linguistic behaviour of the recipient, and may therefore be passed on to other individuals.

The ultimate problem facing historical linguistics is starkly posed by Weinreich, Labov and Herzog in the following way:

> Why do changes in structural features take place in a particular language at a given time, but not in other languages with the same feature, or in the same language at other times? This actuation problem may be regarded as the very heart of the matter. (1968: 102)

But as James Milroy admits (1992: 20), we are no nearer to solving this problem of causation than we are to forecasting whether it will rain in a specific place at a given time. Indeed, the ability to make linguistic forecasts, an ability which would follow from the solution of the actuation problem, may be totally beyond reach. However, there have been significant advances in our understanding of the factors which encourage or inhibit the spread of innovations, and which therefore govern the speed at which linguistic change takes place. These advances have come chiefly through the application to language of social network theory, especially in the work carried out by Lesley and James Milroy in the UK and by William Labov in the US.

Social relations between individuals can be represented by the metaphor of the net, in which the knots stand for individual people and the strings represent the connections between individuals. However, unlike real nets, in which two knots are connected by only one string, social networks reveal that two individuals may be connected by several or many links, such ties consisting of features such as the following: family relatedness, living in the same neighbourhood, having the same place of work, attending the same place of worship, spending leisure time in the same places. Two individuals who share one such link are said to be joined by a *weak tie*, while two who share many links are bound by a *strong tie*.

It is noted that groups of individuals who are mutually linked by strong ties exhibit behaviour in which traditional values are constantly reinforced. This self-reinforcing aspect of the behaviour of closely knit groups extends to language, so that such groups will be marked by traditional forms of speech and will be resistant to changes originating outside the group. However, all strongly tied groups have connections with other individuals and groups, typically by simple or weak ties.

What is more, it follows from this discussion that social change, including linguistic change, can be propagated from group to group only via such weak ties.

The significance of these considerations, from the point of view of language history, is that communities which are dominated by strongly tied sub-groups are notably more resistant to linguistic change than are those communities in which most individuals are linked to others via weak ties (see Milroy and Milroy 1985). Work by Lesley Milroy on the working-class speech of Belfast (reported in Milroy 1987) helps to explain not only resistance to change of urban working-class dialects, but also helps to demonstrate (through the study of the effects of the movement of people into Belfast from the Ulster countryside) that when migration from one area to another takes place this inevitably leads to the breaking of strong ties, to the dominance of weak ties, and at least some delay in the formation of new tightly knit groups. That is, migration leads to the dominance of weak ties in a community, and dominance of weak ties fosters linguistic change. Societies on the move are likely to experience more linguistic change, even substantially more change, than those which remain rooted for long periods of time in the same place.

How are these observations related to the matter of change in Spanish? The principle that movement fosters change can be demonstrated repeatedly in the history of Castilian, and in fact has already attracted our attention on a number of occasions. In discussing dialect contacts (3.1), we have stressed that throughout the Middle Ages and well into the modern period, speakers of Castilian have been on the move, successively resettling areas in the centre and south of the Peninsula, as the Reconquest of Islamic Spain progressed southwards, then continuing the process overseas in the Canaries, the Balkans (see also Chapter 6), and the Americas (Chapter 5). Not only that, but the expansion of Madrid in the latter part of the sixteenth century was achieved by substantial immigration from the north (3.1.3). We have emphasized that the dialect mixing which resulted from these movements of population had certain predictable results (typically, levelling and simplification) on the language of the communities concerned.

What interests us in this section is that the social history of medieval and early modern Castile, involving repeated dissolution of strong ties between members of northern communities, and the creation of new communities (in resettled areas) dominated by weak social ties, leads us to predict a faster than average pace of linguistic change in Castilian.

This rapid pace of change did not pass unnoticed by the great historians of Spanish, but it went unexplained. Menéndez Pidal (1964: 472–82) discussed together the openness to change seen in the Castilian language and certain essentially social changes: the rejection of written Roman law (codified in the *Fuero Juzgo*) in favour of local, customary law; the lessening of social stratification (there were fewer serfs in Castile, and only one degree of nobility, rather than the two that existed in more conservative Leon); the early adoption of Carolingian script (rather than the traditional Visigothic script); political resistance to backward-looking Leon; openness to Moorish customs in matters of dress, etc. It is true that these are social changes which, for the most part, affected the wealthier sector of Castilian society, but we can perhaps infer from them that social change was also occurring at other levels, spurred by the more radical movement of population that occurred in Castilian territory, by contrast with other Romance-speaking areas, including most other Peninsular territories. The movements of population, we can speculate, fostered a society structured in terms of weak ties, along which linguistic innovations were free to spread. These innovations, usually identified as evidence of the 'revolutionary' character of Castilian, appear to have spread successively and rapidly through Castilian society in the period of the early Reconquest. They include the following:[36]

1   Use of /h/ or /Ø/ in the class of words descended from those which contained /f/ in standard Latin (for example, using modern spelling, *hablar*, *ahogar*, etc.), by contrast with the retention of /f/ elsewhere in the Peninsula.

2   Use of /ʒ/ in the class of words descended from those which in Latin contained the consonant groups -c'l-, -g'l-, -lj- (e.g., OCULU > *ojo* 'eye', TEGULA > *teja* 'tile', FOLIA > *hoja* 'leaf') by contrast with the /ʎ/ used in most other areas.[37]

3   Use of /tˢ/ (later /θ/) in the class of words descended from those which in Latin contained -scj- or -sc- followed by a front vowel (e.g., ASCIATA > OSp. *açada* > *azada* 'hoe', MISCERE > *mecer* 'to wag, rock'), by contrast with the /ʃ/ used in other parts of the Peninsula.

4   Loss of the initial phoneme in the class of words whose Latin etyma showed word-initial I- or G- followed by an unstressed front vowel (e.g., *IENUĀRIU (for IANUĀRIU) > *enero* 'January', GENESTA > *hiniesta* 'broom'), by contrast with remaining

varieties of Hispano-Romance, which retain a palatal consonant in this class of words.

It should be noted that many of the cases examined in **3.1.3** and **3.1.4** as instances of simplification and levelling under conditions of dialect contact can also be seen as instances of the enhanced rate of change observable in Castilian, since the resettlements which led to dialect mixture also resulted (we must presume) in the predominance of weak social ties in the new communities, conditions which we know promote rapid change.

In this context, it is worth emphasizing the correlation which exists, among the totality of the present-day varieties of Peninsular Romance, between the geographical latitude to which a given variety belongs and the degree of change to which it has been subjected. Certainly this effect is most notable in the Castilian zone, where least innovation (i.e., greatest conservatism) is seen in Cantabria and increasingly greater degrees of innovation are seen as one progresses through Old Castile, New Castile, and reaches Andalusia, perhaps owing to the progressively larger and more complex movements of population which took place in Castilian territory, by contrast with other Peninsular territories. Nevertheless, similar patterns (of increasing degrees of innovation as one examines more and more southerly varieties) are observable on both flanks of the Peninsula. In Portugal, it is an oft-repeated observation that the dialects of Entre-Douro-e-Minho and of Trás-os-Montes are the most conservative, with increasing degrees of change visible in the central areas (including Lisbon), and with the greatest degree of innovation to be found in the varieties spoken in the Algarve.[38] A similar but not identical pattern can be seen on the eastern side of the Peninsula, where the most conservative varieties of Catalan are to be found in the Pyrenees, especially in northern Lérida, and the most innovatory in the Valencia area.[39]

3.4 Direction of change through society

Linguistic changes that gain ground in society do so by being imitated and adopted by an increasing number of individuals, through face-to-face contacts, and, as we have seen (**3.3**), such imitation necessarily takes place between individuals who are connected by weak social ties. Our concern here is to consider the ways in which changes are transmitted from one part of the social matrix to another, and in this consideration we find further confirmation that change is almost exclusively propagated via weak ties. Pairs or groups of individuals who are linked by strong ties, that is those who are joined by multiplex bonds, of necessity belong to the same segment of the social matrix: they have similar jobs, live in the same locality, may be members of the same family, enjoy the same pastimes, and so on. Because of the mutually reinforcing nature of these relationships, such individuals are overwhelmingly likely to use closely similar varieties of speech. Any feature which belongs to a group with other social characteristics can only reach the group under consideration by travelling along ties which link one group with another, links which must be predominantly simple or weak, since a group of individuals who share many social characteristics with another group are likely to be linked to the latter by the multiplex contacts that these similarities imply.

For an innovation to gain ground within a social group, it has to be adopted by some lead-individual within the group, after which it may be quickly adopted by the other members of the group (Milroy and Milroy 1985). But more important from our point of view are the reasons why innovations pass from group to group, that is, why one individual imitates a feature of the speech of another individual to whom he or she is weakly linked. Although it seems reasonably clear that not all innovations are equally likely to spread (the alternative view is that not all innovations are equally likely to *occur* in a given speech variety, but, having occurred, all have the same potentiality to spread), the main driving force behind the spread of any feature is the relative prestige of the individuals involved. Prestige is, of course, not a linguistic matter, but consists of a number of traits (which we shall not attempt to enumerate) possessed in differing degrees by any specific individual;[40] this prestige may then be associated with any particular linguistic item or set of items used by that individual, increasing its likelihood (in differing degrees) of being imitated by others.

If, as seems to be the case, the main or only reason for the spread of a feature is the prestige associated with it, it should not be forgotten that prestige may be overt or covert, and that social spread may therefore be top-down or bottom-up.

3.4.1 Downward change

The kind of imitation of linguistic innovations which is due to the overt prestige of the individuals already using such innovations is usually viewed as spreading 'down' through society. Thus one is more likely to imitate a feature which is heard to belong to the speech of an individual who is more powerful, rich, etc., than oneself, than to imitate a feature heard in the speech of someone 'lower' than oneself in the social pecking order. This 'downward' spread of linguistic change seems to be common in all societies, and has been amply documented in sociolinguistic studies such as William Labov's now classic study (1966) of the downward spread of post-vocalic /ɾ/ in the previously non-rhotic speech of New York.

3.4.2   Upward change

Scarcely less usual, and evidently important, is the process by which changes are propagated 'upwards' through society, from less to more privileged groups. Certain styles of behaviour, prominent among which are those exhibiting 'street credibility' and worldly wisdom, although they are exhibited by individuals who have a small share in wealth, education, etc., may nevertheless possess prestige, of a covert kind. Such styles, which of course include features of linguistic behaviour, may therefore be viewed positively and imitated not only by those of the same social level, but by those at 'higher' points on the socio-economic continuum. A case in point which is frequently cited in this context is the spread of the diphthong /wá/ through French society following the Revolution, at the expense of /wé/ in words like *roi, moi*. Previously a low-prestige feature of Parisian French, this item became associated with the newly acquired prestige of working-class social styles and was more widely imitated, perhaps out of a sense of solidarity with the ideals of the Revolution (see von Wartburg 1958: 229, and, for the spread of lower-class Parisian features in general, Lodge 1993: 228–9).

A feature of pronunciation which appears to be spreading in this way in current Peninsular Spanish is the weakening of syllable-final /s/ to an aspirate articulation, that is, the pronunciation [aβíʰpaʰ], [éʰtoʰ], [móʰkaʰ] in words like *avispas, estos, moscas*, etc. (see **4.1.7.2.4**). Attested from the sixteenth century in the south of Spain, and presumably in use there rather earlier in humble social groups, this feature begins to be noted in central Spain in the nineteenth century, specifically in working-class Madrid varieties, and was conceivably brought to the capital by immigrants from the south. It surfaces, for example, in the novels of Benito Pérez Galdós, in cases where he is portraying the speech of individuals from this background (Lapesa 1980: 502).[41] Since then, it appears to have advanced somewhat through the social matrix, so that, even if it is still mostly absent from educated Madrid speech, it is no longer confined to working-class varieties.

3.5 Lexical diffusion

So far we have discussed the spread of linguistic features through geographical and social space as if each innovation simultaneously affected every lexical item or syntagma that was eligible for that change (by offering the specific conditions required for such a change to take place). However, such a view is a simplification, and we now need to make clear that innovations proceed through space and through society *word by word*. This is what is meant by lexical diffusion, which emphasizes that during the spread of any change some words are affected before others, or, to look at the process from the other angle, some words are more resistant to change than others. Those which are more resistant to change will usually be those lexical items which signify aspects of reality which are central to the concerns of the community whose speech is potentially open to the change in question. This differential diffusion of sound change has been evident at least since the publication of the *Atlas linguistique de la France* (*ALF* 1903–10); the maps in Jaberg (1959), based upon the *ALF*, demonstrate the way in which, at the beginning of this century, the change by which /k/ (in the reflexes of Latin words containing initial CA-, such as CANTĀRE, CANDĒLA, CAMPU) is replaced by /ʃ/ (standard French *chanter* 'to sing', *chandelle* 'candle', *champ* 'field', etc.), in northeastern and in southern France, has progressed to a different extent in the case of each word examined. The isoglosses which reflect the advance of /ʃ/ at the expense of /k/ do not coincide exactly, and are sometimes markedly divergent, and it is evident that the rate of advance is more rapid in words associated with supralocal concerns and least rapid in the case of words closely related with local lifestyles, such as names of farm implements and farm activities.

  Such lexical diffusion of change is, of course, evident also in Spanish. The isogloss which, in Cantabria, separates retention of initial /h/ in *hacer* 'to do, make' from its deletion (i.e., the isogloss which

separates /haθér/ from /aθér/) is to be found further to the west than
the isogloss which separates these two pronunciations in *hacha* 'axe'
(Penny 1984). The data provided by *ALEA* (1962–73: maps 1548–50,
1553, 1556) reveal a similar word-by-word retreat of /h/ in western
Andalusia. In the words *hiel* 'bile', *hollín* 'soot', *hoz* 'sickle', and *moho*
'mould', /h/ appears in practically all the localities studied in western
Andalusia, sometimes recorded alongside a form without /h/. By contrast with words such as these, which refer to concrete notions, the
abstract *hambre* 'hunger' appears to be much more open to influence
from the standard, showing a large predominance of /h/-less forms, in
the same area of western Andalusia.

What has also become evident through work on lexical diffusion
(see Wang and Cheng 1977, and especially Wang 1969) is that some of
the words eligible for a change may *never* be affected by it. A residue of
unaffected words may be created when two or more competing
changes are taking place in a community in overlapping time periods.
While the first change is in progress, and part but not all of the eligible
words have been affected by it, a second change may affect one of the
conditioning factors which make words eligible for the first change,
thereby removing their eligibility for it. We may illustrate the way in
which a residue is produced by examining the interplay between two
changes in Castilian:

1   The already much-cited change of Latin f to /h/.
2   The process of diphthongization whereby stressed short ŏ of
    Latin, having been modified to mid-low [ɔ], becomes [wé] (PONTE
    > [pɔ́nte] > *puente* 'bridge').

One view of the first change is that it is conditioned by a following syllabic nucleus, which in Latin and Spanish must always be a vowel and
can never be a consonant or a glide.[42] The second change is conditioned only by presence of word stress and is unaffected by any syllable-
initial elements that precede the vowel in question.

Let us begin by examining the circumstance in which the two
changes do not overlap, and there is no residue. In some varieties of
Castilian, the northernmost ones, change (1) must have affected all or
almost all eligible words before change (2) spread into the area. As a
result, all of the words in Table **3.9** (in which f immediately precedes
the syllabic nucleus) had been affected. However, the words of the
pattern shown in Table **3.10**, in which [f] is not pre-nuclear, could not
be affected by this change. When change (2) began to affect stressed [ɔ],

FŪSU	>	[húso]	'spindle'
FONTE	>	[hɔ́nte]	'spring'
FAMINE	>	[hámne]	'hunger'
FEMINA	>	[hémna]	'female'
FĪCU	>	[híku]	'fig'

Table 3.9   Early development in Cantabria of Latin words containing pre-nuclear [f]

FRONTE	>	[frɔ́nte]	'forehead'
FRIGIDU	>	[frído]	'cold'

Table 3.10   Early development in Cantabria of Latin words containing [fr]

it simply converted [hɔ́nte] and [frɔ́nte] to [hwénte] and [frwénte], but did not otherwise affect the patterning of these groups of words.[43] Following the later adjustment [frwénte] > [frénte], these pronunciations have remained unchanged and are today preserved in the rural speech of western Cantabria and eastern Asturias (Rodríguez-Castellano 1946, Penny 1984). In this area, then, all the eligible words have been affected by both changes.

A different scenario is seen in Castilian varieties spoken to the south of Cantabria. There the two changes interfere with one another and produce a residue of words unaffected by change (1). In the Burgos area, as Menéndez Pidal's masterly examination of place-names shows (1964: 226–7), change (1) was later to begin, and began to spread from the north at a time when change (2) had already begun. In this area, there must still have been competition between innovatory [fwénte] and conservative [fɔ́nte] at the time [f] began to give way to [h] in immediately pre-nuclear position, so that the outcome was variation between [fwénte] and [hɔ́nte]. As the alternation between [wé] and [ɔ́] was gradually resolved in favour of [wé], so the variation between [fwénte] and [hɔ́nte] was resolved into competition between [fwénte] and [hwénte].

In the Burgos area, then, the change [f] > [h] has left a residue of unaffected words (*fuente, fuera, fuelle, fuerte, fuego*, etc.), although it has to be added that the competition between these forms and their alternants ([hwénte], [hwéra], [hwéʎe], [hwérte], [hwéɣo], etc.) has still not been resolved. Rural speech in this area (and in many other areas of

Castile, Andalusia, and America) maintains the aspirated variants (using a pronunciation identical with the local pronunciation of words like *juego*), while the labiodental variants have become increasingly identified with urban/educated varieties and were ultimately the forms chosen as the standard ones in the later Middle Ages.[44]

4   Variation in Spain

We have seen in Chapter 2 that all languages exist in a state of orderly heterogeneity, whether one is considering the spatial, the social or the diachronic aspects of variation, and in Chapter 3 we have considered the way in which such organized variation frequently determines the way in which language change proceeds. Many of these general issues have been illustrated with data taken from the Peninsular languages, but in the present chapter we come to a more systematic consideration of the distribution of linguistic features in the Spanish Peninsula. First we shall consider geographical variation, seeking an explanation for the main patterns of distribution of these features across the Peninsula. Then we shall turn to social aspects of variation, where reasons for particular patterns of heterogeneity will be hard to find, but where we shall study some of the many striking instances in which linguistic and social variation are correlated.

4.1 Geographical variation

The present geographical distribution of features in the Peninsula has been determined by two sets of circumstances, namely the existence of a northern dialect continuum, and the territorial expansion of northern varieties which accompanied the reconquest of Islamic Spain. The northern dialect continuum stretches across the northern third, approximately, of the Peninsula, and is part of the Romance dialect continuum which extends from northwestern Spain into France and thence into Belgium, Switzerland and Italy (see sections **1.1.1** and **4.1.2**). Certain varieties from this continuum were projected southwards through the Peninsula, as their speakers resettled newly acquired territories, and were subject to a process of dialect contact and mixture (see Section **3.1**), which involved not only different northern varieties, but also varieties of Mozarabic (**4.1.1**). As this southward expansion progressed, processes of focusing and standardization (see Chapter 7) introduced breaks in the east–west continuum (see **2.5.2**), so that, in the southern two-thirds of the Peninsula, there occurred a superimposition of isoglosses, a development which produced sharp boundaries between a western or Portuguese set of varieties, a central or Castilian set, and an eastern or Catalan range.

4.1.1 Mozarabic

Between the establishment of Latin in the Peninsula and the Islamic invasions, which took place from AD 711 onwards, and with the exception of the Basque-speaking region (then much more extensive than today), the entire Peninsula must have been covered by a dialect continuum. The northern Peninsular dialects are the only segments of this continuum which have survived to the present day. Following the imposition of Islamic power on the southern two-thirds of the Peninsula, the Hispano-Romance dialect continuum did not simply shrink, since Romance dialects continued in use for centuries in Islamic Spain, spoken as everyday vernaculars by Christians, Muslims and Jews. These varieties we now refer to as the *Mozarabic* dialects, and they have no direct modern descendants.[1] They either ceased to be used as their speakers adopted Arabic, following conversion of families to Islam (a process which became important only from the twelfth century onwards, as Islamic Spain was subjected to increasing Islamic fundamentalism), or they contributed to the dialect mixture which was created as the areas where they were spoken became incorporated into the expanding Christian states. Their effects upon such dialect mixtures have not been fully assessed, partly because our knowledge of their features is so limited. The amount of written evidence which reveals the nature of the Mozarabic dialects is exceedingly restricted, because these varieties were spoken in areas where the prestige standard for writing was Arabic, and because they were in use at a period when, as almost everywhere in Europe, there was no orthography capable of reflecting vernacular speech. Occasional Mozarabic texts, mostly poems, and written in Arabic or Hebrew script, together with small numbers of words and phrases contained in Hispano-Arabic texts, and limited evidence of post-reconquest Mozarabic (sometimes isolated words in Latin-alphabet documents, but sometimes entire notarial documents written in Arabic script), combine to provide us with a sketch of some of the phonological, morphological and lexical characteristics of these southern Hispano-Romance varieties.[2]

The Mozarabic dialects formed part of a continuum with the dialects of Christian Spain until the Reconquest disrupted this continuity by overlaying the northernmost Mozarabic dialects with new, mixed varieties, and thereby providing a dialect boundary where none had previously existed. So it is not surprising that southern varieties should show features which were also present in parts, often large parts, of the north. Such distribution implies that the features concerned were to be found both in the north and in the centre and south before the Islamic invasions of the early eighth century, whether these features were innovations which were then advancing or archaisms which were then retreating. Thus, Galmés (1983: 67–116) concludes that the Mozarabic of Toledo showed the following characteristics:

1   Unconditioned diphthongization of Latin stressed short ĕ and ŏ: HERBA > Moz. *yerbāt.o,* derived from **yerba* (like Cast. *hierba,* Leon. *yerba,* Arag. *yerba, yarba,* but unlike Gal.-Ptg. *erva,* Cat. *herba)* 'grass'; HORTA > Moz. *werţa, warţa* (like Cast. *huerta,* Leon. *güerta, guorta,* Arag. *güerta, guarta,* but unlike Gal.-Ptg. *horta,* Cat. *horta)* 'garden'.

2   Diphthongization of Latin stressed short ŏ when followed by a glide arising in the groups -LJ-, -C'L-, -G'L-: OCULU > Moz. *walyo, welyo* (like Leon. *güeyu, guoyu,* Arag. *güello,* Cat. *ull* (< **[wóȷ̯ʎ]),* but unlike Gal.-Ptg. *ollo, olho,* Cast. *ojo)* 'eye'.

3   Distinction of final /-u/ (< Lat. -ŭ), in masc. sing., from /-o/ (< Lat. -ō), in masc. plur., as in Leonese (but by contrast with Galician–Portuguese, Castilian, Aragonese and Catalan).

4   Loss of final vowels: FEBRUĀRIU > Moz. *febrayr, febreyr* (like Cat. *febrer,* Arag. *febrer,* but unlike Gal.-Ptg. *fevereiro, febreiro,* Leon. *febreiru, febreru,* Cast. *febrero)* 'February'.

5   Maintenance of falling diphthongs /ei/ or /ai/ (and perhaps of /ou/): FEBRUĀRIU > Moz. *febrayr, febreyr* (like Gal.-Ptg. *fevereiro, febreiro,* Western Leon. *febreiru,* but unlike Central and Eastern Leon. *febreru,* Cast. *febrero,* Arag. *febrer,* Cat. *febrer)* 'February'.

6   Preservation of /f/ (< Lat. F): FĪLIA > Moz. *filya* (like Gal.-Ptg. *filla, filha,* Western and Central Leon. *fiya,* Arag. *filla,* Cat. *filla,* but unlike Eastern Leon. /híya/, Cast. *hija)* 'daughter'.

7   Maintenance of the Latin initial groups PL-, CL-, FL-: PLANA > Moz.

plana (like Arag., Cat. *plana,* but unlike Ptg. *chã,* Gal. *chá,* Western Leon. *chana,* Central and Eastern Leon., Cast. *llana*) 'flat, plain'.

8 Maintenance of / ʎ/ resulting from -LJ-, -C'L-, -G'L-: OCULU > Moz. *walyo, welyo* (like Gal.-Ptg. *ollo, olho,* Leon. *güeyu, guoyu* (earlier *güellu, güollu),* Arag. *güello,* Cat. *ull,* but unlike Cast. *ojo*) 'eye'.

9 Maintenance of the Latin group -MB-: COLUMBA > Moz. *qolomba* (like Gal.-Ptg. *pombo,* Leon. *palomba* (< PALUMBA), but unlike Cast. *paloma,* Arag. *paloma,* Cat. *colom*) 'pigeon, dove'.

10 Maintenance of the /t/ in the Latin groups -CT-, -(U)LT-, competing with their modification to /tʃ/: CULTELLU + -ARIU > Moz. *qutilyero* 'cutler', LACTŪCA > Moz. *lechuga* 'lettuce' (compare LACTE > Gal.-Ptg. *leite,* Western Leon. *lleiti, tseiti,* Arag. *llet,* Cat. *llet,* versus Central and Eastern Leon. *llechi,* Cast. *leche* 'milk').

11 Use of fem. plur. {-es} < Lat. -ĀS: *magraneš,* pl. of *magrana* 'pomegranate' (compare Lat. CASĀS > Central Asturian *cases,* Cat. *cases,* versus Gal.-Ptg., Leon., Cast., Arag. *casas* 'houses').[3]

In the period between AD 711 and the disappearance of distinctively Southern Hispano-Romance several centuries later, there must have been many innovations which arose at different places and times in the Mozarabic continuum. However, apart from lexical innovations (largely, borrowings from Arabic) few have come to light. As a result, almost all those who have studied the Mozarabic dialects have characterized them as being overwhelmingly conservative. Some have even gone so far as to claim that Mozarabic is so archaic that it presents us with a picture, frozen in time, of what Peninsular Romance was like before 711. Such a view is, of course, untenable, since these varieties of speech, like all other examples of living language, were inevitably subject to change. However, even allowing for the highly imperfect and incomplete picture of Mozarabic which has reached us, there do seem to be reasons for claiming that the pace of change in Southern Peninsular Romance was rather slow. Such relative lack of innovation can be related to the circumstances under which those varieties of which we have knowledge were spoken; although speakers of Romance are known to have existed at all social levels, the Mozarabic dialects which were (albeit partially) reflected in writing were, it would seem, those of urban groups. The evidence we have of post-Reconquest Mozarabic comes almost entirely from urban ghettos in cities such as Toledo (see Hernández 1989), Valencia, and Seville, and these circumstances may have been typical of those in which most Mozarabic-speakers lived in earlier centuries, since what evidence we have suggests that Arabic-speakers preferred the countryside (Entwistle 1962: 111). If it can be confirmed that the Mozarabic we know is the product of urban ghettos, then we have an explanation for its conservatism. Undisturbed urban communities (as we have seen in Section **3.3**) typically consist of networks of individuals whose interrelationships are multiplex, and in societies dominated by such strong social ties it is normal to find resistance to linguistic change.

At all events, it is clear from the evidence presented above that some features which occupied part of the northern dialect continuum also occupied part of the Mozarabic continuum. This continuity of features across the political frontier between Islamic and Christian Spain springs from the fact that all of the features concerned were already widespread in the Peninsula (and often elsewhere) before the existence of the frontier. Indeed, although the frontier was not a total barrier to communication, it is important to note that we have no evidence that any feature was spread from any point in the northern dialect continuum in such a way that it crossed the frontier and was adopted by southern varieties, or vice versa. Thus, the northwestern innovation which consists in the deletion of intervocalic -L- and -N- (e.g., SALĪRE > Ptg. *sair* 'to leave', LŪNA > Ptg. *lua* 'moon') is nowhere attested in Mozarabic, including those varieties spoken in what was to become, as the Reconquest progressed, central and southern Portugal. If these areas now show the results of this deletion, as they do, this results from the successful emergence of this feature from the dialect mixture which resulted from the resettlement of these areas by people from elsewhere, including many speakers of northwestern varieties (those of northern Portugal and Galicia).

All cases of agreement between north and south, it would therefore appear, are cases of preservation of a feature already shared before the Islamic invasion, rather than cases of participation in an innovation which has spread from north to south or from south to north since that time. Each feature that we can examine occupies, naturally, an area which is unique to that feature. Thus we have seen that examination of the Mozarabic of Toledo provides evidence that in an ill-defined central region of the Peninsula (before the local varieties of Romance were submerged in the dialect mixture which followed upon the Reconquest of that area) certain features were in use which were shared with varieties spoken to the north of the frontier. We should not lose sight of the fact that a large number of features were shared by *all* varieties, north and south, although these cases are inherently uninteresting. More interesting are the cases in which a feature known to exist in part of the Mozarabic continuum also appears in part or parts of the northern continuum. The cases listed above (pp. 76–7) demonstrate various kinds of continuity across the frontier. Thus feature (1) (unconditioned diphthongization of Latin stressed short ĕ and ŏ) shows continuity between the Mozarabic of Toledo (together with some other, but not all, Mozarabic varieties) and a broad segment of the northern continuum, from which the westernmost and the easternmost varieties are excluded. Feature (5) (maintenance of falling diphthongs /ei/ or /ai/), and feature (9) (maintenance of the Latin group -MB-) show agreement between most varieties of Mozarabic and a western segment of the northern continuum, while feature (3) (distinction of final /-u/ (< Lat. -ŭ), in the masculine singular, from /-o/ (< Lat. -ō), in the masculine plural) connects the Mozarabic of Toledo with only a small segment of the northern continuum, the part corresponding approximately to Asturias and Cantabria (**4.1.2.2**). By contrast, feature (4) (loss of final vowels) shows continuity only with the far northeast, and feature (7) (maintenance of the Latin initial groups PL-, CL-, FL-) appears in a broader northeastern area (La Rioja, Aragon, Catalonia) as well as in all Mozarabic.

Most revealing are those Mozarabic features which show continuity with two distinct segments of the northern continuum, leaving a central segment occupied by an innovation. This is the case of features (6) and (8) (preservation of /f/ (< Lat. F), and maintenance of /ʎ/ resulting from -LJ-, -c′L-, -G′L-), in which instances the areas of innovation (replacement of /f/ by /h/ or /Ø/, and of /ʎ/ by /ʒ/) are at first small, corresponding only to Cantabria and parts of northern Old Castile. Feature (10) (maintenance of the /t/ in the Latin groups -CT-, -(U)LT-) shows similar distribution of innovatory and conservative results, except that the segment of the northern continuum occupied by the innovation on this occasion includes not only Cantabria and northern Old Castile, but also adjacent parts of Asturias and Leon.

Finally, we find patterns which are in some sense mirror images of those just mentioned, ones in which the Mozarabic development is continuous with two separate segments of the northern continuum, but in which the unaffected northern areas preserve an earlier state of affairs. This is true of feature (2) (diphthongization of Latin stressed short ŏ when followed by a glide arising in the groups -LJ-, -c′L-, -G′L-), since both the northwest and the north-centre show no diphthongization, although the intervening segment (traditionally labelled 'Leonese') does so, as do the varieties of the northeast (Aragon and Catalonia). A similar pattern is seen in feature (11) (use of feminine plural {-es} < Lat. -ās contrasting with feminine singular {-a}); here, if Galmés (1983: 302–17) is right, the (frequent but not exclusive) Mozarabic feminine plural morpheme {-es} connects the Catalan and Asturian segments where the pattern *casa/cases* is also seen. See also Figure **3.2**, and Section **4.1.3**.

4.1.2   The northern Peninsular dialect continuum

There are no dialect boundaries to be observed as one progressively examines the linguistic varieties that occupy the northern third of the Peninsula (see **1.1.1** and **2.1**). Two or more isoglosses rarely, if ever, coincide; at most, the gradient of accumulating differences becomes a little steeper in some places than in others; that is, for a given distance there are more isoglosses to be crossed in some parts of the territory than in others. This intermeshing of varieties implies that any linguistically motivated division of the dialect continuum can be based on no more than a single isogloss at any one time. All other divisions can only be arbitrary, since they will not coincide with any observable linguistic reality. In particular, terms like *Galician, Leonese, Castilian*, etc., when used to distinguish one segment of the continuum from the rest, are motivated entirely by politico-historical considerations, such as where administrative boundaries and other frontiers now fall or once fell. They are at best a necessary convenience (since we often need to refer to portions of what is an amorphous reality), but at worst they are a dangerous fiction (since they suggest linguistic boundaries where none exist).

The sections that follow present a number of case-studies which examine aspects of the geographical variation evident in the northern Peninsula, and which emphasize the continuity which is everywhere observable.

4.1.2.1   Miranda do Douro

The independence of isoglosses from political frontiers and other boundaries is well exemplified by the varieties spoken in the area of Miranda do Douro, a town in northeastern Portugal which is separated from the Spanish province of Zamora by the international frontier, which here coincides with the River Douro/Duero. Many of the isoglosses which run, approximately north–south, through this part of the northwestern Peninsula do not coincide with the frontier, but run some way to the west of Miranda, each following its individual path (see map in Menéndez Pidal 1962a), but then drawing together some way south of the town and thereafter coinciding with the frontier (except where there have been changes in the frontier in recent centuries: this coincidence with the frontier, a result of the resettlements which followed upon the Reconquest, has been considered in Section **2.5.2** and will be studied in more detail in Section **4.1.7**).

Among the features listed by Leite de Vasconcellos (1900–1, 1970: 166) and Carvalho (1958) as characterizing the speech of Miranda, the following show continuity with the speech of Zamora (and districts further east) but differ from the features which characterize varieties spoken further to the west in Portugal:[4]

1   Latin stressed short ĕ and ŏ often become diphthongs (/ie/, /uø/), where /ø/ indicates a front mid rounded vowel: TERRA > *tierra*, BONU > [bwǿnu] (beside [bǿnu]) (compare Ptg. *terra, bom*) 'earth', 'good'. As a consequence of this process, the Mirandês dialects appear once to have had a five-phoneme vowel system, lacking the distinction of mid-low and mid-high vowels which characterizes the Portuguese seven-vowel system, although speakers now appear to have moved towards a seven-vowel system (Carvalho 1958: 102).

2   Diphthongization of Latin stressed short ŏ takes place when it is followed by a glide arising in the groups -LJ-, -C'L-, -G'L-: FOLIA > [fwøλa] 'leaf'.

3   Latin v- merges with B- as a bilabial: vīnu > /bíno/ (compare Ptg. *vinho*), 'wine'.

4   Intervocalic -N- remains unchanged (except in certain suffixes): RANA > *rana* (compare Ptg. *rã*) 'frog'.

5   Geminate -NN- > /ɲ/: ANNU > *anho* (compare Ptg. *ano*) 'year'.

6   The group -MN- > /ɲ/: SOMNU > *sonho* (compare Ptg. *sono*) 'sleep'.

7   Initial L- > /ʎ/: LŪNA > *lhuna* (compare Ptg. *lua*) 'moon'.

8   Geminate -LL- > /ʎ/: CABALLU > *cabalho* (compare Ptg. *cavalo*) 'horse'.

9   Diphthongization of Latin short ĕ occurs in the second- and third-persons singular of the present indicative, and in the imperfect indicative, of the verb *ser* 'to be': /jés/, /jé/, /jéɾa/, etc.

10 The third-person singular of rhizotonic preterites is marked by {-o}: DĪXIT > *dixo* (compare Ptg. *disse*) 'he said'.

This disparity between the isoglosses considered here, on the one hand, and the political frontier, on the other, has traditionally been expressed by claiming that '(Western) Leonese dialects are spoken in northeastern Portugal' (e.g., Menéndez Pidal 1962a: 19; Zamora 1967: 87). However, within the view of geographical variation presented in this book, and elsewhere, it is clear that the dialects of Miranda form part of the Northern Peninsular dialect continuum, and that they have attracted particular attention only because in certain salient respects they show greater similarity with varieties spoken in Spain than with those spoken in the rest of Portugal. Nevertheless, it is important not to lose sight of the fact that greater or lesser similarity of features between any given varieties implies stronger or weaker communication between their speakers, so that the history of communications in this area can be held at least partly responsible for the distribution of isoglosses there.[5]

Menéndez Pidal (1962a: 19–20) has identified what are probably the key factors of the communication history of this area.[6] In Roman times, Miranda belonged to the administrative region (*conventus*) based upon Astorga, to the north, and not to the region whose capital was Braga, to the west. These Roman administrative divisions were probably based upon pre-Roman ethnic divisions, and in turn formed the basis of the medieval ecclesiastical boundaries, which show that Miranda belonged to the diocese of Astorga (and not to that of Braga) until well after the creation of the Portuguese state, in the twelfth century, and the fixing of its political frontier at the River Duero. Even after the ecclesiastical boundaries were redrawn to coincide with the political frontier, contacts continued (and perhaps still continue) to be closer between Miranda and Spain than between Miranda and the rest of Portugal. Although the political frontier has been in place for 800 years, the local isoglosses have still not come to coincide with it, a nice example of the extreme slowness with which political events affect the distribution of linguistic features.

4.1.2.2 Cantabria

The autonomous region of Cantabria, formerly the province of Santander and otherwise known as La Montaña, occupies a segment approximately in the middle of the northern Peninsular dialect continuum, on the northern seaboard. The name *Cantabria*, in Roman and early medieval times, indicated an area somewhat larger than the present autonomous region, including not only La Montaña, but also Campoo,

Amaya, La Bureba and Castilla la Vieja (then small), and stretching, on some accounts, as far as La Rioja in one direction and central Leon in the other (Menéndez Pidal 1964: 482–83). Early medieval Cantabria therefore embraced, among its southern territories, the group of counties which gradually amalgamated as the expanded county of Castile, and whose speech displayed the features which, following their southward extension to Burgos (resettled in AD 884), contributed most substantially to the first Castilian *koiné* (see **4.1.2.3**). However, in the present discussion, we shall limit consideration to the area north of the Cantabrian mountains, the present Cantabria.

Our knowledge of the distribution of linguistic features in this part of the Peninsula has been considerably improved since the appearance of the *Atlas Lingüístico y Etnográfico de Cantabria* (*ALECa* 1995; see also Alvar 1977 [1980], 1981); we previously had to rely on studies of individual localities (Holmquist 1988, Penny 1970a, 1978) and on geographical studies of specific features or groups of features (García González 1978, 1981–2, 1982, Penny 1984, Rodríguez-Castellano 1954). What emerges from these studies is that the speech of Cantabria forms a bridge which links western Peninsular varieties with eastern varieties, and which runs north of the area (northern Burgos) where the most characteristic features of Castilian developed. This bridge bears some resemblance, but on a smaller scale, to the Mozarabic bridge which up to the thirteenth century similarly provided a link of continuity between east and west, except that the Mozarabic bridge was entirely washed away by the southward spread of Castilian features which came as a consequence of the resettlement of such regions as New Castile and Andalusia by communities whose speech was predominantly flavoured by varieties originating in the centre-north. By contrast, Cantabria was not subject to any such resettlement (quite the reverse, it was a constant source of emigration), and the link that its speech provides between east and west was not completely submerged by the tide flowing from the prestige centres further south, since this tide was of the more usual type, consisting of a gradual spread of central Castilian features northwards across the Cantabrian mountains, through face-to-face imitation of features rather than by movement of people. Other parts of this northern bridge, specifically La Rioja and Romance-speaking Navarre, show a greater erosion than the Cantabrian segment, reflecting stronger lines of communication leading northeast from Burgos than those that led northwards. What remains of this link can be traced in the Cantabrian area?

1   The final /-ɾ/ of infinitives is realized as /Ø/ when followed by a
    clitic (e.g., *me, te, lo, nos, se*): [miðíla] *medirla* 'to measure it'; [íβus]
    iros 'to go away' (2nd plur.) (Penny 1970a: 58; 1978: 45–6; 1984:
    maps 24–5). This feature extends from the west (Galician–
    Portuguese) through Asturias into Cantabria and the north of
    Old Castile (but not including the varieties spoken in the town of
    Burgos and its immediate environs, from which the standard lan-
    guage sprang) into La Rioja and Aragon (see Nagore 1977: 21).[7]
    Cantabria also reveals deletion of the final /-ɾ/ of infinitives
    when a definite article heads a following noun phrase (whether it
    is the subject or the direct object of the infinitive). Information
    from neighbouring areas on this sandhi feature is generally
    lacking.

2   A number of Cantabrian varieties display a contrast between final
    /-i/ and /-e/, although in some cases this contrast is now only
    visible through the effects of metaphony (see **4.1.2.5**), in that /-i/
    has historically given rise to metaphony while /-e/ has not (Penny
    1970a: 65; 1978: 47–8; 1984: map 8), after which the two final
    vowels merged. The classes of words displaying /-i/ are singular
    imperatives of -*er* and -*ir* verbs, the masculine singular forms of
    the demonstratives corresponding to standard *este* and *ese*, the
    first-person singular of rhizotonic preterites, together with a
    small and ill-defined group of nouns and adverbs corresponding
    to such standard words as *leche, tarde, noche,* etc. This state of
    affairs continues westward into northeastern Leon and eastern
    and central Asturias, where the phonological distinction between
    these two final vowels is often still evident on the surface (García
    Arias 1988: 45; Granda 1960: 85–114).[8] In the medieval period, this
    contrast of final vowels also extended eastwards into La Rioja
    (Alvar 1976: 61–2; Gulsoy 1969–70; Tilander 1937) and Aragon
    (Alvar 1953: 214; Tilander 1937: 4–5).

3   Distinction between final /-u/ and /-o/ is also fundamental to the
    phonology of Cantabrian varieties. Final /-u/ characterizes a
    large class of masculine singular count-nouns (as well as adjecti-
    val and pronominal forms which concord with such nouns), e.g.,
    /lóβu/ 'wolf', /guénu/ 'good', and in many areas (Penny 1984:
    maps 1–7) this high final vowel causes metaphonic raising of the
    tonic vowel, e.g., /lúβu/, /guínu/ (see Section **4.1.2.5**). By con-
    trast, final /-o/ marks masculine plural count-nouns and mascu-
    line singular mass-nouns (together with agreeing adjectives and

pronouns), e.g., /lóβos/ 'wolves', /guénos/ 'good (masc. plur.)', /késo guéno/ 'good cheese', as well as adjectives and pronouns which refer to feminine mass-nouns, e.g., /jérβa séko/ 'dry grass'.[9] This distinction of final vowels must earlier have occupied the far western segment of the northern Peninsular dialect continuum (Galicia and western Asturias), but its traces are now limited to the metaphonic effects visible in Portuguese; e.g., masc. sing. *porco* /pórku/ vs masc. plur. *porcos* /pórkuʃ/ 'pig(s)'. However, it is better preserved in the rural speech of central and eastern Asturias, and is often accompanied there by similar metaphonic effects, due to /-u/, to those observable in Cantabria (García Arias 1988: 90–6; Granda 1960: 30–85). This contrast between /-o/ and /-u/ extends into northeastern Burgos (González Ollé 1960: 70), and Menéndez Pidal (1964: 168–72) shows that it formerly extended into La Rioja and Aragon (see also Alvar 1953: 50–1), although relics of /-u/ are today few in these latter areas. Any such early contrast in Catalan was quickly submerged in the regular loss of both vowels.

4 The survival of the diphthong /ié/ under conditions in which it is reduced to /í/ in the dialects of the Burgos area provides further evidence of the continuity provided by Cantabria across the north of the area from which standard Castilian sprang. The main circumstances in which the dialects of central Burgos introduced this change were before /ʎ/ (principally in the diminutive suffix *-iello* > *-illo*) and before syllable-final /-s/ (e.g., VESPA > *(a)viespa* > *avispa* 'wasp'), and although the monophthongized form of the suffix (*-illo*) has long since spread northwards into Cantabria, there are frequent residues there of lexical items containing /ié/ which in the standard show /í/. Thus, the Cantabrian descendants of VESPA typically retain the diphthong (Penny 1970a: 60; 1978: 55): /griéspa/, /biéspra/, /abriéspa/, /abiéspa/; as do a few other words: /niéspra/ < MESPILU 'medlar tree'; /piésku/ < *PESCU < PERSICU 'peach'. This result cannot, of course, be seen at either the eastern or the western extremities of the northern Peninsular dialect continuum, since in these areas the diphthong /ié/ is unknown (Latin tonic ĕ remains a monophthong, /é/ or /ɛ́/), but the Cantabrian result forms part of the bridge which joins Asturias and upper Aragon, where /ié/ survives in the relevant forms.[10] What is more, the band represented by diphthongized forms of the descendant of VESPA is quite a wide one;

ALPI (1962: map 19) reveals such forms not only in northern Palencia and northern Burgos, but also in the southern part of Burgos. For northeastern Burgos, see also González Ollé (1960: *aviespa, riestra*).

5   There are likewise relics in Cantabria of the diphthong /ué/ (<Latin ŏ), under conditions in which the dialects of Burgos show the simple vowel /ó/, namely when followed by a glide arising in the groups -LJ-, -c'L-, -G'L-: *cuejo* (standard *cojo*) 'I grasp' < COLLI(G)O, *bisueju* (standard *bisojo)* 'cross-eyed' < BIS + OC(U)LU; and when followed by -CT-: *nuechi* (standard *noche)* 'night' < NOCTE. More frequent cases of diphthongization under these conditions are to be seen in Asturias (García Arias 1988: 67–8), and in Aragonese (Zamora 1967: 216–18), while in the Middle Ages such cases were quite numerous across the whole area under consideration here, including the far north of Burgos and La Rioja (Menéndez Pidal 1964: 139–43).

6   Although most of the Cantabrian lexical items which are reflexes of Latin words containing the groups -LJ-, -c'L-, -G'L- today show /x/ as the descendant of these groups (e.g., OC(U)LU > *ojo*, sometimes /úxu/ 'eye'), there is a small number of items which show /ʎ/ or /ǰ/: /bíʎu/, /bíǰu/ (< *VICLU < VITULU 'calf'), /dáʎu/ (< DAC(U)LU) 'scythe', /máǰu/ (< MALLEU) 'mallet', /páǰu/ (probably derived from PALEA) 'hay-store' (Penny 1970a: 82–3; 1978: 66–7). These are also the general results of -LJ-, -c'L-, -G'L- to be seen both to the west and east of Cantabria (e.g., OC(U)LU > Gal. *ollo,* Ptg. *olho,* Leon. *güeyu,* Arag. *güello,* Cat. *ull)*. Although almost submerged today by the advancing standardizing tide, Cantabrian forms like /béǰu/ help to demonstrate that there was once a closer similarity between the varieties which stretch across the north of the area in which Castilian has its roots.[11] As is most usually the case, La Rioja is the least resistant link in this northern chain, and although there too the early result of -LJ-, -c'L-, -G'L- was /ʎ/ (Alvar 1976: 54–6), the introduction of /ʒ/ (later /x/) from the Burgos area was probably accomplished before the end of the Middle Ages.[12]

7   The distribution in Cantabria of items which descend from Latin words displaying initial F- followed by vowels other than tonic ŏ reveals that the pronunciation /h/ (sometimes /x/) has receded from eastern Cantabria and from the coast even in the west, in the face of the advance of the /Ø/ pronunciation typical of Burgos

(Penny 1984: map 11). However, where Latin F- was followed by tonic short ŏ, later /ué/ (e.g., FŎNTE, FŎLLE, FŎRTE, FŎRAS), or where /ué/ arose from Latin UI or UE (e.g., FUĪ, FUERUNT), the sequence /hué/ was much more resistant to standardization and has widely survived in the Cantabro-Pyrenean area (and elsewhere): /huénte/ 'fountain, spring', /hueʎe/ 'bellows', /huérte/ 'strong', /huéra/ 'outside', /huí/ 'I was, I went', /huéron/ 'they were, they went'.[13] Because the initial aspirate of these words is necessarily bilabialized (by the following bi-labio-velar glide [w], the normal realization of /u/ under these circumstances), these pronunciations are variously reported as *juente* (i.e., [hwénte] or [xwénte], ignoring the labial quality of the initial consonant, and portraying solely its velar quality), as [ʍwénte] (paying attention to both the bilabial and the velar qualities), or as [ɸwénte] (reporting the bilabial quality but ignoring the velar). However recorded, this feature stretches from central Asturias (where it therefore exists beside the phoneme /f/ which appears in many words such as *facer/fader* 'to do', *fumu* 'smoke', *faba* 'haricot bean'; see García Arias 1988: 51, 106), through eastern Asturias, and Cantabria (Penny 1984: maps 12, 22), into La Rioja, Navarre and Aragon (*ALEANR* 1979–83: maps 818, 1414, 1471, 1472).[14]

8 A feature which is usually characterized as 'western', the non-reduction of the Latin group -MB-, can perhaps be added to the list of features belonging to the Cantabrian bridge. In Catalan, Aragonese, and in standard Castilian, -MB- has undergone assimilation to /m/ (e.g., PLŪMBU > Cat. *plom,* Arag., Cast. *plomo* 'lead'), but in the west this group has remained unchanged (PLŪMBU > Ptg. *chumbo,* LAMBĒRE > Leon. *lamber* 'to lick'). It would seem that this innovation, by which /mb/ was reduced to /m/, reached the Burgos area in Visigothic times (from the northeastern region of the Peninsula, where it may have resulted from the implantation of a central-southern variety of regional Latin; see Menéndez Pidal 1960 and Section **4.1.2.4**); having become established in the varieties spoken in the Burgos area, the /m/ of words like *plomo, lamer* became the form adopted by the Castilian *koinés* created in areas of resettlement following the Reconquest, and thereafter a feature of standard Castilian. However, this innovation fell short of entirely demolishing the bridge which passes from Asturias, through Cantabria and northeastern Burgos into La Rioja. Cantabrian varieties preserve a number of words which

retain /mb/ (see Penny 1970a: 80; 1978: 65; 1984: 132 and map 17), as do the varieties spoken in the Mena valley (northeastern Burgos; see González Ollé 1960), and although /mb/ appears in La Rioja today in just a handful of terms (Zamora 1967: 337), its presence was much more marked in the Middle Ages: it characterized the language of Gonzalo de Berceo and of the notarial and other documents written in this area (Alvar 1976: 52–3). Torreblanca (1984–5) shows that with regard to this feature and others, and contrary to what is claimed by Menéndez Pidal (1964: 286–7), medieval La Rioja did not constitute a linguistic island, but showed continuity with the area of La Bureba (northeastern Burgos). What we can just perceive today, then, is an area of continuity in the retention of /mb/ stretching from Galicia to La Rioja across the top of the central Burgos area (but including the northeastern part of that province). Examples of this retention are now relatively few in the Cantabrian segment of this arc, and almost non-existent in its Riojan extension, as a result of the lexical diffusion, from Burgos, of forms with /m/ which has been taking place for centuries.[15]

We have been arguing here that there is strong evidence of shared dialectal features which provide continuity right across the top of the Spanish Peninsula, a continuity of features which connects the eastern and western varieties of Hispano-Romance in a manner similar to the way in which they were formerly connected by means of the Mozarabic varieties (see 4.1.1). In other respects, this northern bridge is, of course, like any other array of geographically related varieties: it consists of a spectrum of interlocking dialects, randomly traversed by a series of isoglosses. These isoglosses are fairly well spaced in Cantabria (see Penny 1984), showing the usual smooth gradient of accumulating change typical of long-settled areas undisturbed by immigration. In places, however, the gradient of variation becomes steeper (that is, the isoglosses are seen to run closer together, a feature which is usually due to increased difficulty of communication across the part of the territory in question; see Section 2.5 and Figure 2.3). One such case occurs in the area of eastern Asturias close to western Cantabria. Here García González (1981, 1981–82) maps a number of isoglosses and finds that they run north–south approximately parallel with the River Purón, separating the dialects spoken in eastern Llanes, and in all of Ribadedeva, Peñamellera Alta, and Peñamellera Baja from the varieties spoken in the rest of Asturias, and linking them with varieties spoken in Cantabria. The isoglosses in question mark the separation between the following features (western results precede eastern): /ǰ/ vs /x/ as results of -LJ-, -C'L-, -G'L- (e.g., *vieyu* vs *vieju* < VECLU < VETULU 'old'); /ʃ/ vs /x/ as results of -x- (e.g., *coxu* vs *coju* < COXU 'lame'); retention vs loss of / -d- / in feminine participles (e.g., *cerrada* vs *cerrá* 'closed'); regular diphthongization of Latin ŏ when followed by a glide arising in the groups -LJ-, -C'L-, -G'L- (e.g., *jueya* vs *hoja* < FOLIA 'leaf'); loss vs retention of the final vowel of the suffix *-inu* (e.g., *camín* vs *caminu* 'road, track'); singular and plural dative clitics i~*yos* vs *li(s)*; possessives *mió(s), tó(s), só(s)* vs *mí(s), tú(s), sú(s)* (e.g., *la mió casa* vs *la mí casa* 'my house'). García González finds no reason for this bunching of isoglosses, and in an area like that of northern Spain, where movements of population within the zone are rare, such a relatively sharp dialectal transition needs further study, with the aim of discovering the factors which have impeded east–west communication in the area, and which have therefore disrupted the expected linguistic accommodation processes.[16]

Most of the features discussed in the previous paragraphs are conservative features, since we have been considering the resistance of this northern zone to innovations spreading northwards from Burgos. Cantabria is also an area which we would predict to be linguistically more conservative than territories further south, since it is an area which has suffered little or no inward migration; in consequence, we can expect that its rural communities (at least) will be characterized by the strong social ties typical of such settled social groups, conditions which we have seen (Section **3.3**) to favour resistance to innovation. However, undisturbed areas and peripheral zones (and within the Peninsula, Cantabria is obviously peripheral from a purely geographical point of view) are not always conservative, as we have already seen (in **1.1.1**). One way in which the varieties of Cantabria are markedly less conservative than the standard is in the development of a complex system of vowel harmony. This innovatory system, in which the appearance of high or mid vowels is determined by the tongue-height of the tonic vowel in the phonological word concerned (and by some other phonological factors), is described in Penny (1969), and has attracted a good deal of theoretical attention (see Goldsmith 1987; Hualde 1989; McCarthy 1984; Spencer 1986; Steriade 1987; Vago 1988; Wilson 1988).

4.1.2.3   **Old Castile**
The northern part of Old Castile falls within the northern Peninsular
dialect continuum, but like the rest of Castile it is a region which has
attracted relatively little variational study. Although a dialect atlas, with
a sociolinguistic component, is planned for New Castile (see García
Mouton and Moreno 1994), no such plans exist for Old Castile, and we
are dependent upon scanty data for the area which interests us here.
The one published volume of the Peninsular linguistic atlas (*ALPI* 1962)
uses a very sparse network in Castile, and although studies from the
first decades of the twentieth century (see García de Diego 1916) made
clear that Castile presented no exception to the rule of geographical
variation, the view has persisted that Castile is linguistically rather uniform, so that a manual such as Alonso Zamora Vicente's *Dialectología
española* (1967) contains no chapter on Castilian dialects to match those
on Leonese, Aragonese, Andalusian, Judeo-Spanish, etc.

Dialectal variation within Castile is however beginning to attract
attention and a number of studies have appeared which are directed at
third-person clitic pronoun reference. García González (1981) examines the values of *lo*, and finds that this pronoun is the one used to refer
anaphorically to mass-nouns, whether masculine or feminine (e.g., *esta
leche hay que beberlo* 'this milk must be drunk') not only in Asturias and
Cantabria (see **4.1.2.5**), but also in Vizcaya and Alava, in all of Burgos
and Palencia, in eastern Leon, and in northern Valladolid. However, an
isogloss separates this area from La Rioja, where a different agreement
system is in use, in which *lo* cannot refer to feminine mass-nouns, but
only to masculine nouns, whether count-nouns or mass-nouns.[17]
These findings are broadly confirmed by Klein (1979, 1980, 1981a,
1981b), who contrasts the case-determined use of third-person clitics
(in which *lo(s), la(s)* are used for direct object reference and *le(s)* only for
indirect object reference) with their semantically determined use (in
which the semantic properties of the referent determine the selection
of the clitic, such that *lo* is selected for mass-noun referents, whether
masculine or feminine, while *le(s)* and *la(s)* are used respectively to refer
to masculine and feminine count-nouns). Two separate Castilian zones
are studied and it is found that the semantically determined usage
belongs to the west of the northern Meseta (Valladolid), while the case-
determined type is the one used in the east (La Rioja and Soria),
although one facet of the semantically determined usage (namely the
use of *le* for animate direct objects) has gained ground in the east

	SINGULAR		PLURAL	
	M	F	M	F
Direct object	lo	la	los	las
Indirect object	le		les	

Table 4.1 Case-determined or etymological system of clitic pronoun reference

(where, it is presumed, *le* was previously restricted to indirect-object functions).

Further broad confirmation of this distribution of clitic systems in Old Castile comes from Fernández-Ordóñez (1994), who reports in detail on a massive but still incomplete survey of the values of third-person clitics in Old and New Castile, Extremadura, Asturias, Cantabria, and the Basque Country. She identifies a series of systems, and assigns them to specific areas, describing some zones as 'transitional'. A large (western and northern) area of Old Castile uses these clitics in the semantically determined manner described above, while the case-determined system is most usually found on the eastern side of the northern Meseta.

Some explanations for the semantically determined system of clitic usage have been hazarded.[18] Fernández-Ordóñez (1994) explains this system as due to influence exerted by Basque–Castilian bilinguals upon the case-determined system and to successive reanalyses by monolingual speakers. Whether or not this explanation can be shown to be true, it is evident that the Old Castilian segment of the northern Peninsular dialect continuum is a battlefield in which the two clitic systems are in contention. On the one hand we have the case-determined or etymological system, shown in Table **4.1**. In this system, inherited directly from Latin, difference of case (direct vs indirect object) is consistently marked by the form of the pronoun, in both genders and both numbers. That is, *leísmo*, *laísmo* and *loísmo* are entirely absent:[19]

Lo(s) vi *(a mi(s) amigo(s))*	[+direct, +animate, +count, +masc]
El reloj me **lo** *rompí*	[+direct, -animate, +count, +masc]
Le(s) mandé una carta *(a mi(s) amigo(s))*	[-direct, +animate, +count, +masc]
La(s) vi *(a mi(s) amiga(s))*	[+direct, +animate, +count, -masc]
La cabeza **la** *tengo sucia*	[+direct, -animate, +count, -masc]
Le(s) mandé una carta *(a mi(s) amiga(s))*	[-direct, +animate, +count, -masc]

COUNTABLE				NON-COUNTABLE
Singular		Plural		
M	F	M	F	
le	la	les	las	lo

Table 4.2   Semantically determined system of clitic pronoun reference

On the other hand, part of Old Castile uses a semantically based system, which in its simplest form takes the shape shown in Table **4.2**. In this semantically based system, there is no contrast of forms corresponding to contrasts of function; each form pronominalizes both direct and indirect objects. In other words, users of such a system display total *leísmo* and *laísmo*, and no distinction is made between animate and inanimate, or between human and non-human, referents; e.g.:

Le(s) vi (a mi(s) amigo(s))   [+direct, +animate, +count, +masc]
El reloj me le rompí   [+direct, -animate, +count, +masc]
Le(s) mandé una carta (a mi(s) amigo(s)) [-direct, +animate, +count, +masc]
La(s) vi (a mi(s) amiga(s))   [+direct, +animate, +count, -masc]
La cabeza la tengo sucia   [+direct, -animate, +count, -masc]
La(s) mandé una carta (a mi(s) amiga(s)). [-direct, +animate, +count, -masc]

The pronoun *lo* in this system is reserved for non-countable referents; e.g.:[20]

Este pan hay que echarlo   [+direct, -count, +masc]
Esta leche hay que echarlo   [+direct, -count, -masc]

We have already noted that the semantically based system is dominant in eastern Cantabria, adjacent parts of the Basque Country, Burgos, Palencia, eastern Leon, and Valladolid. Very similar systems are also used in western Cantabria and in Asturias, with the difference that although *lo* is used there to pronominalize mass-nouns of either gender, there is nevertheless a distinction of case between pronouns which refer to count-nouns; typically *lu/los* and *la(s)* are used for direct objects, while indirect objects are pronominalized by means of *li(s)~le(s)* (western Cantabria), or *i~yos*, etc. (Asturias) (see García González 1981, Penny 1978: 80).

We have also seen that the case-determined system is the one which dominates the eastern side of the northern Meseta (La Rioja, Soria). This system extends into much of New Castile (Fernández-Ordóñez 1994) and into Andalusia, and was the type which dominated the various *koinés* which emerged during the settlement of America.

However, the *koinés* which emerged in southern Old Castile and in northern New Castile were more complex in this regard. The best explanation of what occurred in Segovia, Madrid, Toledo, etc., was that interdialect creation took place (see **3.1.2**), giving rise to hybrid systems of pronoun reference. A number of such systems are observable in present and past varieties from the centre of the Peninsula. The most common interdialect system was one which had most of the features of the semantically based system but into which was introduced a gender distinction in the case of non-countable referents (e.g., *esta leche hay que echarla,* rather than the *echarlo* which is typical of the fully semantic system), retaining *lo* only for masculine mass-noun referents. Such a system, characterized as it is by *leísmo* and *laísmo* in the case of all count-noun objects, is the type which came to be dominant in the written varieties of Golden Age Castile, and which widely persists today in non-standard varieties spoken in Old Castile, including among educated speakers from these areas.[21] Since then, another, different, hybrid system has come to dominate the standard, one in which (in addition to the introduction of *la* to pronominalize feminine mass-nouns) case distinctions have been introduced between pronouns which refer to feminine count-nouns (direct-object *la(s)* vs indirect-object *le(s)*), and between those that refer to non-human (sometimes non-animate) masculine count-nouns (*lo(s)* vs *le(s)*), while preserving the caseless use of *le(s)* for masculine human (sometimes, more broadly, animate) referents.

The system represented in Table **4.3**, now the prestige system in much of Spain, is one of many interdialectal systems in use in Old Castile and in northern New Castile which emerged in different places through contact between the case-determined system originally dominant in eastern Old Castile (Table **4.1**) and the semantically governed system of north and western Old Castile (Table **4.2**).

4.1.2.4 The Pyrenees

The Pyrenean area provides us with an opportunity to examine the relationship between the distribution of isoglosses and a major topographical feature. A study of geographical variation in this area

	Countable					Non-countable	
	Singular			*Plural*			
	M	**F**		**M**	**F**	**M**	**F**
	+H	−H		+H	−H		
Direct object	le	lo	la	les	los	las	lo	la
Indirect object	le			les				

The columns reflect properties of the noun being pronominalized (+H indicates a human referent, −H a non-human referent; M and F indicate Masculine and Feminine referents respectively), while the two rows reflect the role of the pronoun in its clause.

Table 4.3 Hybrid or interdialectal system of clitic pronoun reference, now standard

confirms that, as we found in the case of the Miranda area, isoglosses do not in many cases coincide with a political frontier, but it also allows us to see that, contrary to naive expectation, isoglosses do not necessarily coincide with mountain ranges either.

We shall focus on the extent of spread of three groups of features which are evident in overlapping areas centred upon the Pyrenees. These features belong principally to the rural speech of these areas, but in a few instances a change has come to be used in one or more of the Peninsular standards.

1   The reduction, through assimilation of the second element to the first, of groups consisting of a sonorant followed by a voiced plosive (e.g., -MB- > /m/, -ND- > /n/, and, less frequently, -LD- > /l/ or /ʎ/). The change -MB- > /m/ was extended to areas from which Castilian originated and was thereafter spread as part of the Castilian set of features (e.g., LUMBU > *lomo* 'back, ridge'), while both -MB- > /m/ and -ND- > /n/ affected the northeastern Peninsular area from which Catalan sprang and were then extended southwards as part of the Catalan expansion (e.g., COLUMBĀRIU > *Colomer* (surname), DEMANDĀRE > *demanar* 'to ask').

2   The voicing of a plosive when grouped with a preceding sonorant (e.g., -MP- > /mb/, -NT- > /nd/, -NC- > /ng/, -RT- > /rd/, etc.).

3   The retention of the Latin voiceless plosives -P-, -T-, -K- in intervocalic position, by contrast to their voicing (-P- > /b/, -T- > /d/, -K- > /g/) in a vast surrounding territory comprising northern

Italy, the Alps, France (except the Pyrenean area in question), and most of the Peninsula.

Debate about the origins of changes (1) and (2) has been intense, and Menéndez Pidal (1964: 286–306; 1960: lix–lxxxvi) makes a strong case for an Italic origin, arguing that the kind of Latin brought to northeastern Spain from the third century BC onwards was highly dialectal, preserving many features which originated not in the Latin of Rome but in the contemporary Umbrian and Oscan speech of central and southern Italy. He emphasizes that feature (1) above is attested in ancient Umbrian texts and is evident today in central and southern Italy and in the Pyrenean zone, in both of which areas change (2) also occurs, contained within the area occupied by change (1).

Although Menéndez Pidal's account was not (and could not be) couched in terms of sociolinguistic theories of language change, it squares well with more recent accounts of the linguistic consequences of colonization processes (e.g., Trudgill 1986: 127–61, concerned with colonial English, but in principle applicable to colonial Latin or colonial Spanish). When the spread of Latin to the Iberian Peninsula began in the late third century BC, variation of speech between groups of settlers must have been marked, reflecting the marked linguistic variation which must have existed in the areas from which they came, central and southern Italy. At this period, the Latin of Rome (with its inevitable internal variation) was still in the process of extending its features into these territories, where its Italic competitors, Umbrian and Oscan, had hitherto been spoken unchallenged. It can therefore be regarded as highly likely that the speech forms brought to northeastern Spain during and in the wake of the Roman conquest of the Ebro valley (Lerida, Saragossa, Huesca, 218–206 BC) were highly varied, and that at least some varieties contained features which were common to Oscan and / or Umbrian rather than to the Latin of Rome. Within this dialect mixture, we would expect the normal processes of *koinéization* to take place, reducing variation through levelling and simplification (see Section **3.1**), not always with results which coincided with the still-emerging standard language. Hypothetical pronunciations like /lúmmu/ or /lómmu/ (corresponding to standard LUMBU), which arguably underlie both the present-day central and southern Italian dialect forms and those of northeastern Spain (later including both standard Castilian and Catalan), are quite as understandable as the appearance of *yeísmo* in much of the Spanish Peninsula as well as in most of Spanish America (see Sections **4.2.1** and **5.1.2.1**), or the appearance of post-nuclear /-r/ both in western England and in most of north America (by contrast with standard British English, which has deleted it).

Whatever their origin, the Pyrenean spread of these features was examined by W. D. Elcock (1938), who aimed at establishing the isoglosses which delimit the territorial extent of each of the three phonological features under discussion here. If further proof were needed (see Section **3.5**) that linguistic innovations are diffused word by word, rather than affecting all eligible words alike, then the maps which accompany this study provide it in abundance; each word mapped reveals a different position of the isogloss concerned. But equally importantly, Elcock shows that these isoglosses frequently run north–south cutting at right angles through both the mountain chain and the political frontier, and therefore revealing continuity of features between France and Spain in many parts of the Pyrenees, but frequent discontinuity between neighbouring valleys on the same side of the mountains.

Thus, he shows (map 9) that the -T- of VITELLU 'calf' has been maintained as a voiceless plosive both in a large area of Gascony ([betét], [betéc], [betétʃ]), just as happens in some upper Aragonese valleys ([betjéʎo], [betjéto], [betjétʃo]).[22]

Map 19 shows that both features (2) and (3) are to be found both in southern Gascony and in upper Aragon. URTICA 'nettle' shows voicing of T after a sonorant, and retention of voiceless C in intervocalic position: [urtíko], [hurtíko] on the north, and a wide variety of southern forms (from west to east): [ʃorðíɣa], [orðíɣa], [ʃorðíka], [sorðíka], [tʃorðíka], [ʃorðíka], [tʃorðíka], [iʃorðíka], [iʃorðíɣa].

Map 27 (descendants of BRANCA, meaning '(tree) branch' on the north, but 'stem and ear (of wheat)' to the south) shows continuity across the Pyrenees in the voicing of a plosive after a sonorant: Béarnais [bráŋgo], upper Aragonese [bráŋga], the latter now restricted to two islands, one separated from the frontier.

Since every isogloss implies that those on the same side of it are in closer communication than those who are separated by it, Elcock explores the historical circumstances which allowed speakers on the northern flanks of the mountains to remain in closer contact with their southern counterparts than either enjoyed with people who lived in the lowlands on each side. He shows that until the nineteenth century the many tracks crossing the Pyrenees were in regular use. The traditional economic basis of Pyrenean life was transhumant cattle-raising; each summer, those from south and north would meet in the high pastures, and medieval pastoral conventions record the arrangements they reached in order to share these resources and avoid conflict. In the absence, until the sixteenth century, of powerful nation-states on either side of the mountains, the Pyrenees scarcely formed a frontier, and even after the appearance of centralized states, at war with one another, the Pyrenean people continued to cooperate: treaties guaranteeing trade between neighbouring valleys on either side continued to be made, seeking to defend the interests of the people of this area as a whole against outside interests. This state of affairs continued until the mid-eighteenth century, when closer but separate links began to be forged between the mountain-dwellers on the southern side and their lowland neighbours (and likewise on the north), and some of the advantages of belonging to a large nation-state began to be felt even at its margins. Only the heightened nationalism resulting from the French Revolution brought real separation between north and south, and the frontier was then definitively fixed, becoming real only in the nineteenth century. Throughout that century, links were tenuously maintained through smuggling, but the twentieth century brought economic depression to the southern side, with consequent emigration and depopulation. If the Pyrenees finally became a barrier to communication, this was a modern event, and the pattern of geographical variation of language reveals the centuries-old contact between north and south.

More recent research (Guiter 1983) bears in part upon the matter of dialectal transition across the Pyrenees, and no doubt reflects the convergence of isoglosses upon the frontier, as this became a more effective barrier to communication in the fifty years since Elcock's study. Guiter uses dialectometric techniques to calculate the degree of difference between twenty-six points located along the Pyrenean–Cantabrian chain from Galicia to Catalonia and in southern France (Gascony and Languedoc). The distance between any two adjacent points is necessarily large, but the distribution of twenty-seven features reveals a concentration of isoglosses which separate Gascon varieties on the north from Aragonese on the south; this concentration Guiter terms a 'high level linguistic frontier', but since the points he selects are some distance from the political frontier, we cannot conclude how

far the isoglosses concerned have come to coincide with the political
boundary.

4.1.2.5   Metaphony and mass-noun reference

4.1.2.5.1   *Metaphony*

Some of the varieties that make up the northern Peninsular dialect continuum display a feature called *metaphony*, a phonological process whose
output has sometimes come to play a morphological role, serving as the
basis for gender contrasts, number contrasts, and for the contrast
between countable and non-countable referents. Metaphony also occurs
widely in Italy; Maiden (1985–6, 1987), Politzer (1957), and Tuttle
(1985–6) study its operation there, while Penny (1994) compares Italian
with Peninsular metaphony and finds a common origin. Other discussions of the nature and history of metaphony can be seen in Alarcos
(1964), Alonso (1962b), Neira (1962), Penny (1970b), Schürr (1958, 1976).

Metaphony is a process in which the tonic (i.e., stressed) vowel of
a word is raised (usually by one degree of aperture) through anticipa-
tory assimilation to a high vowel (/i/ or /u/) which appears in the final
syllable of the word. High tonic vowels are therefore not susceptible to
metaphony, while the low vowel /á/, which belongs neither to the
front nor to the back series, may be attracted upwards and forwards
(towards /é/) or upwards and backwards (towards /ɔ́/).[23] In the areas
where metaphony appears today, the vowel system within which it
operates is (like that of standard Castilian) one which has five vowels
organized in three degrees of aperture, as in Table **4.4**. In the geographical areas concerned, under conditions of metaphony (namely,
where the final syllable of the word contains unstressed /i/ or /u/),
mid vowels become high and the low vowel becomes mid (/e/ or /o/).
Word-final /i/ is less frequent than /-u/, so we shall begin by considering metaphony caused by the latter vowel:[24]

$$
\begin{array}{llll}
\text{underlying /é/ \dots /u/} & \rightarrow & \text{/í/ \dots /u/:} & \text{/péru/} \rightarrow \text{/píru/ 'dog'} \\
\text{underlying /ó/ \dots /u/} & \rightarrow & \text{/ú/ \dots /u/:} & \text{/lóbu/} \rightarrow \text{/lúbu/ 'wolf'} \\
\text{underlying /á/ \dots /u/} & \rightarrow & \text{/é/ \dots /u/:} & \text{/gátu/} \rightarrow \text{/gétu/ 'cat'} \\
& \text{or} & \text{/ó/ \dots /u/:} & \text{/gátu/} \rightarrow \text{/gótu/ 'cat'.}
\end{array}
$$

Since final /u/ is associated with nouns which are characterized as [+sin-
gular, +masculine, +countable], and with adjectives and pronouns
which refer to such nouns, the presence of metaphony is inevitably
associated with these syntactic/semantic features. Likewise, since the

	Front	Central	Back
High	/i/		/u/
Mid	/e/		/o/
Low		/a/	

Table 4.4   Vowel system underlying metaphony in northern varieties

appearance of final /o/, /a/ and /e/ (vowels which do not cause metaphony) is *never* associated with these features, absence of metaphony helps to identify nouns whose features include any one or more of [-masculine], [-singular], [-countable]. Thus, /píru/ 'dog', which is [+masculine, +singular], is contrasted with /péra/ 'bitch', which is [-masculine], and with /péros/ 'dogs' and /péras/ 'bitches', which are [-singular]. Similarly, /pílu/ 'strand of hair', which is [+countable], contrasts with /pélo/ 'hair (the substance)', which is [-countable]. It can be seen that the contrast between metaphonized (raised) and unmetaphonized tonic vowel is not the only element which expresses the syntactic/semantic contrasts concerned, since there is also a corre-lated contrast of final vowel. Only a few dialects, which have allowed final /-u/ and /-o/ to merge, have proceeded to full morphologization of metaphony, and then in rather restricted circumstances. Where these final back vowels fall together (in a vowel with varying realizations, here subsumed under the symbol /U/ [= non-low back vowel]), the alterna-tion of tonic vowels can carry the contrast between [+countable] and [-countable]: /pílU/ 'strand of hair' vs /pélU/ 'hair (the substance)'.

Final /-i/ (see **4.1.2.2(2)**) occurs in a limited set of words: singular imperatives of *-er* and *-ir* verbs, the masculine singular forms of the demonstratives corresponding to standard *este* and *ese*, the first-person singular of strong preterites, together with a small group of nouns and adverbs corresponding to such standard words as *leche, tarde, noche,* etc. Because of this restricted occurrence, metaphony caused by /-i/ only gives rise to morphological contrasts in a restricted number of cases. For example:

underlying /é/ ... /i/ → /í/ ... /i/: /ésti/ → /ísti/ 'this'
underlying /ó/ ... /i/ → /ú/ ... /i/: /kóri/ → /kúri/ 'run (imper.)'
underlying /á/ ... /i/ → /é/ ... /i/: /táɾdi/ → /téɾdi/ 'late; afternoon'.

It will be seen that alternation between metaphonized and unmeta-phonized vowels has come to play a minor syntactic/semantic role in the dialects concerned. Although the alternation of tonic vowels is rarely the only exponent of syntactic/semantic contrasts, the presence of raised (metaphonized) vowels is associated with the following features: [+masculine] (/ísti/ vs /ésta/); [+singular] (/ísti/ vs /éstos/; /térdi/ vs /tárdes/); [+imperative] (/kúri/ vs /kóre/ '(s)he runs (indic.)'). Full morphologization of these contrasts only occurs in those varieties which have allowed final /-i/ and /-e/ to merge, presumably in recent times, with a range of phonetic values here subsumed under the symbol /I/ (= non-low front vowel, typically raised [ę] or [i] or some articulation between these points), and then only in the second-person singular forms of -er and -ir verbs: /kúrI/ 'run (imper.)' vs /kórI/ '(s)he runs (indic.)'.

For speakers of metaphonizing dialects, whatever the antiquity of the metaphonic process (and it appears to be ancient), it remains a productive one. This can be seen in the fact that metaphony is applied by speakers to words containing the diphthongs which result from the tonic ĕ and ŏ of Latin:[25]

/abjértu/ (< APERTU) > /abjírtu/ 'open'
/nuétʃi/ (< NOCTE, with modification of the final vowel) >
        /nuítʃi/ 'night'
/guébu/ (< OVU) > /guíbu/ 'egg'.

It will be evident that the dialects which display metaphony are northern varieties which have not been subjected to the more intense levelling and simplification which occurred in areas of dialect mixture further south, and which have preserved phonemic contrast between final /u/ and /o/ and between final /i/ and /e/.[26] The majority of Peninsular dialects, including standard Castilian, do not permit high vowels in final unstressed syllables and therefore cannot display metaphony.[27]

Currently, metaphony belongs to the traditional speech of a number of areas. It is best seen in the dialects of central Asturias, in what are now two separate areas, one on the coast at the Cabo de Peñas and the other in the mountainous central-southern part of the Principality, separated by the varieties used in and around Oviedo (see Díaz 1957, Galmés 1960, García Álvarez 1955, Neira 1955: 3–6, 1962, Rodríguez-Castellano 1952: 54–62, 1955, 1959). It is rather vestigially present in eastern Asturias (Garvens 1960) and in western Cantabria (Penny 1978: 153–5), where raising of the affected tonic vowels is always less than a full degree of aperture. Further east, in the Pasiego

	Front	Central	Back
High	/i/		/u/
High-mid	/e/		/o/
Low-mid	/ɛ/		/ɔ/
Low		/a/	

Table 4.5 Vowel system underlying metaphony in Portuguese

varieties of central-southern Cantabria, there is a further coherent area of metaphony (Penny 1970a: 383–96, with map).

It appears likely that the metaphony of northern Spanish varieties is genetically related to that of Portuguese, despite the lack of geographical continuity between the two areas (Galician lacks metaphony as defined here; Vázquez and Mendes da Luz 1971, I: 111–12). Early medieval Portuguese probably contrasted final /-o/ and /-u/ (despite the representation of these two vowels by a single letter, <o>; Williams 1962: 121), and since /-u/ occurred in the singular form of a large class of masculine nouns, pronouns and adjectives, while /-o/ occurred in the corresponding plurals and /-a/ occurred in corresponding feminines, metaphony had the effect of marking differences of gender and number by means of the aperture of the tonic vowel, and these contrasts of aperture survived the merger of final /-u/ and /-o/ (Vázquez and Mendes da Luz 1971, I: 255–9).

It has to be remembered that, in Portuguese, metaphony operates upon a vowel system of seven phonemes, ranged in four degrees of aperture (Table **4.5**). And since metaphony consists in the assimilatory raising of tonic vowels by one degree of aperture, it is to be expected that, under appropriate conditions, low-mid vowels will be raised to high-mid position, while high-mid vowels will become high.

In fact, metaphony in Portuguese is seen to operate most regularly upon underlying tonic /ɔ/, which emerges as /ó/ in the case of many masculine singular forms, but remains as /ɔ́/ in corresponding masculine plurals and in feminines:

/pɔ́rku/ (< PORCU) > /pórku/ *porco* 'pig'
/pɔ́rkos/ (< PORCŌS) > /pɔ́rkuʃ/ *porcos* 'pigs'
/pɔ́rka(s)/ (< PORCĀ(S)) > /pɔ́rka(ʃ)/ *porca(s)* 'sow(s)'

However, not all masculine singulars displaying the pattern /ɔ/ ... /u/ show raising of the tonic, while there are substantial numbers of nouns and adjectives whose tonic vowels behave like those of Ptg. *porco, -os*, but which have adopted this pattern analogically, since their tonic vowel is not underlying /ɔ/, but /ó/:

/formózu/ (< FORMŌSU) > /formózu/ *formoso* 'beautiful (masc. sing.)'
/formózos/ (< FORMŌSŌS) > /formɔzuʃ/ *formosos* 'beautiful (masc. plur.)'
/formóza(s)/ (< FORMŌSA(S)) > /formɔza(ʃ)/ *formosa(s)* 'beautiful (fem. sing./plur.)'

Other relevant tonic vowels (/ɛ/, /é/, /ó/) show more sporadic and even less regular metaphonic effects, and /í/, /ú/ and /á/ are never affected. And although Portuguese metaphony serves to enhance contrasts of number and gender, it is never correlated with the contrast between countable and non-countable concepts. Thus, among the rare cases of metaphonic raising of mid-high tonic vowels, we find the 'neuter' pronouns *isto* and *tudo*, whose underlying forms contain /é/ and /ó/ respectively (Lat. ISTUD, TŌTUM, proto-Portuguese /éstu/, /tótu/). Since these words ('this', 'all') can never refer to countable concepts, it follows that there is no connection (contrary to what happens in Asturian and Cantabrian varieties) between presence of metaphony in a word and the presence of a [+countable] semantic component.

4.1.2.5.2   *Mass-noun reference*

It will be apparent, from the discussion of metaphony as it appears in the northern Peninsular dialect continuum, that these dialects frequently make a morphological contrast between forms associated respectively with [+countable] and [-countable] concepts. This contrast is most clearly (but not exclusively) observable in the case of words (nouns, adjectives, pronouns) which have a back vowel in their final syllable. Within this (large) class, a word which refers to a single item (a person, a thing) which in the real world is individualizable or countable displays specific morphological properties: final /-u/, presence of metaphony. By contrast, any word which refers to a plurality of items or to any non-individualizable or non-countable item (such as a substance in indeterminate quantity, or an abstract item) shows different morphological properties: final /-o/, absence of metaphony.

Rather rarely, this contrast is displayed in the noun itself, and is naturally confined to masculine singulars. We have already examined cases of such contrast like:

un /pílu/	'a strand of hair'	([+countable])
/pélo/	'hair (the substance)'	([-countable])
un /kísu/	'a[n individual] cheese'	([+countable])
/késo/	'cheese (the product)'	([-countable]).[28]

More usually, the contrast is seen through pronoun reference or adjective agreement. Irrespective of the form of the noun, if it has the syntactic-semantic properties [+masculine, +singular, +countable], then any pronoun or adjective which agrees with that noun (provided that the pronoun or adjective is not one which ends in a consonant or /-e/ or /-i/) will be marked by final /-u/ and by metaphony. On the other hand, if any one of those properties is not associated with the noun, then the pronoun or adjective will be marked by some other final vowel (/-o/ or /-a/) and will lack metaphony. Thus:

A:	*un hombre* /guínu/	'a good man'	([+masculine, +singular, +countable])
	un pan /guínu/	'a good loaf'	([+masculine, +singular, +countable])
B:	*una mujer* /guéna/	'a good woman'	([-masculine, +singular, +countable])
	pan /guéno/	'good bread'	([+masculine, -countable])
	los que son /gúenos/	'those who are good'	([+masculine, -singular, +countable])
	las /guénas/	'the good ones'	([-masculine, -singular, +countable])

A further, related, characteristic of dialects from the central part of the northern continuum is that, in the case of nouns which have the properties [-masculine, -countable], any agreeing adjective or pronoun (of the appropriate class) will have /-o/ in its final syllable and will (therefore) lack metaphony (see Penny 1970b):

la hierba está /séko/	'the grass is dry'
lo que esté /séko/	'whichever [sc. grass] is dry'
la tierra /akéʎo/	'that earth'
esta leche, hay que beber/lo tó/	'this milk must all be drunk'.

For full discussion of these agreements in northern Spain, see García González (1989).

4.1.3   The broken southern Peninsular dialect continuum

While it is possible to recognize an unbroken dialectal continuity across the northern third of the Peninsula (**4.1.2**), it is no longer possible to do so in the remaining, central and southern, portions of Spain and Portugal. Today, there are three dialect continua in the southern two-thirds of the Peninsula: one which comprises central and southern Portugal from the Atlantic to (approximately) the Spanish frontier; a second which comprises the band of Catalan speech down the Mediterranean coast from approximately Tarragona to Alacant/Alicante; and a third which comprises the territory in between the first two. This three-fold division of the Peninsula contradicts the general principle that, at least at the level of everyday speech, sharp dialectal boundaries do not exist. In the north of Spain, we observe the general Romance pattern of interlocked dialects without sudden transitions (see **4.1.2**). But along the Portuguese–Spanish border between the Duero and the Atlantic, and along a line which runs irregularly southwards through the provinces of Castellón, Valencia, and Alicante, we *can* observe sharp dialectal boundaries. An explanation is therefore called for and will be attempted (in section **4.1.4**) after we have looked at the facts.[29]

The three dialect continua under consideration are separated by a number of superimposed isoglosses, which can be summarized as in Table **4.6**.

1   Down the central axis of the Peninsula, Latin stressed ĕ is seen to be regularly diphthongized to /ie/ (TĔRRA > Cast. *tierra*), contrasting with the product (/e/) of Latin stressed ē or ĭ (CATĒNA > Cast. *cadena*). By contrast, in both lateral zones we find /ɛ/ from Latin ĕ (TĔRRA > Ptg., Cat. *terra*), again contrasting with /e/ from Latin ē (CATĒNA > Ptg. *cadeia*, Val. *cadena*).[30]

2   In comparable fashion, the central dialect continuum of the central and southern Peninsula is characterized by showing /ue/ as the product of Latin tonic ŏ (PŎRTA > Cast. *puerta*), contrasting with /o/ from Latin tonic ō or ŭ (> Cast. *boca*). Both lateral zones again display a monophthong (/ɔ/) from Latin ŏ (PŎRTA > Ptg., Cat. *porta*), in contrast with /o/ from Latin ō or ŭ (BUCCA > Ptg., Cat. *boca*).

3   In the central area, the contrast between earlier voiceless /s/ and voiced /z/ has been lost, so that, for example, the internal

	West	Centre	East
1	/ɛ/ vs /e/ t[ɛ]rra vs cad[e]ia	/ie/ vs /e/ tierra vs cadena	/ɛ/ vs /e/ t[ɛ]rra vs cad[e]na
2	/ɔ/ vs /o/ p[ɔ]rta vs b[o]ca	/ue/ vs /o/ puerta vs boca	/ɔ/ vs /o/ p[ɔ]rta vs b[o]ca
3	/s/ vs /z/ grossa vs casa	/s/ (alone) gruesa = casa	/s/ vs /z/ grossa vs casa
4	/s/ grossa = caça	/s/ vs /θ/ gruesa vs caza	/s/ grossa = caça
5	/ʃ/ vs /ʒ/ coxa vs cerveja	/x/ caja = mujer	/ʃ/ vs /ʒ/ caixa vs rajar
6	/b/ vs /v/ ~ /β/ saber vs cavalo	/b/ (alone) saber = caballo	/b/ (alone) or /b/ vs /v/ saber vs cavall
7	/f/ filha	/h/ ~ /Ø/ hija	/f/ filla
8	/t/ noite	/tʃ/ noche	/t/ nit
9	/ʎ/ filha	/x/ hija	/ʎ/ filla
10	casa-cases	casa-casas	casa-cases

Table 4.6   Central Peninsular innovations

consonant of Cast. *gruesa* (< GROSSA) is identical to that of Cast. *casa* (< CASA), whereas Portuguese and Catalan words of the *casa* class have voiced /z/, in contrast with the voiceless /s/ of Ptg. *grossa*, Cat. *grossa*.

4   A feature related to the preceding one is that most central areas maintain a contrast between two voiceless sibilants, /s/ and /θ/, whose antecedents merge on the two flanks of the Peninsula (as well as in the south of the central zone, namely in part of Andalusia). Thus, Castilian distinguishes the internal consonant of *gruesa* from that of *caza*, while Portuguese *grossa* and *caça*, despite the contrast in spellings, contain the same phoneme, as is also the case in Catalan *grossa* and *caça*.

5   In a manner similar to that of point 3, the central zone has allowed
    the merger of earlier /ʃ/ and /ʒ/, later modifying the result of
    this merger to /x/. Thus medieval Castilian *caxa* /káʃa/ and
    muger /muʒér/ now have the same internal consonant /x/
    (/káxa/, /muxér/). However, on both sides of the Peninsula, this
    phonemic contrast is preserved unchanged, so that Ptg. *coxa* and
    Cat. *caixa* maintain /ʃ/, while Ptg. *cerveja* and Cat. *rajar* show
    unchanged /ʒ/.
6   The two medieval Castilian voiced labials /b/ (spelt *b*) and /β/
    (spelt *v/u*) have merged into a single phoneme /b/ (although
    both *b* and *v* continue to be used in the spelling of the words con-
    cerned). Thus medieval Cast. *saber* (with /b/) and *cavallo* (with
    /β/) (later respelt *caballo*) now have the same internal consonant,
    /b/. However, Central and Southern Portuguese maintains the
    medieval contrast (in this case between bilabial /b/ and labioden-
    tal /v/, while much (but not all) of Southern Catalan (i.e.,
    Valencian) similarly contrasts /b/ with either /β/ or /v/.
7   In the case of the reflexes of F-, there is again a three-fold division
    of the territory comprising the southern two-thirds of the
    Peninsula. In both lateral zones, Latin initial F- has been retained
    essentially unchanged: Lat. FĪLIA > Ptg. *filha*, Cat. *filla*. However,
    it is well known that Castilian (for reasons which are still open to
    dispute; see Lloyd 1987: 212–23, Penny 1972b, 1990) first replaced
    Latin F- with an aspirate /h/, and then allowed the latter to be
    dropped. The first of these innovations came to occupy the whole
    of the central dialect continuum under consideration here, abut-
    ting sharply upon the Central-Southern Portuguese area and
    upon the Southern Catalan region, along the boundaries outlined
    above. The second Castilian innovation (/h/-dropping) has not
    yet covered the entire central zone. All of Old and New Castile are
    affected, as are Aragon, Murcia, and eastern Andalusia, so that
    today there is an isogloss (coinciding with the others discussed in
    this section) separating an /f/-retaining area (Castellón, eastern
    Valencia, most of Alicante) from an area whose speakers use no
    initial consonant in the relevant words (Cat. *filla* vs Cast. *hija* [=
    /íxa/]). However, on the other side of the Peninsula, /h/-drop-
    ping has not reached all levels of society, so that along the
    Spanish–Portuguese frontier, in rural speech, there is an isogloss
    which separates (Portuguese) /f/-retention (e.g., Lat. FARĪNA

'flour' > *farinha* on the western side of the line, but FARĪNA > /harína/ on the eastern side). The area of /h/-retention (in rural speech) includes much of western Andalusia (Huelva, Seville, Cádiz, Málaga, Córdoba provinces) together with Extremadura (Cáceres and Badajoz). Moving northwards, there is then a break in the /h/ area (so that /h/-dropping reaches the Portuguese frontier between the Tagus and the Duero) before we reach a residual and fast-fading area of /h/-retention in the west of Valladolid (La Ribera).

8   A similar three-fold division of the central and southern Peninsula (with agreement between the western and eastern sectors) emerges when we observe the various forms of words which descend from those containing CT in Latin. On both flanks, the dental consonant is retained (e.g., Lat. NOCTE > Ptg. *noite*, Cat. *nit*, Lat. FACTU > Ptg. *feito*, Cat. *fet*), while in the centre a palatalization process changes CT to /tʃ/ (e.g., Lat. NOCTE > Cast. *noche*, Lat. FACTU > Cast. *hecho*).

9   We can observe an identical pattern in the case of words descended from Latin items containing the sequence /lj/ (e.g., FOLIA), or /kl/ or /gl/ (e.g., OC(U)LU, TEG(U)LA): on the two flanks, we see an identical result, /ʎ/ (Lat. FĪLIA > Ptg. *filha*, Cat. *filla*, Lat. OC(U)LU > Ptg. *olho*, Cat. *ull*, Lat. TEG(U)LA > Ptg. *telha*, Cat. *tella*), while the centre shows a different result, namely /x/ (Lat. FOLIA > Cast. *hoja*, Lat. OC(U)LU > Cast. *ojo*, Lat. TEG(U)LA > Cast. *teja*).

10 The plural of nouns in *-a* takes the form *-es* (e.g., sing. *casa*, plur. *cases*), and second-person singular verb forms appear with *-es* where their Latin antecedents showed *-ās* (e.g., pres. indic. *cantes*, imperf. indic. *cantabes/cantaves*), not only throughout the Catalan-speaking area, but also in central Asturias, and in a number of now isolated pockets in the western Meseta. There is also good evidence of this feature in Mozarabic (see **4.1.1** and Galmés 1983: 302–17 + map). Although the distribution of this feature is not identical to that of other features discussed in this section (Galician–Portuguese lacks it, as do the dialects of western Asturias), it should be included here, since its current distribution strongly suggests that there was once an unbroken area in which Latin *-ās* was preserved as *-es*, stretching from the Mediterranean to central Asturias, via the Mozarabic-speaking areas.

4.1.4   The expansion of Castilian features

The explanation for the facts set out in **4.1.3** can be found in the political history of the Peninsula. The expansion of Castile, from its small
tenth-century central-northern origins, led to the development of a
large Peninsular state which by the fifteenth century stretched from the
Cantabrian coast to the Atlantic and the Mediterranean. As a result of
this expansion, speakers from the region of Old Castile and other
northern areas resettled in territories further and further south as these
were reconquered from Islamic Spain. This movement led to a
complex state of dialect contact (see **3.1** for the mechanisms involved)
among a range of northern varieties spoken alongside a range of
southern or Mozarabic dialects. As accommodation processes (**3.1.1**)
led to reduction of variants, it was the Mozarabic (southern) features
which largely disappeared in favour of northern features; and since
several of the Mozarabic features were ones which extended across the
whole Peninsula, and were shared with the westernmost (Galician–
Portuguese) and easternmost (Catalan) varieties (see **4.1.1**), the disappearance of these features from the area of Castilian expansion implied
the breaking of an earlier east–west dialect continuum. As the
imported features became dominant in the centre-south of the
Peninsula, their prestige gradually ensured that they expanded towards
the boundaries of the state, so that the isoglosses which reflect their
distribution eventually coincided, in the west, with the Portuguese–
Spanish frontier, and, in the east, with the line which demarcated the
areas settled by Catalan speakers (see Penny (1999) for elaboration of
this point).

  Expansion of central-northern features into the centre-south was
not the only process of this kind to occur in the Middle Ages, since
exactly similar processes were occurring down both flanks of the
Peninsula. These expansions of northwestern and of northeastern features will be discussed in **4.1.7.1** and **4.1.7.3**.

4.1.5   Eastern innovations

A number of new features have at different times spread from east to
west across the Peninsula without occupying the whole territory. In
some cases, these innovations originated elsewhere in the Romance

	West	Centre	East
1	*cantei*	*he cantado*	*he cantat*
2	/ei/	/e/	/e/
	primeiro	*primero*	*primer*
3	/ou/	/o/	/o/
	pouco	*poco*	*poc*
4	/mb/	/m/	/m/
	pomba	*paloma*	*coloma*
5	/nd/	/nd/	/n/
	demandar	*demandar*	*demanar*
6	/l-/	/l-/	/ʎ-/
	lombo	*lomo*	*llom*

Table 4.7   Eastern Peninsular innovations

world (they may show up in Gallo-Romance, for example) and appear to have spread into the Peninsula via the eastern Pyrenees. Others must have had their origin in the speech of the northeast Peninsula and belong only to (part of) Hispano-Romance. At all events, the features under consideration are today delimited by isoglosses that run approximately north-south. In the northern third of the Peninsula, these isoglosses form part of the northern dialect continuum (**4.1.2**) and are typically scattered, but in their trajectory through the central and southern Peninsula they converge, some of them meeting at the Portuguese–Spanish frontier (e.g., features 1–4 in Table **4.7**), and then coinciding with the western isoglosses set out in Table **4.6**. Others (for example, features 5–6 in Table **4.7**) converge with the eastern isoglosses of Table **4.6** and help to form the sharp boundary between Castilian and Catalan which runs down through Castellón, Valencia and Alicante provinces to the Mediterranean.

   Table **4.7** presents a selection of salient features which are distributed in the two ways just described. They are then discussed in the remainder of this section.

1   The Latin perfect (CANTĀVĪ, etc.) expressed both perfective and perfect aspects in the past (see Comrie 1976: 53). That is, in terms of approximate English translation equivalents, it meant both 'I sang' (in a period of past time unconnected with the moment of

speaking), and 'I have sung' (in the past, but with present relevance). In most areas of Romance, CANTĀVĪ survives with the first of these two values (e.g., Old Catalan *cantí*, Castilian *canté*, Galician–Portuguese *cantei*), but already in spoken Latin it was being replaced in its perfect value by the analytic construction HABĒRE CANTĀTUM, a form which reaches most of the Peninsula with this value (Cat. *he cantat*, Cast. *he cantado*). However, in the western third of the Peninsula, this change has not occurred, and the descendants of CANTĀVĪ, etc., continue to express both perfect and non-perfect values (e.g., Ptg. *cantei* 'I sang, I have sung') (Willis 1965: 209–11). It is true that Galician and Portuguese possess compound perfect constructions (e.g., literary Ptg. *hei cantado*, Ptg. *tenho cantado*), but these are not functional equivalents of the Castilian or Catalan compound perfects (or their French, Italian, etc. counterparts). Ptg. *hei/tenho cantado* expresses a past state which continues at the moment of speaking ('I have been singing').[31] The perfect value of the descendants of CANTĀVĪ is found not only in Galicia and Portugal, but also in a wider area of the Peninsular northwest, including Asturias and Cantabria, and has been widely transmitted to American Spanish, where (for example) *Ya lo hice* frequently has the same value ('I've already done it') as standard Peninsular *Ya lo he hecho*.

2   The spoken Latin diphthong /ai/ (which often arose through metathesis of the sequence consonant + palatal glide, bringing the glide into contact with a preceding /a/, e.g., PRĪMĀRIUM > /primairo/) underwent change to /ei/ and then to /e/ in Central Romance areas. These innovations spread into and across the Peninsula, but the second (/ei/ > /e/) failed the reach the western flank, so that /ei/ remains (e.g., *primeiro*) in Galicia, western Asturias, far western Leon, and Portugal.[32]

3   In exactly parallel manner to the changes just discussed, Latin /au/ was modified to /ou/ and then /o/ in much of the Romance-speaking world (although not in southern Gaul, where Occitan retains /au/). These changes spread across the Peninsula from east to west (apparently in tandem with the changes /ai/ > /ei/ > /e/), but the last stage again failed to reach the western Peninsula, which widely retains /ou/ (as in PAUCU > *pouco*).[33]

4   As we have seen in **4.1.2.2**, retention of /mb/, by contrast with its reduction to /m/, is one of the features which helps us to identify the northern dialectal bridge which links the northwestern

Peninsula with La Rioja and Aragon, via Asturias, Cantabria and northeastern Burgos (see also Penny 1997). The place of origin of the change MB > /m/ seems to lie in the Pyrenees, spreading from there to Catalan and Aragonese and extending westwards to the central Burgos area. The consonant group is retained throughout the Galician–Portuguese area (e.g., PALUMBA > *pomba*), and in the rural speech of western Leon, Asturias and Cantabria. It was also characteristic of the pre-Reconquest southern Peninsula (see **4.1.1**), but has been swept from this area (except for its Portuguese segment) by the expansion of Castilian features from the centre-north (see **4.1.4**).

5 Although the Latin group -ND- has an exactly similar structure to that of -MB- (namely, nasal plus homorganic voiced plosive), and although in the east -ND- is modified in an exactly parallel manner (namely, to /n/, e.g., Latin DEMANDĀRE > Cat. *demanar*), the geographical extent of each of these innovations is very different. Whereas the change -MB- > /m/ extends far to the west, now reaching the Portuguese border, the change -ND- > /n/ barely progresses beyond the Catalan-speaking area (it once spread into Aragonese territory), and the isogloss separating its area from that of retention of the group (e.g., Latin DEMANDĀRE > Cast., Ptg. *demandar*) now coincides (in Castellón, Valencia, and Alicante) with those other isoglosses which sharply mark off Southern Catalan (i.e., Valencian) from Central and Southern Castilian (see **4.1.3**).

6 Latin initial L- produces a palatal result (/ʎ/) in the northeast of the Peninsula (e.g., Lat. LUMBU > Cat. *llom*), an innovation which extends into Roussillon and some way into the central Pyrenees, in the province of Huesca. It also extends southwards, covering the entire Catalan-speaking area, including the Balearic Islands. The remainder of the Peninsula retains L- unchanged (e.g., Lat. LUMBU > Cast. *lomo*, Ptg. *lombo*), and once again the isogloss separating innovation from retention coincides with those other isoglosses which today serve to sharply divide the Catalan area from the Castilian area, running irregularly down, as we have seen, through the provinces of Castellón, Valencia and Alicante.

4.1.6 Western innovations

In keeping with the view that Western Hispano-Romance is more conservative than that of the centre or east, there are fewer innovations

	West	Centre	East
1	/tʃ/ ~ /ʃ/ *chorar*	/ʎ/ *llorar*	/pl/, /kl/, /fl/ *plorar*
2	/Ø/ *lua*	/n/ *luna*	/n/ *lluna*
3	/Ø/ *dor*	/l/ *dolor*	/l/ *dolor*
4	perf. aux. *ter* *tenho cantado*	perf. aux. *haber* *he cantado*	perf. aux. *haver* *he cantat*

Table 4.8   Western Peninsular innovations

that can be observed to have spread eastwards from a western focus.
Among the most salient western innovations are those listed in Table
4.8.

1   The treatment of the Latin word-initial consonant clusters PL-,
CL-, FL- shows wide variation across the Peninsula. The deepest
level of innovation belongs to the northwest, where (through a
process whose details are not fully agreed) PL-, CL-, and FL- were
modified to /tʃ/ (e.g., PLŌRĀRE > *chorar*, CLAMĀRE > *chamar*,
FLAMMA > *chama*). This result extends into western Asturias and
far western Leon, and was spread down through the whole of
Portugal (see **4.1.7.1**), although in recent centuries the affricate /tʃ/
has been modified to fricative /ʃ/ (without change of spelling) in
Central and Southern Portuguese, including the standard variety.

By contrast, the whole central block of the Peninsula, from
Cantabria to Andalusia and Murcia, shows a less radical innovation, PL-, CL-, FL- > /ʎ/ (e.g., PLŌRĀRE > *llorar*, CLAMĀRE >
llamar, FLAMMA > *llama*). As in the case of the spread of /tʃ/
down the west of the Peninsula, it is evident that the innovation
/ʎ/ was spread from north to south down the centre, since in
both cases there is evidence that the pre-Reconquest (Mozarabic)
speech of these southern areas retained PL-, CL-, FL- unchanged
(Galmés 1983: 86, 174, 201, 232).

A third area of the Peninsula, originally comprising the
northeast (La Rioja, Aragon and Catalonia), and linked in this
regard with Gaul, showed regular retention of PL-, CL-, FL- (e.g.,

PLŌRĀRE > *plorar*, CLAMĀRE > *clamar*, FLAMMA > *flama*). In this case, it cannot be accurately said that the northeastern result (/pl/, /kl/, /fl/) was spread southwards, since the area settled by Catalan-speakers down the Mediterranean coast was one where speakers (i.e., Mozarabic-speakers) already used unmodified /pl/, /kl/ and /fl/.

2   Treatment of Latin intervocalic -N- reveals a bipartite division of the Peninsula, by contrast with the tripartite division just discussed. Throughout the western third of the Peninsula (Galicia and Portugal), -N- gave rise to nasalization of the preceding vowel and was then effaced (e.g., LANA > Ptg. *lã*). In the case of some vowel combinations, a palatal nasal consonant was reinserted (e.g., VĪNU > Ptg. *vinho*), but in a large number of cases there is no surviving trace of the nasal (e.g., LŪNA > Ptg. *lua*) (see Williams 1962: 70–4, Sampson 1999: 186–97). This feature presumably had its origins in the northwest, since there is no evidence of it in the Mozarabic speech of (central and southern) Portugal. Today it occupies all of Galicia and Portugal, but was absent from Miranda do Douro (see **4.1.2.1**) until standardizing pressures introduced it there. The rest of the Peninsula retains /n/ (e.g., LŪNA > Cast. *luna,* Cat. *lluna*).[34]

3   An identical division of the Peninsula can be observed in the case of the treatment of Latin intervocalic -L- . Loss of the lateral has become normal in all Galicia and Portugal (e.g., DOLŌRE > Ptg. *dor*), except Miranda, but it is retained throughout the rest of the Peninsula (e.g., DOLŌRE > Cast., Cat. *dolor*).

4   We have seen (in **4.1.5(1)**) that perfect aspect is most usually expressed, in the west, by forms (e.g., Ptg. *cantei* 'I have sung' < CANTĀVĪ) which also express perfective aspect ('I sang'), but that compound tenses also exist, with 'progressive' value (approximately 'I have been singing'). The auxiliary used in such compound forms (Gal.-Ptg. *haver*) was cognate with that used for perfect aspect in the centre and east (Cast. *haber,* Cat. *haver*), but this auxiliary is now infrequent and is reserved for literary registers. In other registers, Gal.-Ptg. *haver* has been replaced by innovatory *ter* (< TENĒRE 'to hold'), and, although this innovation is also widely found in Golden-Age Castilian, it has largely retreated from the centre and now serves to distinguish Western Hispano-Romance from Central and Eastern.

4.1.7 Southward expansion of northern features: the Reconquest and its linguistic effects

Up to this point in this chapter, we have been concerned with variation across the Peninsula, identifying the main isoglosses which run (approximately) north–south and contribute both to the northern dialect continuum and to the separation of the three great southern blocs. In order to account for the latter, we have had to take into consideration the spread of features from the north towards the south, within each of the three major zones, but here we look in more detail at the resettlement processes that underlie and explain such developments.

In the aftermath of the Islamic conquest of much of the Peninsula in AD 711–18, a number of independent Christian states slowly emerged in the unconquered north. This zone included approximately the northern quarter of the Peninsula, but the independent band of territory was broader in the west, where it soon reached down to the Duero, than in the east, where it was narrowed to the foothills of the Pyrenees. The main early centre of resistance to Islamic power was Oviedo (in Asturias), but others soon appeared at Santiago de Compostela, Burgos, Pamplona, Girona/Gerona, etc., centres which were strung out along the Romance dialect continuum whose existence we infer for that period (just as we know it to have existed later, and as it still exists today).[35] Each of these statelets was able to expand its territory over the centuries, sometimes at the expense of its neighbours, most usually at the expense of Islamic Spain, and in the wake of this expansion there usually came movement of population within each state, with people from the north resettling areas to the south, as these were acquired.

The linguistic effects of these movements were no doubt complex: features which belonged to specific segments of the northern dialect continuum were carried south into areas where they were previously unknown, and where they entered into competition with features used by the surviving Romance (i.e., Mozarabic) speakers of those areas. This southward movement of population was constant throughout the period of the Reconquest (eighth–fifteenth centuries), and at each stage produced different cases of dialect contact (see **3.1** for the expected outcomes of such contact).[36] The linguistic results of this process, taken together with the gradual hardening of political frontiers in the Peninsula, were the creation of three vertical dialect continua, one in the west (Portugal), one in the centre (Old Castile, New Castile, Extremadura, Andalusia and Murcia, increasingly also including southern Aragon), the third in the east (the Catalan-speaking part of the Kingdom of Valencia). Of course, the northern segments of each of these north–south dialect continua dissolved into the northern (east–west) dialect continuum already discussed (see **4.1.2**), but their southern segments came to be sharply delimited one from another as a result of the process discussed in **4.1.3**.[37]

Certain broad characteristics are shared by these three north–south continua. In the first place, in all three cases, innovations accumulate as one progresses further and further south. That is, the southernmost varieties in each continuum show the greatest degree of change, and this openness to linguistic change is perhaps due to the fact that contact among competing varieties was most intense in these areas immediately after their reconquest. What is known of the consequences of loosened social networks (namely, encouragement of change; see **3.3**) and of dialect contact (that is, levelling and simplification; see **3.1**) is in keeping with the development of the southern varieties in each of the three vertical continua: they are more innovatory than their northern counterparts, and the kinds of changes exhibited are most frequently of a simplifying kind.

Secondly, it should be noted that innovations that arose in the southern zones of each of these continua (whether they arose as a result of dialect contact or for any other reasons) did not generally flow back to the north. That is to say that it was southern innovations, each occupying (as always) a different territory from that occupied by every other innovation, that served to create each north–south continuum.

A third generalization about the Peninsular dialect continua is perhaps also in order. As a result of the social and political history of the Peninsula in the early Middle Ages (the appearance of independent Christian states strung from west to east across the north of the Peninsula and the southward expansion of their populations during the Reconquest), the degree of linguistic difference is greater between east and west than between north and south: on any north–south journey one crosses many fewer isoglosses than on an east–west journey of the same length.

Each of the north–south dialect continua will now be examined, in turn.

4.1.7.1   Galician and Portuguese

Until the eleventh century, Galicia and Portugal (that is, the part of it thus far reconquered, approximately down the Duero) were territories belonging to the Crown of Leon (to which Castile, on the eastern flank, also belonged). It seems that, as the frontier with Islamic Spain was pushed southwards, the territory between the Minho/Miño and the Duero was principally settled by people from what is now Galicia, and that northwestern features (characterizing the western end of the northern dialect continuum) were consequently carried down the Atlantic side of the Peninsula. These would include loss of intervocalic -N- and -L-, use of /tʃ/ in words like *chorar* (< PLŌRĀRE), etc. (see **4.1.6**).

The daughters of Alfonso VI of Leon (1065–1109) were given these territories as fiefdoms, Urraca receiving Galicia, which she governed with her husband Raymond of Burgundy, while Teresa and her husband Henry of Burgundy (cousin of Raymond) received Portugal. While Galicia always thereafter remained integrated in the Crown of Leon (later dominated by Castile), Henry of Burgundy pursued an independent policy, dramatically extending his territory southwards. Henry's son Alfonso (Afonso Henríquez) secured full independence from Leon in 1143 and became the first King of Portugal. The result of this political change turned the Minho into a state frontier, making movement of people across it less frequent and making it more difficult for innovations to cross in either direction. Features which were shared by Galician and Portuguese varieties in the twelfth century most frequently continued to be shared in later periods; this is the case of deletion of intervocalic -L- and -N- (as in *sair* < SALĪRE, *lua* < LŪNA), or the inflected infinitive construction.[38] By contrast, innovations which arose later on either side of the frontier generally did not cross to the other territory. So, for example, devoicing of voiced sibilants and their merger with their voiceless counterparts (/ʃ/, /ʒ/ > /ʃ/; /s/, /z/ > /s/; /tˢ/, /dᶻ/ > /tˢ/, later /θ/ or /s/, a northern innovation affecting varieties stretching from the western Galician coast to the central Pyrenees), does not spread south of the Minho (Table **4.9**).

Innovations which arose in the south of Portugal often do not spread to the whole of Portuguese territory, and so cannot reach Galicia. A case in point is the merger of dental with alveolar sibilants, with dental outcome (exemplified by the identical internal consonants today found in standard Portuguese *passo* and *braço*, on the one hand, and in *rosa* and *prazer*, on the other), which almost certainly has southern origins identical with those of Andalusian *seseo* (see **4.1.7.2.1**). It

Medieval Galician–Portuguese		Portuguese		Galician	
/ʃ/	*roxo* (< RUSSEU)	/ʃ/	*roxo*	/ʃ/	*roxo*
/ʒ/	*queijo* (< CASEU)	/ʒ/	*queijo*		*queixo*
/s/	*passo* (< PASSU)	/s/	*passo*	/s/	*paso*
/z/	*rosa* (< ROSA)	/z/	*rosa*		*rosa*
/tˢ/	*braço* (< BRACCHIU)	/s/	*braço*	/θ/ ~ /s/[a]	*brazo*
/dᶻ/	*prazer* (< PLACĒRE)	/z/	*prazer*		*prazer*

[a] Certain western varieties of Galician exhibit *seseo* (merger of /s/ and /θ/ in (predorsal) /s/), while the majority maintain the distinction (see Zamora 1986: 1–10).

Table 4.9 Development of sibilants in Galician–Portuguese

reaches only the southern two-thirds of Portugal, therefore including the important urban centres of Coimbra and Lisbon, whose varieties underlie the Portuguese standard, but leaves large northern Portuguese areas unaffected.[39]

Similarly, the deaffrication of /tʃ/ to produce /ʃ/ in words like *chorar* (< PLŌRĀRE) 'to weep', *chegar* (< PLICĀRE) 'to arrive', etc., is a Southern Portuguese phenomenon (perhaps related to the similar deaffrication of Castilian /tʃ/ in parts of Andalusia)[40] which extends far enough northwards to include the Lisbon and Coimbra areas (and therefore enter the standard) but does not reach northern Portugal (or Galicia).

Again, reduction of the diphthong /ou/ to /o/ (or its replacement by /oi/, e.g., *ouro* (< AURUM) > /óro/ or /óiro/ 'gold') is a Southern Portuguese feature (shared with much of the centre and east of the Peninsula; see Table 4.7) which has penetrated all of southern and central Portugal (thereby affecting the standard) but not the north, or Galicia.[41]

More complex is the case of the merger of /b/ (< -B-, -P-) and /β/ (< -B-, -V-). This merger (into a single voiced non-nasal bilabial /b/) is characteristic of all northern varieties of Hispano-Romance, from the Atlantic to the Mediterranean, including Galician and northern Portuguese varieties. This distribution suggests that this merger (and the related absence of labiodental /v/) is quite ancient, antedating the twelfth-century separation of Portugal from the Crown of Leon.[42]

4.1.7.2   Castilian and Andalusian

Just as Portuguese can be a regarded as a southern offshoot of varieties originating in the northwest of the Peninsula, so Andalusian can best be considered as a southward extension of varieties originating in the centre-north. In both cases, northern features were extended southwards largely as a result of the displacement of speakers from north to south as they settled new territories in the wake of the Reconquest. Similarly, in both cases, innovations which arose in these southern territories could be transmitted northwards. The great difference between the linguistic development of the two territories is that whereas Lisbon lies far enough south to be affected by a large number of southern Portuguese innovations (which were then incorporated in the Portuguese standard), central-southern innovations most usually did not reach the trend-setting cities of central Castile, Toledo and Madrid, and therefore did not usually become part of standard Spanish.

On the other hand, southern features of both Portuguese and Castilian were prominent in the varieties which were established in the Americas from the late fifteenth century onwards, so that Brazilian Portuguese more closely resembles Southern Peninsular Portuguese than other varieties of Peninsular Portuguese, just as American Spanish inherits many of the characteristics of Andalusian varieties (see **5.1**).

The most salient southern innovations in the central Peninsular bloc (i.e., the most noticeable features of Andalusian Spanish) include the following.

4.1.7.2.1   Seseo *and* ceceo

In much of Andalusia, the four medieval sibilant phonemes $/t^s/$, $/d^z/$, $/s/$ and $/z/$ have merged into a single voiceless dental fricative $/\underset{\sim}{s}/$, which today appears with or without interdental colouring (fronting of the tongue body so that the sound acquires some of the acoustic qualities of interdental $/\theta/$), respectively $[\underset{\sim}{s}^\theta]$ and $[\underset{\sim}{s}]$. To the non-Andalusian speaker of Castilian, it seems that the Andalusian speaker who pronounces $[\underset{\sim}{s}^\theta]$ is using a sound, similar to Castilian $/\theta/$, in circumstances where the Castilian speaker expects not only $/\theta/$ (e.g., $[ká\underset{\sim}{s}^\theta a]$ for *caza*) but also $/s/$ (e.g., $[ká\underset{\sim}{s}^\theta a]$ for *casa*). Since to the outsider this kind of pronunciation appears to be an 'abuse of the letter *z* (i.e., *zeta*)' (more properly, of the sound represented by *z*), it is named *ceceo*. In the second case, the non-Andalusian hears a sound ($[\underset{\sim}{s}]$) somewhat like his own $/s/$, not only where he is expecting $/s/$ (e.g., $[ká\underset{\sim}{s}a]$ for *casa*) but also

Medieval phoneme	Medieval spelling	Modern spelling and meaning	ceceo	seseo
/tˢ/	caça	caza 'hunt'	[káṣ̬ᶿa]	[káṣa]
/dᶻ/	deẓir	decir 'to say'	[deṣ̬ᶿír]	[deṣír]
/s/	passo	paso 'step'	[páṣ̬ᶿo]	[páṣo]
/z/	caẓa	casa 'house'	[káṣ̬ᶿa]	[káṣa]

Table 4.10 *Seseo* and *ceceo* in Andalusian Spanish

where he is expecting /θ/ (e.g., [káṣa] for *caza*). This style of pronunciation is deemed to be an 'abuse of the letter *s*' and is consequently labelled *seseo*.

Table **4.10** summarizes and exemplifies these mergers. Their origin is much disputed, but it is likely that there were two phases of merger, following routine deaffrication of /tˢ/ and /dᶻ/ to /ṣ/ and /ẓ/. The first (merger of dental-alveolar /s/ and /z/ respectively with dental /ṣ/ and /ẓ/) is characteristically Andalusian, while the second (merger of voiced and voiceless sibilants with voiceless outcome, here bringing /ṣ/ (< /s/ and /ṣ/) and /ẓ/ (< /z/ and /ẓ/) together as /ṣ/) is eventually felt in all Castilian varieties.

The first of these mergers is perhaps best described as the outcome of the dialect contact which must have arisen due to immigration into post-Reconquest Seville (just as occurred in other recently reconquered areas). As we have seen (**3.1**), one of the expected effects of contact among mutually intelligible language varieties is preference for the simplest among competing variants. Thus, if any group of speakers, however small, had allowed dento-alveolar /s/ and /z/ to merge with dental /ṣ/ and /ẓ/, this merger would be likely to be extended to the whole community (see Penny 1987, Tuten 1998).[43]

Seseo, then, probably has its origins in late-medieval Seville, gaining ground in the sixteenth century and spreading not only to other areas of Andalusia but also (because of the vital role played by Seville in overseas settlement) to the whole of Spanish America (see **5.1.1**). Because of its establishment in many cities, including among educated urban speakers, *seseo* has acquired full acceptability in the Spanish-speaking world, and competes equally with the central/northern Peninsular norm (which distinguishes /káθa/ *caza* from /kása/

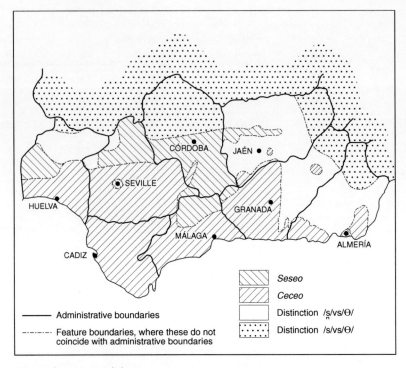

Figure 4.1   *Seseo* and *ceceo* in Andalusia

casa). On the other hand, *ceceo* is more limited in geographical and social extent. It appears to have developed in the seventeenth or eighteenth centuries, in coastal regions of Andalusia, and now stretches from southern Huelva through Cádiz, Málaga and southern Granada to Almería. Although it is the usual pronunciation of this area, including major cities such as Cádiz and Málaga, *ceceo* has not acquired full social acceptance; educated speakers from these areas tend to move from *ceceo* to *seseo* and back according to the formality of the social circumstances in which they find themselves.

It is to be noted (as can be seen from the map in Figure **4.1**) that considerable areas of Andalusia (although not a large proportion of the Andalusian population) show neither *ceceo* nor *seseo*, but distinguish an interdental /θ/ from an /s/ (of whatever phonetic kind).[44]

4.1.7.2.2   Yeísmo

Another innovation which took root in early modern Andalusia was the merger of the palatals /ʎ/ and /j̆/, in favour of non-lateral fricative and affricate articulations: [ĵ], [ʒ], [dʒ], etc. Since the predominant real-ization ([ĵ]) of the merged phoneme is identical to that of standard /ĵ/ (e.g., in *mayo*), this innovation is labelled *yeísmo*. It is to be observed in almost the whole of Andalusia, the exceptions being certain pockets of retention of the /ʎ/–/ĵ/ contrast in the southwest (parts of Huelva, rural Seville and Cádiz).

Although this merger may have had its remote origins in the far north of the Peninsula (Penny 1991b), its success in the Spanish-speaking world is undoubtedly due to its adoption by urban speakers in Andalusia in the wake of the Reconquest, despite the fact that it is not unambiguously attested there until several centuries later. This adop-tion, once again, can be regarded as the predictable preference for a simpler variant (one phoneme rather than two) in a situation of dialect contact (see **3.1.4**).

However, unlike many other southern Castilian (i.e., Andalusian) features (e.g., *seseo*), *yeísmo* did flow back northward, in recent cen-turies. Perhaps as a result of Andalusian immigration into Madrid, this feature began to gain ground there in working-class speech, as can be seen in the late nineteenth-century novels of Benito Pérez Galdós, and then began to move up through society in successive generations until in the late twentieth century it reached all but a small number of the most conservative varieties of Madrid speech. During the same century, *yeísmo* spread from Madrid to other cities of central and north-ern Spain and has become part of the dominant urban speech pattern throughout the Peninsula, even though many geographically interme-diate (predominantly rural) varieties maintain the older pattern, distin-guishing the two phonemes in such minimal pairs as *mallo* 'mallet' and *mayo* 'May' (for details see Alonso 1967a). Like other Andalusian fea-tures, *yeísmo* became characteristic of Spanish in the Americas (see **5.1**), and although not universal there (since many Andean areas main-tain /ʎ/), it forms part of the phonology of the large majority of American-Spanish speakers.

4.1.7.2.3 *Maintenance and loss of /h/*
As we have seen (in **3.1.3.2**), /h/-dropping began in Old Castile in the later Middle Ages and began to spread rapidly after its adoption by speak-ers in Madrid in the later sixteenth century. Until the sixteenth century, then, Andalusia remained unaffected by this change, and pronunciations like /hámbre/, /hílo/, /húmo/ (*hambre, hilo, humo* < FAMINE, FILU, FUMU) continued in use. Likewise, the /h/ (phonetically [ʍ]) of words

like *fuego, fuente, fui* (< FŎCU, FŎNTE, FŪĪ) remained unchanged and was not replaced by /f/. Two changes have taken place since that time, one geographical, the other diastratic or social. On the one hand, /h/-less pronunciations have become the norm for all speakers in eastern Andalusia (the province of Jaén, the eastern half of Granada, and most of the province of Almería), while western Andalusian varieties have maintained /h/ (at least in informal speech), in common with Extremadura and other, northern, areas. On the other hand (as just implied), in western Andalusia /h/-dropping has progressed down the social scale, so that retention of /h/ now typifies unguarded rural and working-class speech.

Those speakers who maintain /h/ have merged this phoneme with the reflex of medieval /ʃ/ and /ʒ/ (see **3.1.3.1**), usually with glottal outcome ([h]), so that *hambre, hilo, humo, fuego* for such speakers contain the same initial phoneme as *jugo* (medieval /ʃúgo/ *xugo* < SŪCU), *juego* (medieval /ʒuégo/ *juego* < IŎCU), *jinete* (medieval /ʒinéte/ *ginete* < Ar. *zenêtī*). This popular Western Andalusian feature, like a good number of others, was spread to the Canaries and to large areas of America, where it maintains a similar social status to the one it enjoys in Andalusia (see **4.1.8** and **5.2.1**).

4.1.7.2.4   *Weakening of /-s/*
Weakening of syllable-final /s/, whether within the word (as in *es̱te*), at the end of a word before a pause (as in *son éstos̱*), or at the end of a word before a word-initial consonant (as in *estas̱ casas*), is a further character-istic of southern Castilian. Like *yeísmo*, its remote origins may lie in the far north, where small rural pockets of similar /-s/-weakening still exist (Penny 1991b), but, as in that case, the success of this feature is due to its acceptance by urban speakers in reconquered areas of southern Spain.

Weakening of /s/ manifests a range of degrees of intensity. The lowest degree of intensity is represented by simple glottalization or aspiration of /-s/, modifying it to [ʰ]. This style of pronunciation (e.g., [éʰtaʰ kásaʰ] = *estas casas*) is the most widespread geographically and socially; it continues northwards into all of New Castile, Extremadura and Murcia, and appears in the speech of all social classes. It appears to be gaining increasing currency in Madrid (where its existence is already noted in the working-class characters of Benito Pérez Galdós's late nineteenth-century novels) and is now reported (Williams 1987: 114–18) in urban varieties in Old Castile (see **4.2.3**).

A further degree of weakening is seen when the aspirate adopts some of the features of the following consonant, as when the aspirate takes on the voice feature and sometimes the nasal quality of a following nasal consonant: [mí^ɦmo], [mí^ɦmo] = *mismo*. Such assimilation of the syllable-final consonant to the following consonant may be total, leading to a long or geminate consonant: [aβíᵖpa] = *avispa*; [áᵏko] = *asco*. Such total assimilation, although frequent, is less widespread than simple aspiration (it is not common outside western Andalusia, and tends to be avoided by educated speakers).

Assimilation between the two consonants concerned may go further, in that the second may take on the voiceless nature of the first (original voiceless /s/, or its voiceless successor [ʰ]), while the first adopts the place of articulation of the second, so that the two merge as a single voiceless consonant: [la ɸákaʰ] = *las vacas*; [lo θeβáneʰ] = *los desvanes*; [dihúʰto] = *disgusto*, where the voiceless fricatives [ɸ], [θ], [h] respectively maintain the place of articulation of the original second consonant, /b/, /d/ and /g/. This kind of articulation, which only occurs in the sequences cited, is more restricted, geographically and socially, than the simple assimilation exemplified by [aβíᵖpa] or [áᵏko].

The most radical weakening of all, typical of eastern Andalusia but also occasionally observed in western Andalusia, is the complete elimination of syllable-final /s/, with the consequence that traditional markers of number (in nouns and adjectives) and person (in the verb) are eliminated: [étɔ] = *estos*; [lɔ mímɔ] = *los mismos,* although presence of an original /s/ may be marked by the devoicing of syllable-initial /b/, /d/ or /g/: [læ ɸǽkæ] = *las vacas*, vs. [la βáka] = *la vaca* (Penny 1986). We shall see in the following section how Eastern Andalusian varieties remedy this lack of consonant marking by transferring the morphological load to the vowels of the phrase concerned.

In western Andalusian areas where morpheme-final /-s/ survives as an aspirate (e.g., [laʰ kása⁽ʰ⁾] *las casas*, this /s/ may be pronounced as an aspirate even where it is syllable-initial (in accordance with the resyllabification rule of Spanish phonology).[45] Thus, although this pronunciation is more stigmatized than other types of /-s/-reduction, a phrase like *las olas* is frequently articulated [la-hóla⁽ʰ⁾]. This kind of articulation is also heard in words like *nosotros* (which can be analysed as /nos#ótros/): [no-hó-tro⁽ʰ⁾], just like *los otros* [lo-hó-tro⁽ʰ⁾].

The various results of /-s/-weakening can be listed as in Table **4.11**, where any combination of /s/ and another consonant (e.g., /sf/) is to be understood as occurring either within a single word (where

		Aspiration	Assimilation		Loss
/sp/	*los perros*	[loʰ péro⁽ʰ⁾]	[loᵖ péro⁽ʰ⁾]		[lɔ pérɔ]
	avispa	[aβíʰpa]	[aβíᵖpa]		[aβípa]
/sb/	*las vacas* .	[laʰ βáka⁽ʰ⁾] [laⁿ βáka⁽ʰ⁾]	[laᵝ βáka⁽ʰ⁾]	[laᶲ ɸáka⁽ʰ⁾]	[læ ɸǽkæ]
	desván	[deʰβáŋ] [deⁿβáŋ]	[deᵝβáŋ]	[deᶲɸ áŋ]	[deɸ áŋ]
/sm/	*las manos*	[laʰ máno⁽ʰ⁾]	[laⁿ máno⁽ʰ⁾]	[laᵐ máno⁽ʰ⁾]	[læ mǽnɔ]
/sf/	*las fotos*	[laʰ fóto⁽ʰ⁾]	[laᶠ fóto⁽ʰ⁾]	[laᶲ ɸóto⁽ʰ⁾]	[læ ɸɔ́tɔ]
	asfalto	[aʰfálto]	[aᶠfálto]	[aᶲɸálto]	[aɸálto]
/st/	*los toros*	[loʰ tóro⁽ʰ⁾]	[loᵗ tóro⁽ʰ⁾]		[lɔ tɔ́rɔ]
	estos	[éʰto⁽ʰ⁾]	[éᵗto⁽ʰ⁾]		[étɔ]
/sd/	*los días*	[loʰ ðía⁽ʰ⁾]	[loᵟ ðía⁽ʰ⁾] [loⁿ ðía⁽ʰ⁾]	[loᶿ ðía⁽ʰ⁾]	[lɔ ðíæ]
	desde	[déʰðe]	[déⁿðe]	[dé¹ðe]	
/sn/	*asno*	[áⁿno]	[áⁿno]	[áⁿno]	
/ss/	*los sesos*	[loʰ séso⁽ʰ⁾]			[lɔ sésɔ]
/sl/	*los lomos*	[loʰ lómo⁽ʰ⁾]	[loⁿ lómo⁽ʰ⁾]	[lo¹ lómo⁽ʰ⁾]	[lɔ lɔ́mɔ]
/sr/	*los reyes*		[lo¹ réje⁽ʰ⁾]		[lɔ réjɛ]
/stʃ/	*las chicas*	[laʰ tʃíka⁽ʰ⁾]			[læ tʃíkæ]
/sj/	*mis yernos*	[miʰ jérno⁽ʰ⁾]	[miⁿ jérno⁽ʰ⁾]		[mɪ jɛ́rnɔ]
	las llamas	[laʰ jáma⁽ʰ⁾]	[laⁿ jáma⁽ʰ⁾]		[læ jǽmæ]
/sk/	*los quesos*	[loʰ késo⁽ʰ⁾]	[loᵏ késo⁽ʰ⁾]		[lɔ késɔ]
	asco	[áʰko]	[áᵏko]		
/sg/	*los gatos*	[loʰ ɣáto⁽ʰ⁾]	[loˠ ɣáto⁽ʰ⁾] [loⁿ ɣáto⁽ʰ⁾]	[loˣ xáto⁽ʰ⁾]	[lɔ xǽtɔ]
	disgusto	[diʰɣúʰto]	[diˠɣúᵗto] [diⁿɣúᵗto]		[dihúᵗto]
/sx/	*los jarros*	[loʰ háro⁽ʰ⁾]			[lɔ hǽrɔ]
/s#V/[a]	*las olas*	[la hóla⁽ʰ⁾]			

[a] The symbol #V here indicates any vowel at the onset of a following word, and implies that /s/ is resyllabified from syllable-final to syllable-initial.

Table 4.11 Results of /-s/-weakening

such a word-internal sequence exists) or across the boundary between closely linked words.[46]

This phenomenon, like many other Andalusian features, was extended to America, although not so universally as in the case of *seseo* or even *yeísmo*. We shall see (**5.1.2**) that it is characteristic of those areas most culturally distant from the chief administrative centres of the Spanish Empire, namely Mexico City and Lima. It is most strongly evident in the Spanish of the southwestern United States, in central America and the Caribbean, and in the countries of the Southern Cone.

4.1.7.2.5 *Andalusian vowel-systems*

The complete loss of syllable-final (including word-final) /s/, typical of eastern Andalusia, has potentially dramatic effects on the morphological structure of those varieties, since (as in standard Spanish) word-final /s/ carries a heavy morphological load: it marks the contrast between plural and singular in nouns, adjectives, etc., and marks the contrast between second person and third person in the verb. Eastern Andalusian varieties have, however, made good this potential deficiency by transferring the morphological load from the consonant to the vowels of the forms in which the /s/ originally occurred. The mechanism employed was the following.

In all varieties of Spanish (as in many other languages) a vowel phoneme which appears in a syllable blocked by a consonant has a somewhat lower tongue-height than the same phoneme when it appears in a free syllable (i.e., when no consonant follows the vowel concerned in the same syllable). Thus, the first and last /o/ of *los toros* is articulated a little lower than the final /o/ of *el toro*. In the large majority of varieties of Spanish, this slight variation carries no information (it is sub-phonemic) and therefore passes unnoticed by speakers. However, as /-s/ headed towards elimination and was finally deleted in parts of southern Spain, tongue-height became the only way of distinguishing singular from plural and second person from third. That is to say, a purely phonetic difference (of tongue-position) provided the basis for a series of phonological splits, /e/, /o/ and /a/ dividing respectively into /ɛ/ and /e/, /ɔ/ and /o/, /æ/ and /a/.[47] These splits have come to affect not solely the final syllable of the words concerned, but *all* the syllables, so that a measure of vowel harmony has been introduced: if the final syllable contains /ɛ/, /ɔ/ or /æ/, then the other syllables of the word may not contain /e/, /o/ or

	Front	Back
High	/i/	/u/
Mid-high	/e/	/o/
Mid-low	/ɛ/	/ɔ/
Low	/æ/	/a/

Table 4.12   Eastern Andalusian vowel-system

/a/. The result, in eastern Andalusia (Jaén, Granada, Almería, most of Málaga and Cordoba and adjacent parts of Seville province; Alvar 1996a: 145), is a rectangular eight-vowel system (notably different from the triangular five-vowel system used throughout the rest of the Spanish-speaking world): see Table **4.12**. Some examples of these contrasts can be found among the illustrations of /-s/-weakening in Table **4.11**, in the column headed 'loss'. Further examples, organized by the tonic phoneme, are:

/píto/	pito	/múla/	mula
/pítɔ/	pitos	/múlæ/	mulas
/pélo/	pelo	/kósa/	cosa
/pélɔ/	pelos	/kɔ́sæ/	cosas
/pǽlɔ/	palos	/pálo/	palo[48]

4.1.7.2.6   *Merger of /-r/ and /-l/*

Syllable-final (including word-final and phrase-final) liquids are most frequently neutralized in Andalusian varieties, with varied results. The origin of this change, as always, is difficult to determine, but as in the case of *yeísmo* and /-s/-weakening may have its distant source in immigration from the far north (Penny 1991b). But as in those cases, it was no doubt the social conditions of post-Reconquest Andalusia which determined the propagation of this feature: contact between speakers of many mutually intelligible varieties which produced a multiplicity of competing variants, a competition from which the simplest variant normally emerged the winner (see **3.1** and Trudgill 1986).

In syllable-final position, then, many speakers of Andalusian Spanish make no distinction between, say, *harto* 'satisfied' and *alto* 'high', or *arma* 'weapon' and *alma* 'soul'. The realization of the neutralized phonemes is very varied, ranging from the flap [ɾ] or approximant [ɹ] ([áɾto] ~ [áɹto] = *harto* and *alto*) to lateral [l] ([álto] = *harto* and *alto*), with a number of possible intermediate articulations, such as [ɺ], which exhibit both rhotic and lateral qualities. Aspirated articulations are also frequent (e.g., [káʰne] *carne*), as is deletion of these neutralized phonemes, especially in word-final (including phrase-final) position. In this position, the solution [l] is the most frequent outcome in the eastern provinces (eastern Cordoba, Jaén, Almería and most of Granada) and in northern Huelva, while deletion is the commonest outcome in the rest of Andalusia (Alvar 1996a: 247–8).

In the case of this development (unlike *seseo* and *yeísmo*) there is no phonemic merger, since /r/ and /l/ continue to be contrasted in Andalusian Spanish in syllable-initial position (e.g., *paro* 'strike' vs *palo* 'stick'), including those cases where word-final /-r/ or /-l/ becomes syllable-initial because the following word begins with a vowel: those speakers who merge the phonemes with a rhotic result (e.g., [eɹ-pé-lo] *el pelo*) nevertheless use a lateral when the word-final phoneme becomes syllable-initial (e.g., [e-ló-tro] *el otro*).

This neutralization, like many of the features discussed here as centred upon Andalusia, is not limited to the eight provinces of Andalusia. Many areas of New Castile display it, as do Murcia, Extremadura and southern Salamanca (*ALPI* 1962: 17, 74). With regard to its social appreciation, it is associated especially with rural and uncultured speech, but has also made some headway in urban varieties, without gaining social acceptability.

This feature was evidently carried to America as part of the speech of early colonists, since it is revealed in many parts of the overseas empire by sixteenth-century misspellings. Despite this, it is today limited to the islands and coastal areas of the Caribbean and to the Pacific coast (**5.1.2.3**).

4.1.7.2.7 *Third-person pronoun reference*
Andalusian Spanish differs from that of Old and New Castile in its personal pronoun system. Whereas most speakers in those areas have adopted *leísmo* (the use of the pronouns *le* and *les* to designate masculine personal direct objects; see **4.1.2.3**), Andalusian Spanish maintains the older case-determined system of reference, which distinguishes between *le(s)* (indirect object pronouns, unmarked for gender), on the one hand, and *lo(s), la(s)* (direct object pronouns, masculine and feminine respectively), on the other. Table **4.1** (p. 91) reflects the Andalusian system; the examples based on it are repeated here for convenience:

Lo(s) vi (a mi(s) amigo(s))	[+direct, +animate, +count, +masc]
El reloj me lo rompí	[+direct, -animate, +count, +masc]
Le(s) mandé una carta (a mi(s) amigo(s))	[-direct, +animate, +count, +masc]
La(s) vi (a mi(s) amiga(s))	[+direct, +animate, +count, -masc]
La cabeza la tengo sucia	[+direct, -animate, +count, -masc]
Le(s) mandé una carta (a mi(s) amiga(s)).	[-direct, +animate, +count, -masc]

4.1.7.2.8   *Modes of address*

Most Peninsular Spanish distinguishes, for example, *vosotros / -as sois* (to express solidarity) from *ustedes son* (to express distance or respect) 'you (pl.) are'. However, many Western Andalusian varieties have lost this contrast (as also occurs in Canarian and American Spanish; see **4.1.8** and **5.1.1.2**). In much of Huelva and Seville, in Cádiz and Málaga, and in parts of Cordoba and Jaén, the only pronoun available is *ustedes*, most typically accompanied by a third-person-plural verb, so that *(ustedes) son* in these varieties is equivalent to both standard *(vosotros/ -as) sois* and standard *(ustedes) son*.[49] However, unlike Canarian and American Spanish, these Western Andalusian varieties also allow *ustedes* to appear with a second-person-plural verb: *ustedes sois* (whether or not through hypercorrection (**1.5**) is unclear). In the same areas, the plural object pronoun (direct and indirect) for reference to the second person is correspondingly *se* (e.g., *ustedes se van* = both standard *(ustedes) se van* and *(vosotros/-as) os vais*). Like *vosotros/-as*, the pronoun *os* is not used in this area.

4.1.7.3   Catalan and Valencian

Northern Catalan varieties represent the eastern extremity of the northern Peninsular dialect continuum (see **4.1.2**), so that (*pace* Badía 1951: 53–4) there is no boundary in this area between Catalan varieties and other Peninsular varieties spoken further to the West.[50] As in the parallel cases of Galician–Portuguese and Castilian, speakers of these varieties carried them southwards (and to the Balearic Islands) in the wake of the medieval territorial conquests made by the Crown of Aragon, forming a new north–south continuum. These resettlements produced the same kind of dialect contact (with all the predictable effects that contact no doubt produced; see **3.1**) as occurred in reconquered territories further west. However, with hindsight it is possible to say that in the dialect mix from which the Balearic varieties of Catalan emerged it was the features which were typical of the eastern part of Old Catalonia (including Barcelona) which were most successful, while the mix from which the Valencian varieties emerged was resolved in favour of features typical of the western part of Old Catalonia (including Lleida/Lerida). There may be a demographic reason for these outcomes (predominance of settlers from east and west Catalonia in the Balearics and in Valencia, respectively), but this has not so far been clearly demonstrated (or falsified). In any case, features belonging to the majority of settlers are not expected necessarily to predominate in the *koiné* which emerges under the conditions of dialect contact, unless they have the advantage of simplicity (see **3.1**).

In accordance with these outcomes, the main feature which separates Southern Peninsular Catalan (i.e., Valencian, spoken in a broad coastal band stretching through the provinces of Castellón, Valencia, and Alicante) from the Balearic varieties is the retention in Valencian, as in Northwestern Catalan, of five contrasting atonic vowels (/i/, /e/, /a/, /o/, /u/, as in *primer, segur, amic, morir, durar*), while Balearic varieties, like those of eastern Old Catalonia, most frequently reduce atonic vowels to only three (/i/ in *primer*, /ə/ in *segur* and *amic*, /u/ in *morir* and *durar*).

With regard to the transition between Catalan as a whole and Castilian, there are close similarities between this transition and the one that can be observed on the other side of the Peninsula between Castilian and Portuguese (**4.1.7.1**). The isoglosses that separate Southern Catalan from Castilian essentially coincide over a distance of some two hundred miles, forming a sharp boundary which begins at a point north of the river Ebro, and runs approximately parallel to the Mediterranean and reaches the sea below Alicante (see **4.1.3–4**, especially Table **4.6**).[51]

4.1.8   The Canaries

The Canary Islands were discovered by Europeans in the fifteenth century, and were incorporated into the Crown of Castile during that century. The islands were settled by people largely from western Andalusia, although it is evident that there were also contingents from Galicia and Portugal, Leon, and Castile proper. (Note that the Kingdom of Granada, comprising what is now much of eastern Andalusia, was still to be reconquered and remained outside the Crown of Castile at this time, so that it could not contribute to the initial colonization process.) At all events, out of the mix of Spanish varieties which came into contact in the Canaries there emerged new varieties predominantly characterized by features stemming from Seville, Cádiz, Huelva, and other western Andalusian regions. As a result, Canarian speech has much in common with Western Andalusian varieties, since it displays the following features:[52]

1 *Seseo* (**4.1.7.2.1**) is typical of Canarian speech, most usually with the non-fronted realization ([s̺]) of dental /s̺/. However, the fronted variant ([s̺θ], often identified by outsiders as a Castilian /θ/) is heard in rural Tenerife. More strikingly, in the western Canaries (Gomera, La Palma) the merger of voiced and voiceless sibilants (see **3.1.3.1**) has not occurred, so that a voiced dental fricative /z̺/ here represents medieval /dᶻ/ and /z/, in words like *racimo, decir* / *queso, casa*, while words which in the medieval period displayed /tˢ/ or /s/ here have /s̺/: *caza, mecer* / *pasar, eso* (Lapesa 1980: 519; ALEICan, 1975–8). These pronunciations, like similar ones reported in Extremadura, are important for establishing the chronology of the merger of the voiced and the voiceless sibilants, a merger which began in the north of the Peninsula and spread into southern Spain after the mid-sixteenth century (**3.1.3.1**). Clearly, this devoicing process had not reached western Andalusia (or many other southern regions) at the time of the settlement of the Canaries.

2 Although *yeísmo* (**4.1.7.2.2**) is today almost universal in Andalusia, it is precisely in southwestern Andalusia (Huelva) that the major pockets of distinction between /ʎ/ and / ǰ / are to be found. It is perhaps therefore not surprising that the /ʎ/–/ ǰ / contrast is widely observed in Canarian Spanish, although *yeísmo* dominates in Gran Canaria and in Santa Cruz de Tenerife (ALEICan, 1975–8: maps 904, 930, 954).

3 The aspirate /h/ (**4.1.7.2.3**) is widely maintained in the Canaries, in unpretentious speech, as in western Andalusia, Extremadura, etc. As in these areas, /h/ not only descends from Latin F- (*humo, fuego*) but also represents the product of merged medieval /ʃ/ and /ʒ/ (*caja, mujer*) (ALEICan, 1975–8: maps 927, 973, 980, 1011, 1198).

4 Weakening of /-s/ is typical of the Spanish spoken throughout the Canaries. It is of the Western Andalusian type (see **4.1.7.2.4**), in

which /-s/ survives as an aspirate (e.g., [éʰte] *este*) or is assimilated to the following consonant (e.g., [íʰla] [íˡla] *isla*) (Oftedal 1985: 51–8; *ALEICan*, 1975–8: maps 905–6, 912–13). However, treatment of syllable-final /s/ does not lead to the expanded vowel-system of the type observed in eastern Andalusia (**4.1.7.2.5**).

5   Merger of syllable-final /-r/ and /-l/ (**4.1.7.2.6**) is also typical of Canarian Spanish (e.g., [hálto] *harto*), with a similar range of outcomes to those observed in Andalusia, including occasional aspirate articulations, especially before nasals (e.g., [káʰne] *carne*).

6   Third-person pronoun reference is of the Southern Spanish and American Spanish type, in which *le(s)* is reserved for indirect-object function, and *lo(s)* continues to function in accordance with its etymology, signalling direct-object referents, both personal and non-personal (see examples in **4.1.7.2.7**).

7   In most Canarian varieties, modes of second-person plural address are like those of western Andalusia and America, with loss of *vosotros/ -as* and of the historically second-person plural verb-forms (**4.1.7.2.8**), so that, for example, *(ustedes) van* is equivalent to both standard *(vosotros) vais* and standard *(ustedes) van*. However, in the western Canaries (La Gomera, El Hierro, parts of La Palma) *(vosotros) vais* continues in use.

Although, as we have seen, Canarian Spanish shares many of its features with Andalusian Spanish, it has at least one phonetic feature which appears to be unique. Magne Oftedal (1985) describes lenition (in the form of voicing) of intervocalic /p/, /t/, /tʃ/ and /k/ in the speech of Gran Canaria. These phonemes appear as [b], [d], [dʒ] and [g] respectively, whenever the phoneme occurs between vowels, whether word-initially (e.g., [la báta] *la pata*) or word-internally (e.g., [debórte] *deporte*). Taken together with loss of word-final /-s/ in the varieties he describes, he is able to claim that Canarian Spanish offers word-initial consonant mutation in the Celtic manner: [la gála] *la cala* vs [la kála] *las calas*. For a similar claim in connection with Eastern Andalusian, see Penny (1986).

Canarian Spanish also shares a number of features, especially vocabulary, with northwestern Peninsular varieties. One such consists of the values of the preterite and perfect verb-forms, which differ from those used in the rest of the Peninsula, but coincide with those used in Galicia, Leon, Asturias, and Cantabria, as well as in Spanish America. For further discussion, see **5.1.3.2**.

4.2 Social variation

Since the middle of the twentieth century it has become abundantly
clear that, in all languages, variation in certain linguistic features is correlated with sociological variables such as age, social class, educational
background, sex, and so on (**1.1.2**). Studies of this kind of co-variation
have not been abundant in the Spanish-speaking world, where sociolinguistic study has most frequently been directed towards matters of language contact and code-switching, especially in bilingual areas such as
Catalonia, the Basque Country, Galicia, the Andes, or the US
Southwest. It follows that no comprehensive account of social variation in Spain can yet be attempted, although there are perhaps
sufficient data to allow us to present a number of case-studies of such
variation. In all the cases concerned, we are dealing with changes in
progress, which are working their way through the Spanish-speaking
community and which may or may not eventually become universal.
We do not have evidence of the rarer instance of stable variation
without ongoing change.

4.2.1 *Yeísmo*

We have already had cause to look at this merger of /ʎ/ and /ǰ/
(which brings together sets of words such as *pollo, mallo* with sets
including *poyo, mayo*, most usually with non-lateral results) from a
geographical point of view (in **4.1.7.2.2**, **4.1.8**), and we shall meet it
again in connection with American Spanish (**5.1.2.1**). We have noted
that in recent centuries this feature has spread from a southern
Peninsular base (western Andalusia) to New Castile, including most
notably to Madrid, from where it has spread to urban centres in the
north of Spain. Although we do not have recent sociolinguistic
studies of this variable, it is reasonably clear that, in the urban speech
of the northern half of Spain, the variant [ʎ] (in phonemic contrast
with /ǰ/) only occurs with any frequency among the oldest age-
groups and the 'highest' socio-economic classes, and is effectively
absent from the youngest groups and from working-class speech,
where only variants such as [ǰ] (representing both /ʎ/ and /ǰ/) are in
use.

4.2.2 Loss of /-d-/

In Section **1.2** we presented a model of diachronic variation (see Table **1.1**) in which treatment of /d/ in the sequence *-ado* was given as an example of the way in which a range of competing variants (here [d]~[ð]~[ᵒ]~[Ø]) changes over time, usually by the successive loss of older variants and the introduction of new variants. It was also noted (**1.4**) that historically successive variants may also appear synchronically in co-variation with such sociological variables as age or social class. Such synchronic co-variation applies to the case in hand, and has been studied in detail, for Valladolid, by Lynn Williams (1987: 65–8). In this presumably typical city of Old Castile, he found that, whereas in reading style there was a heavy preponderance of [-áðo] (with some cases of [-áᵟo]) in participles of this pattern, in conversation [-áo] and [-áṳ] were dominant in all social classes. And unlike what has been reported else-where, women in Valladolid show more resistance than men to the inno-vatory variants, in this case [-áo] and [-áṳ]. Similar observations could no doubt be made all over the Spanish-speaking world, certainly all over Spain, although some American varieties (such as those of Mexico) appear to be more resistant to loss of /d/ in words of this pattern.

4.2.3 Aspiration of syllable-final /s/

We have noted (**4.1.7.2.4**) how weakening of /-s/ gained ground in Andalusia, probably in the late medieval period, and then spread north-wards through New Castile, reaching Madrid no later than the nine-teenth century. It is now clear (Williams 1983a, 1987) that this phenomenon has gained a footing in Old Castile, specifically in the working-class speech of Valladolid. In that city, eighteen- to twenty-six-year-olds make frequent use of velarized or aspirated articulations of /s/ before /k/ (e.g., [áˣko], [áʰko] *asco*). Weakening does not occur before consonants other than /k/, and is a strong marker of social class, being limited to those of working-class status, both males and females.

4.2.4 Neutralization of atonic vowels

Standard Spanish has a system of five vowel phonemes in unstressed syl-lables (except in word-final syllables, where only three occur): *recįbir, temer, cantar, morir, durar*). In educated speech, this five-fold contrast is adhered to everywhere, but in less educated social strata (especially, but not exclusively, in rural environments) there is abundant evidence of merger between the two front vowels (/i/ and /e/) and the two back vowels (/o/ and /u/) respectively. This merger is manifested not by consistent preference for, say, /i/ instead of /e/, or /o/ instead of /u/, but in hesitation between these pairs of vowels. The precise realization of the atonic vowel(s) in a given word may be determined by such factors as dissimilation of high front vowels (/i/.../í/ > /e/... /í/: /θeβíl/ ~ /seβíl/ *civil*, matching /serβír/ *servir*), assimilation of tongue-height before a high tonic vowel or before a glide (/o/.../í/ > /u/.../í/: /murír/ *morir*, /o/.../ú/ > /u/.../ú/: /sultúra/ *soltura*, /e/...[j] > /i/...[j]: /liθión/ ~ /lisión/ *lección*, /e/...[w] > /i/...[w]: /mínguar/ *menguar*), and hypercorrection no doubt has a role to play (/sigír/ for *seguir*, /abereguár/ for *averiguar*, etc.). Not quite so widespread, but abundant among less educated speakers in central and northern Spain and throughout America, is the related merger of atonic /i/ and /e/ in [j] and that of /o/ and /u/ in [w] when they precede another (usually tonic) vowel: [tjátro] *teatro* like [pjára] *piara*, [kwéte] *cohete* like [kuérða] *cuerda*. This non-distinction between atonic /i/ and /e/, like that between /u/ and /o/, is evident in written Spanish from the earliest medieval times to the seventeenth century, when it appears that in the standard language a selection was made between competing forms, often on the basis of the spelling of Latin. Thereafter, *recibir* and *vivir* were preferred to frequent *recebir* and *vevir* (cf. Lat. RECIPERE, VIVERE), and *seguir* was standardized at the expense of *siguir* (cf. Lat. SEQUOR), although these choices were not always consistently made (e.g., *lección* but *afición*).

However, although such resolutions took place in the standard, and in educated speech (thereby establishing five distinct vowel units in atonic syllables), the older state of affairs persisted at other linguistic and social levels. In rural and some urban varieties, therefore, both in the Peninsula and in America, and in Judeo-Spanish, the system of atonic vowels is best described as having only three phonemes (/ɪ/ - /a/ - /ʊ/), in which /ɪ/ may be realized as either [i] or [e], and /ʊ/ as [u] or [o], according to such factors as those outlined above (dissimilation, etc.).

4.2.5   Reinforcement of word-initial /ue/

Morpheme-initial /ue/ in all varieties of Spanish is normally reinforced by an element of audible friction, most usually velar, sometimes

bilabial: [ᵞwe], [ᵝwe] (Navarro Tomás 1961: 64). This element is evident
in all words like *huerta, huele, huevo, deshuesar, ahuecar*, etc., and in the
medieval and Golden Age periods it was evidently acceptable for it to
be pronounced as a consonant with full friction (mainly [ɣwe]), and no
doubt as a plosive [g] following a nasal or a pause, since in those periods
we frequently find spellings like *güerta, güele, güevo, desgües(s)ar, agüecar*.
Two further developments sprang from this state of affairs. On the one
hand, since [ɣwe] and [βwe] were felt to be equivalent realizations of
the same phonemes, it was also possible to apply the pronunciation
[ɣwe] to words which historically demanded [βwe]; this is indicated by
spellings of the type *güeno, güelta, agüelo* (for more usual *bueno, vuelta,
avuelo*, now *abuelo*). On the other hand, the fact that [ɣ] appeared in the
diphthongized forms of certain verbs (*güele, güelve/güelto*) could lead to
the appearance of [ɣ] in the related undiphthongized forms (*goler,
golver*). However, from the seventeenth century, the pronunciation
[ɣwe] in words like *huerta, huele, huevo* has been increasingly confined
to rural and uneducated speech, and the use of [ɣwe] in *bueno, vuelta*,
etc., is particularly heavily stigmatized. Despite this, [ɣwe] in all these
words continues to be widespread in rural Spain and America, as well
as having become normal in Judeo-Spanish (**6.3.5(3), 7.3(8)**).

5   Variation in Spanish America

The large majority of Spanish-speakers today, perhaps 300 million of them, are to be found in the Americas, in a vast area which stretches from the southwestern United States to the far south of the southern continent, not to mention the large cohorts of Hispanophones to be found in major US cities such as New York. We find, as we expect, geographical variation across this area, although mutual intelligibility among varieties is rarely threatened, and certainly not among educated and urban speakers.

Until recently, detailed linguistic studies of American Spanish have most usually been focused on the language of individual countries, and the linguistic atlases so far published continue to be oriented in this way (see *ALEC* 1981–3, *ALESuCh* 1973, *ALM* 1990–4, Navarro Tomás 1974). Even excellent surveys of the language of the whole of Spanish America, such as John Lipski's (1994) or the collaborative work edited by Manuel Alvar (1996b), are, at least in part, internally organized on a country-by-country basis. The frequent implication (although disavowed in the best studies) is therefore that the features described have boundaries which are co-terminous with those of the country concerned. This is not so; in accordance with normal distribution, each feature observed in Spanish America occupies its own area, which rarely if ever coincides with the area of any other feature, let alone with political boundaries. That is to say that we are dealing here, as in northern Spain and many other parts of the world, with a dialect continuum which is intersected by the frontiers which separate one republic from another. This intersection may be less arbitrary than that which occurs in other parts of the world, such as post-colonial Africa or the Middle East, but it is nevertheless true that, where we have sufficiently detailed information, it can be seen that isoglosses rarely coincide with political frontiers.[1]

A further generalization is in order here. With the exception of lexical innovations (loans from Native American languages or from

American English, novel derivative words, etc.), there are exceedingly few features observed in American Spanish which do not also belong to some variety or varieties of Peninsular Spanish, and which are there-fore likely to have their origins in Spain. The exceptional cases, mostly recessive, are ones which are observable among bilingual speakers of Spanish with a Native American language, such as the glottal plosives used at word boundaries (e.g., [mi ʔího] *mi hijo*) in Yucatán Spanish by populations whose first language is one of the Maya-Quiché languages (Lope Blanch 1996: 85), or the three-vowel system used in the Andes by speakers whose first language is Quechua (Lipski 1994: 189, 321).

As in the case of other areas of the world, including Spain, it is among rural varieties of Spanish America that one observes the great-est degree of variation. Urban varieties, and particularly middle-class urban varieties, show rather greater similarity across the Spanish-American world. Whereas earlier studies of Latin American Spanish (like dialect studies in other parts of the world) were most frequently focused on rural speech, information about urban educated Spanish is now more abundantly available. The 'Proyecto de estudio coordinado de la norma lingüística culta de las principales ciudades de Iberoamérica y de la Península Ibérica' (the 'Norma Culta' project, for short) began in 1964 as an undertaking of the Programa Interamericano de Lingüística y Enseñanza de Idiomas (PILEI), and has led to a series of publications describing educated speech in a number of cities in the Spanish-speak-ing world, with several others in progress.[2]

However, it is almost certainly true to say that, at all social levels, the degree of geographical variation within American Spanish is con-siderably less than the variation observable within Peninsular Spanish (as measured by the number of isoglosses which lie between two points the same distance apart). This lessened degree of variation within American Spanish is no doubt the effect of the colonization process which brought Spanish-speakers from Europe, and has its counterpart in the linguistic effects of other colonizing endeavours. Within the Romance language family, there is a considerably greater degree of geographical variation in the territory (namely Italy) from which the ancestor of those languages was originally spread than in the provinces which became Latin-speaking (France, Spain, Romania, etc.). Similarly, it is well known that British English is far more geo-graphically (and socially) varied than the English spoken in the former British colonies (the US, South Africa, Australia, New Zealand, etc.). The reasons for these effects are beginning to be understood, and lie principally in the phenomenon of *koinéization* (see **5.1.1**): the mixing of mutually comprehensible dialects implicit in the colonization process leads to the avoidance of the most marked features of the contributing dialects (see Trudgill 1986: 127–61).[3]

5.1 Geographical variation

A historical curiosity which contrasts World Spanish with World English is that, at the level of pronunciation, it is the consonant system which in Spanish accounts for the large majority of the instances of variation, whereas in English variation is centred on vowel pronunciation. This contrast between the two languages, at the world level, no doubt stems from variation within their respective base territories: almost all varieties of Peninsular Spanish can be seen to share the same five-vowel system and the same allophonic variation within it (the only major exception is the eight-vowel system of some Eastern Andalusian varieties; see **4.1.7.2.5**), whereas British English varieties differ from one another mostly on the basis of their vowel structures. It follows that, in the discussion of phonological variation in American Spanish, we shall be exclusively concerned with consonants.[4]

Early-twentieth-century discussions of American Spanish often focused on the putative impact of Native American languages in creating variation in the Americas. One of the most extreme cases was that of Pedro Henríquez Ureña (1921), who denied the Andalusian contribution to the characteristics of American Spanish and accounted for its internal geographical variation in terms of the different impact of specific Native American languages in different areas. However, further information about the distribution of features in New World Spanish has revealed a poor geographical match between the features at issue and the areas where the indigenous languages concerned are or were spoken. Consequently, this kind of explanation has had to be abandoned, and it is today recognized that the impact of Native American languages on Spanish is confined to the vocabulary, with only few exceptions. Some of these exceptions are innovatory and may extend to syntax (e.g., in the bilingual region of Paraguay, where Guaraní is considered to have influenced certain aspects of Spanish syntax). In other exceptional cases, Native American languages are thought to have a conservative influence on Spanish, as when the phoneme /ʎ/ is retained in Andean Spanish (by contrast with other areas where it has merged with /ǰ/; see **5.1.2.1**) perhaps because the pre-Hispanic languages of this area show /ʎ/ in their inventories of phonemes.

At least some innovations (apart from lexical borrowings from Native American languages, from English, etc.) have had their origins in the Americas, and have therefore never formed part of Peninsular Spanish.[5] However, as noted above, most of the features which separate one variety of American Spanish from another are also to be found in the Peninsula, where they often also separate one variety from another. This implies that the distribution of features in American Spanish can often be reasonably sought in the processes of immigration from Spain and the patterns of dialect mixing which sprang from these processes. In this respect, the spread of Spanish to America can be viewed as a continuation of the process which, during the Middle Ages, as we have seen (**4.1.7.2**), led to the extension of central northern varieties of Hispano-Romance down through the centre of the Peninsula, into New Castile, Andalusia, etc., in the wake of the Christian Reconquest of Islamic Spain. This process was still continuing (in the Kingdom of Granada, finally conquered in the same year that Columbus set sail westwards) as the settlement of America began. The extension of Spanish to America is in part also a continuation of the process which led to the spread of Spanish to the Canaries (see **4.1.8**), since a significant proportion of those who participated in the settlement of America came from families who had first settled in the Canaries (see Lipski 1994: 55–61).

Only slightly different is the settlement process, in the Ottoman Empire and around the Mediterranean, of the Jews who were expelled (also in 1492) from the newly constituted Kingdom of Spain. These events will be considered in Chapter **6**.

In all these cases, it is crucial to understand, as far as possible, the geographical and social origins of the settlers (**5.1.1**), as well as the social patterns which were established in the newly settled territories (**5.1.2**). We have already considered (**3.1**) the linguistic effects to be expected from the mixing of mutually intelligible dialects which occurs under these circumstances.

5.1.1 American Spanish and Andalusian Spanish

The traditional, 'common-sense' view of the relationship between American Spanish and Peninsular Spanish is that the former is in some

sense a continuation of Andalusian Spanish, while central and northern Peninsular varieties represent a slightly different, more conservative outcome of the medieval language. This view is based upon the
observation that Spanish-American speech is characterized (among
other features) by *seseo* (**5.1.1.1**), the same feature heard in much of
Andalusia (**4.1.7.2.1**), rather than by distinction of /s/ and /θ/
(**3.1.3.1**), and by the use of a single second-person plural pronoun
(*ustedes*) (**5.1.1.2**), as heard in much of western Andalusia (**4.1.7.2.8**),
rather than by contrast between formal *ustedes* and familiar *vosotros*.
Similarly, observers note that speakers of American Spanish use the
masculine singular personal pronoun *lo* both for personal and non-personal referents, as happens in Andalusia (**4.1.7.2.7**), rather than the
standard central and northern Peninsular system, which uses *le* for personal referents and retains *lo* only for non-personal referents (**4.1.2.3**).
What is more, many (although not all) American-Spanish speakers

- merge /ʎ/ and /ĵ/ (in [ĵ], [ʒ], etc., as in [ĵáma], [ʒáma] *llama*),
- weaken syllable-final /-s/ (e.g., [éʰto⁽ʰ⁾] *estos*),
- glottalize or pharyngealize the *jota* (/x/) to [h] or [ʰ] (e.g., [húɣo],
  [ħúɣo] *jugo*),
- and allow syllable-final /-r/ and /-l/ to merge, just as most
  Andalusians do (see **4.1.7.2.2**, **4.1.7.2.4**, and **4.1.7.2.6**).

The assumed explanation of these similarities was that it was predominantly Andalusians who settled in the American Empire in the
decades and centuries after Columbus's discovery.

However, this 'common-sense' view was challenged, in the earlier
part of the twentieth century, by Pedro Henríquez Ureña (1921, 1932).
Using information concerning some 10,000 early colonists, he was able
to observe that only a minority (about a third) was from Andalusia,
with most of the remainder drawn from all over the other regions of
the Crown of Castile and from further afield. He therefore concluded
that the similarities between American and Andalusian Spanish were
due to processes of parallel development on each side of the Atlantic.
Since, when Henríquez Ureña was writing, the chronology of the linguistic processes concerned was far from secure – most were then
thought to have taken place considerably later than is now thought –
this was a not unreasonable conclusion.

Beginning two decades later, the effect of Peter Boyd-Bowman's
extensive researches (1956, 1963, 1964, 1968, 1972, 1973) has been to
provide a firm factual underpinning for a return to the old common-
sense view. On the basis of the biographies of some 40,000 early

emigrants to America, he has shown that Andalusian participation in (and influence over) the colonization process was instrumental in establishing a distinctively Andalusian flavour in the language of the first settlements. Additionally, he has enabled us to confirm a specifically western Andalusian, even Sevillian, character in this colonial speech.

Although Boyd-Bowman confirmed that Andalusians constituted a minority of emigrants in the sixteenth and seventeenth centuries, his work, together with that of other scholars (e.g., Menéndez Pidal 1962b, Frago Gracia 1995), has enabled scholars to identify a number of factors which are likely to have enhanced the chances of Andalusian speech-patterns becoming the dominant ones in the new colonies. Three of these factors are particularly persuasive:

1   Although after the first two decades Andalusians did not form an absolute majority, they almost certainly continued to form the largest single cohort, compared with groups from areas such as Extremadura, New Castile, Old Castile, and the Basque Country.

2   In the period immediately following 1493, Andalusians formed an overwhelming majority of emigrants to the new settlements, in the Caribbean (Boyd-Bowman 1973: 3). They were therefore in a position to set the linguistic tone of these new towns, where later emigrants were bound to stay on their way to other colonies. The importance of this 'founder principle' has been pointed out in other colonial contexts, e.g., in the establishment of Australian English.

3   Of the women who emigrated during the first seventy years, the majority were Andalusians, and a significant proportion of these were from Seville. It scarcely needs to be pointed out that women are likely to have a greater impact on the speech-patterns of their children than are their husbands.

Less important, perhaps, were the following factors, which involve linguistic accommodation on the parts of adult speakers. They may nevertheless have had some ancillary importance in the spread of Andalusian features to America:

4   Wherever in the Peninsula would-be emigrants came from, they had to make their way to the Casa de la Contratación in Seville in order to gain permission to emigrate and secure a passage. This was a lengthy process and emigrants were obliged to wait for months, and often as long as a year, in the port cities of Seville, Cádiz, or Huelva. We can predict that many emigrants would have begun the process of accommodation to Andalusian (particularly

Sevillian) speech-patterns well before they ever reached America (see **3.1.1**). It may also be speculated that those who had decided to take the risk of emigration would by temperament be adaptable, not least in their speech.

5   The voyage to the Caribbean took several months, during which time emigrants were in daily contact with the sailors who manned the ships. These sailors were drawn, predominantly or exclusively it would seem, from the ports of western Andalusia: Seville (whence ocean-going ships set out), Cádiz, Palos, Huelva, etc.

We should in any case bear in mind that demographic considerations are not the most important ones in the question of the emergence of *koinés* from situations of dialect contact (see **3.1**). As new dialects form, through selection of competing variants from the multiplicity available in communities formed by mixtures of people from different geographical regions, we expect to observe preference for those variants which offer greatest structural simplicity (see **3.1.4**). The simplest variants may not originally have belonged to the largest group making up the new society. However, it should be noted that in the new Spanish-American societies, it was the Andalusian contingent whose dialects most frequently offered a simpler variant than those contributed by the speech of other Peninsular regions. This is true of a good number of salient Andalusian features: *seseo* (**5.1.1.1**), *yeísmo* (**5.1.2.1**), the merger of syllable-final /-r/ and /-l/ (**5.1.2.3**), the use of *ustedes* as the sole form of second-person plural address (**5.1.1.2**), use of the third-person singular personal pronoun *le* exclusively for indirect-object reference (rather than the more opaque system of *leísmo* used by speakers from the northern Peninsula; see **4.1.2.3**).

In the following sections (**5.1.1.1–2**), we shall look at those features of American Spanish which have Andalusian origins and which have become universal in New World Spanish. Other American Spanish features which arguably have Andalusian origin, but whose distribution is limited to lowland areas (see **5.1.2**), will be discussed in Sections **5.1.2.1–5**.

5.1.1.1   Seseo

It is now all but certain (see Frago 1993: 307–73) that, already at the time of the European discovery of America, the first phase of the reduction of sibilants had taken place in Seville and other parts of western Andalusia. In **4.1.7.2.1**, we saw that reduction of the sibilants in Andalusia takes place in two phases: the first consists of the merger of the dental fricatives /ṣ/ (from earlier /tˢ/) and /ẓ/ (from earlier /dᶻ/) with the (dento-)alveolar fricatives /s/ and /z/ respectively. When, somewhat later, interested observers from outside Andalusia note these changes, they label them *çeçeo* and *zezeo* respectively.[6]

The second phase of the process, bringing /ṣ/ and /ẓ/ together as /ṣ/, spread into Andalusia from the north no later than the sixteenth century and possibly earlier. This development is part of the process whereby all voiced sibilants merged with their voiceless counterparts, one which has become universal in Castilian, as well as in Galician, Asturian and other northern Peninsular varieties (see **3.1.3.1**).

Both of these changes were carried to America. The first no doubt characterized the speech of all western Andalusians, who formed a decisive component in the first settler communities in the New World (see **5.1.1**). The second change rapidly became the norm in all varieties of Peninsular Spanish in the century after the Discovery, and was similarly carried to America. Since, in this case, the change belonged to all classes of emigrants from all the component regions of the Crown of Castile, and since it is a simplifying innovation, there would have been little resistance to it in the dialect mixtures which were gradually being resolved into *koinés* in the various American settlements.[7]

The result of these successive innovations was that the four medieval Castilian sibilants /tˢ/, /dᶻ/, /s/, /z/ were reduced to a single phoneme, typically a voiceless dental slit-fricative (/ṣ/), in all varieties of American Spanish.[8] That is to say that *seseo* is all but universal in Spanish America, since the fronted variant of Andalusian /ṣ/, namely [ṣ̺], is only rarely reported in America. This fronting (or *ceceo*), today characteristic of southern Andalusian varieties (see **4.1.7.2.1**) and some Canarian varieties (**4.1.8**), appears to have arisen too late to be spread to America.

5.1.1.2 Second-person plural address

A further striking way in which a feature belonging to western Andalusian varieties has been extended to America is in the loss of the contrast between informal and formal modes of address in the plural. Although this contrast is universally observed in Spanish in the case of a single addressee (informal *(tú) eres* or *(vos) sos* vs formal *(usted) es*; see also **5.1.2.5**), and although the parallel plural distinction (informal *(vosotros/-as) sois* vs formal *(ustedes) son*) is observed in the whole of

Spain outside western Andalusia (see **4.1.7.2.8**), all American Spanish varieties, apparently without exception, have abandoned the formal vs informal distinction and use *(ustedes) son* for all plural addressees.

This unanimity is striking in two ways. Firstly, the form of the pronoun *ustedes* results, as is well known, from a contraction of the phrase *vuestras mercedes*. However, this particular contraction is only one of several competing contractions, from which the form *ustedes* emerged triumphant among all speakers in Spain only in the eighteenth century (Lapesa 1980: 392). Its present universal use in America argues for a much earlier acceptance of this form of address in western Andalusia than in the rest of Spain. Secondly, we should note that, unlike what frequently happens in western Andalusia, the pronoun *ustedes* in America is always accompanied by (or is represented by) a third-person verb. The Andalusian collocation *(ustedes) sois* is completely unknown on the other side of the Atlantic, where such verb forms only ever have singular value (**5.1.2.5**).

5.1.2 Settlement and communication patterns and their linguistic effects

The route that Columbus took in his first voyage of discovery was from Palos (in the province of Huelva), via the Canaries, to Cuba and La Española (its name anglicized to Hispaniola, an island now comprising the two states of Haiti and the Dominican Republic). This route, followed by later discoverers and conquerors, became the normal line of communication between Spain and America and was extended to the northern mainland, when Hernán Cortés gained control over the Aztec Empire between 1519 and 1521 and founded Mexico City, and to the southern continent, following Francisco Pizarro's conquest of Peru (1532–5) and the establishment of Lima as the capital of the newly acquired territory. The Spanish end of this line quickly became the city of Seville, which was granted a monopoly of trade with the American Empire and fiercely protected this monopoly, ensuring that all traffic (of people or goods) between Spain and America was funnelled through its port or through the other western Andalusian ports that it controlled, such as Cádiz and Huelva.

Along the western arms of this branching line of communication were established the first Spanish-speaking settlements in the Americas, in Cuba and La Española, in Veracruz and Mexico City, in

Cartagena and Lima, etc. Places along these routes remained in relatively close communication with Spain, which could be reached in journeys of eight or ten weeks, mostly by sea. By contrast, travellers from settlements established elsewhere in the expanding Empire often required overland journeys of months before they could reach the main line of communication, typically at one of the points just mentioned. A case in point is the territory which later became Argentina: settlement began there in the mid-sixteenth century, by colonists from Peru, and the territory continued to be administered from Lima until the establishment of a separate Viceroyalty in Buenos Aires in 1776. In this period, direct travel by sea between Spain and Argentina was rarely possible, and travellers had to make the enormously long land and river journey across the southern continent, including the Andes, and up the coast to Lima, then linking with the well-established route back to Seville.

What is the linguistic significance of these facts? Ramón Menéndez Pidal (1962b) has examined the way in which, in late medieval and early modern Spain, two rival linguistic norms were established within the Crown of Castile. The most powerful prestige centre in medieval Castile was Toledo, later displaced by Madrid when the latter became the capital in 1561.[9] This norm was characterized by such features as *leísmo* (see **4.1.2.3**), and maintenance of the contrast between dental and alveolar sibilants (see **3.1.3.1**). However, this norm was rivalled by another, based upon the linguistic varieties which emerged in Seville. This city, already perhaps the largest in the Peninsula when it was recaptured from the Moors in 1248, grew in economic and cultural significance during the later Middle Ages, and was then enormously enriched by its control over all trade with the American Empire (see above). The features of this Sevillian norm (*seseo, yeísmo,* weakening of syllable-final /s/, merger of *vosotros* and *ustedes,* etc.) have been considered in **4.1.7.2**.

On this basis, we can envisage (no doubt with some simplification) that, in each Spanish-American settlement, there was a struggle between the Madrid norm and the Seville norm. In those localities which were centres of political power (and therefore of linguistic prestige), and in those localities which were in relatively easy communication with the latter, the features of the Madrid norm would have had some weight and could be expected to oust at least some features of the Seville norm. By contrast, in those localities which were distant from the prestige centres, Sevillian features would go more or less unchecked.

Therefore, it can be claimed that the pattern of settlement and of communications within Spain's American Empire can be seen to determine, at least in part, the linguistic development of Spanish America.[10] In each town and city in the New World, a slightly different dialect mixture came about, as a result of the different geographical and social origins of the settlers there, and as a result of the extent to which the Sevillian norm was checked by the Madrid norm.

We have already seen (**5.1.1**) that the earliest and most crucial contributions to these mixtures came from speakers of western Andalusian varieties. However, in some centres there would have been considerable input into the mixture from speakers originating in the centre and north of the Peninsula. This would be the case in the cities from which the Empire was administered (principally Mexico City and Lima, and to a lesser extent in the major Caribbean towns). Mexico City and Lima became, by the middle of the sixteenth century, the seats of the viceregal courts and of the colonial administration. Only a little later, the first American universities were founded, in the same two cities, where the Church also set up the headquarters of its powerful missionary effort. Likewise, these cities were a magnet for trade with Europe. As a result, among the population of these cities were crown officials, priests and nuns, academics, traders, etc., drawn from all over Spain, but more likely to aspire to the Madrid norm than to the Sevillian norm. In these places, then, we can predict that the Andalusian flavour would be less likely to totally dominate the dialect mixture, and that the speech of these places, like those in immediate contact with them, would be somewhat closer to the norms of central Spain.

Away from these cultural centres and from the lines of communication which connected them with Spain, the relative rarity of prestigious speakers of central and northern Peninsular varieties would help to ensure that the Andalusian features in the local dialect mixture would go relatively unchallenged. It is for this reason, in all probability, that we find a much more marked Andalusian character in the language of the Southern Cone (Argentina, Uruguay, Paraguay, and to a lesser extent Chile), in central America (despite the fact that it is nearer to Spain than is Peru), in certain other less-frequented parts of the Caribbean (e.g., Venezuela), and in those parts of Spanish America which later became absorbed by the United States.

A principle of classification of Spanish-American varieties which one frequently encounters is their division into highland varieties, on the one hand, and lowland or coastal varieties, on the other. In this way, the speech of the Mexican plateau and of Andean Colombia, Ecuador, Peru, and Bolivia are contrasted with the speech of the Antilles, central America, Venezuela, the countries of the Southern Cone, and the coastal areas of the countries first named. We shall see that some features of American Spanish are indeed distributed in approximately this way: weakening of /-s/ (**5.1.2.2**); merger of /-r/ and /-l/ (**5.1.2.3**); weakening of word-final /-n/ (**5.1.2.4**). It was once claimed that this division was a consequence of the destinations preferred by Spanish settlers: that emigrants from lowland Andalusia preferred to settle in coastal areas, while those from the Castilian Meseta preferred the highland areas of America. However, no data have ever been presented which would support this notion. Neither has any other convincing rationale been provided to account for this distribution of linguistic features, apart from the ideas presented earlier in this section, so that the highland/lowland distinction should be seen as a consequence of the paradoxical fact that speakers in the inland areas of Spanish America often had closer contacts with the central Spanish linguistic norm than those in the coastal regions did, because most of the important political centres were in highland areas.

In the following sections (**5.1.2.1–5**), we shall consider certain key features of American Spanish whose distribution can be seen to respond to the patterns of settlement outlined in this section (**5.1.2**). The phonetic features (**5.1.2.1–4**) will be discussed in descending order of the number of Spanish-American varieties affected by them.

5.1.2.1   *Yeísmo*

Merger of /ʎ/ and /ĵ/ with non-lateral results is as dominant in America as it is in the Peninsula (**4.1.7.2.2**), since the main Spanish-American varieties that retain the contrast are restricted to those of the Andes (highland areas of Bolivia, Peru, Ecuador and (until recently) Colombia; Lipski 1994: 188, 319, 248, 210; Alonso 1967a). It is probable that retention of /ʎ/ (and its contrast with /ĵ/) is related to the factors just outlined (in **5.1.2**), but it has to be said that absence of this feature from Mexico weighs against this interpretation, as does its presence in lowland Bolivia and in Paraguay.

A probably relevant circumstance which has been identified in this case is the fact that there is a good degree of coincidence between the area where /ʎ/ is retained in American Spanish and the area where Native American languages display /ʎ/ among their phonemes. This is not to say that /ʎ/ is retained merely in the Spanish of bilinguals; in the areas identified above, lateral pronunciation (/ ʎ /) is reported to belong to people of all social and educational backgrounds. At the least, the indigenous languages concerned (Quechua and Aymara) have had a role in maintaining a contrast which is recessive in every other part of the Spanish-speaking world.

In the various territories where *yeísmo* has become established, the phonetic result of the merger is very varied. The commonest pronunciation, the voiced mid-palatal fricative [ĵ], is also the most frequent in the Peninsula, but in Spanish America (as in Spain) there are many alternatives, and the range of variants is greater in America than in the Peninsula. While highland Mexico and Colombia have [ĵ], many Caribbean and central American varieties, as well as those of the Pacific coast, show a sound with much weaker friction, sometimes little more than a glide [j], especially weak after the palatal vowels /e/ or /i/: [kasʲʲa], or even [kasía] *casilla*.[11] By contrast, Argentina and Uruguay have a much more tense (and instantly recognizable) prepalatal groove fricative [ʒ], which in Buenos Aires is most frequently devoiced to [ʃ]: [ʒamár]~[ʃamár] *llamar* (Fontanella de Weinberg 1978).

Where the historic phonemic contrast between lateral and non-lateral palatals is maintained (i.e., in the Andean area), the lateral has sometimes been modified to a (non-lateral) prepalatal groove fricative /ʒ/, distinct from the mid-palatal /ĵ/, which is often weakened to [j]. This occurs in the central highlands of Ecuador (Lipski 1994: 248): [ʒamár] *llamar*, [jerno] *yerno*.

5.1.2.2   Weakening of syllable-final /-s/

Just as Spain is divided between those varieties which maintain /s/ as a sibilant in the syllabic coda (most varieties in the northern half of the Peninsula) and those that weaken it in some way, typically to [h] or [Ø] (those varieties used in the Canaries, in Andalusia, Extremadura, and Murcia, and increasingly in New Castile, see 4.1.7.2.4), so Spanish America is also divided. However, in the New World, the division between /-s/-retaining and /-s/-weakening areas is more complex. In some measure, this division corresponds to the degree of closeness of contact between central Spain and the specific American area concerned: those areas which, because of their political and economic importance in the Empire, attracted prestigious speakers of central Castilian varieties are the ones which retain /-s/ most frequently (most of Mexico, much of Colombia, Ecuador, Peru and Bolivia). By contrast, the countries in and around the Caribbean, the Pacific coast, and the countries of the Southern Cone show intense weakening or loss of this phoneme. As we have seen (**5.1.2**), it is likely that in Mexico City and Lima, and in the areas in closest contact with these powerful centres, the colonial dialect mixture produced varieties which were somewhat closer to the central Peninsular norm than was the case in areas which were more distant from such influences, where southern Peninsular pronunciations were able to dominate the mix.

A difficulty inherent in this argument lies in the pronunciations of /-s/ used in Lima. Today, many speakers in Lima weaken syllable-final /s/ to [h], but do not eliminate it (Lipski 1994: 321–2). However, the data reported by Lipski suggest that this may be a recent development. Middle-class speakers show some tendency to aspirate /s/ word-internally, but not word-finally before a pause or a vowel, while younger speakers also sometimes use [h] in the latter environments. Aspiration in a variety of contexts only becomes frequent in working-class varieties. This distribution has all the appearance of recent change from below (see **3.4.2**), and it is therefore likely that, until recent generations, Lima formed part of the /-s/-retaining part of Spanish America.

At all events, weakening of /-s/ is typical of the lowland, island and coastal communities of Spanish America. A good example of this contrast between highland and lowland treatments of /-s/ is provided by Mexican Spanish: by far the greater part of the country comprises highland areas, where /-s/ is retained intact (or as a particularly salient sibilant), while the Pacific coast (e.g., Acapulco), the Gulf coast (e.g., Tabasco and Veracruz), and southern areas adjacent to Belize and Guatemala show weakening in varying degrees (see Lipski 1994: 280–3). Within the various lowland areas of Spanish America, it is in the Antilles and in certain central American countries (e.g., Nicaragua) that the greatest intensity of /-s/-weakening occurs.

As in southern Spain, the realizations of weakened /-s/ are varied, but the range of variation in American Spanish is less than in the Peninsula. There are only infrequent reports of the kinds of assimilation of the aspirate to the following consonant (and of this consonant to the aspirate) which so frequently occur in Andalusia (see **4.1.7.2.4**).[12] In most of the American areas where /-s/-weakening occurs, there appears to be a hierarchy of reduction. From most frequent to least frequent, typical realizations are as follows:

- aspiration of syllable-final /s/ word-internally, word-finally (before a word-initial consonant), and phrase-finally: [éʰtaʰ muhéreʰ] *estas mujeres*.

- aspiration of syllable-final /s/ word-internally and word-finally (before a word-initial consonant), with deletion in phrase-final position: [éʰtaʰ muhére].
- aspiration of syllable-final /s/ word-internally, with deletion word-finally (before a word-initial consonant) and in phrase-final position: [éʰta muhére].
- deletion in all these positions: [éta muhére].
- aspiration of word-final /s/ before a word-initial vowel (with or without deletion of aspiration in internal syllable-final position): [é⁽ʰ⁾ta hóβra] *estas obras*.
- deletion of word-final /s/ in all positions, including before a word-initial vowel: [éta óβra] *estas obras*.
- extension of aspiration to word-initial /s/: [éta heɲóra] *esta señora*.

This hierarchy is not only a frequency hierarchy, but may be correlated with social variants such as socio-economic class, so that, in the lowland areas where this feature occurs, speakers of middle-class background are less likely than members of the working class to use variants at the bottom of the list.[13]

5.1.2.3   Neutralization of syllable-final /-r/ and /-l/

As in southern Peninsular Spanish (see **4.1.7.2.6**), syllable-final rhotics and laterals in some varieties of American Spanish are subject to neutralization and/or weakening, including loss. The varieties concerned are all ones used in lowland areas of Spanish America (as defined in Sections **5.1.2** and **5.1.2.2**), but not all such areas show these processes (for example, they are absent from Argentinian Spanish; Lipski 1994: 168), and, where they occur, they are often confined to working-class or rural speech (for example, in Santiago de Chile; Silva-Corvalán 1987). This feature is strongest in the Caribbean, especially in Cuba, the Dominican Republic (Henríquez Ureña 1940), and Puerto Rico.

Although we are once again undoubtedly dealing with a feature which was transferred to America by migrants from southern Spain, the details of the process are not quite identical on the two sides of the Atlantic. Whereas in Spain the dominant solutions are merger in [ɾ] ([áɾɣo] *algo* = [káɾne] *carne*) or elimination (especially in word-final position), the most frequent outcomes in American Spanish are merger in [l] ([álɣo] = [kálne]) or assimilation ([áᵛɣo] = [káⁿne], especially typical of Cuba), although elimination is not uncommon, and in the Dominican Republic certain rural, recessive, varieties show vocalization of these segments ([áịɣo] = [káịne]), a variant which has no counterpart in European Spanish.

5.1.2.4 Treatment of word-final /-n/

Weakening of syllable-final consonants also extends to /-n/, but in this case the process does not affect the consonant in word-internal positions, but only in word-final (sometimes also morpheme-final) position.[14] Here the process takes the form of velarization of the nasal, which may then lead to nasalization of the preceding vowel, and to loss of the consonant (with or without loss of the nasal quality of the now word-final vowel): [kántaⁿ], [kántãⁿ], [kántã], [kánta], *cantan*.[15]

When the following morpheme begins with a vowel, the normal Spanish resyllabification rule ensures that the nasal consonant, unless deleted, will become syllable-initial, the only circumstances in which a velar nasal appears outside syllable-final position: e.g., [me-ðã-ɲás-ko] *me dan asco*. Since this process, for many speakers, is limited to word-final position, it can be claimed that it gives rise to a new phonemic contrast in these varieties (viz. /n/ vs /ŋ/), on the basis of such celebrated, if rather artificial, minimal pairs as:

| /pán#amerikáno/ | [pá-ŋa-mé-ɾi-ká-no] | *pan americano* |
| /pánamerikáno/ | [pá-na-mé-ɾi-ká-no] | *panamericano.* |

However, since nasalization of the preceding vowel is most frequently present (e.g., [pã-ŋa-mé-ɾi-ká-no]), it is likely to be this nasality which carries the burden of the meaning-difference.

The same weakening of word-final /-n/ is a well-known aspect of southern Peninsular varieties of Spanish (as well as of northwestern varieties), and was no doubt carried to America by migrants from those areas (defined in Sampson 1999: 170–1). As in the case of other processes of consonant-weakening we have seen (those affecting /-s/, /-r/ and /-l/; see **5.1.2.2–3**), the Spanish-American areas affected are especially the lowland/island/coastal zones, although in this case the countries of the Southern Cone are unaffected and retain alveolar /n/, while velarization does occur in some highland areas (Ecuador and Peru; Lipski 1994: 248, 319).

5.1.2.5 *Voseo* and *tuteo*

These terms refer to competing modes of second-person singular familiar address. *Voseo* indicates use of the tonic pronoun *Vos* (and/or historically second-person plural verb forms) for this purpose, although the associated object pronoun is always *te* and the related possessives are *tu* and *tuyo*: *(Vos) cantás/cantáis, lo hice para vos, a vos te vi en la calle, (Vos) estabas en tu casa, esto es tuyo.* By contrast, the term *tuteo* refers to the use of the tonic pronoun *Tú* (and/or historically second-person singular verb forms) in the same role: *(Tú) cantas, lo hice para ti, a ti te vi en la calle, (Tú) estabas en tu casa, esto es tuyo.*

At the time of the European discovery of America, modes of singular address in Spanish were complex (see Penny 1991a: 123–5). Until the fourteenth century, the late Latin system had survived more or less unchanged: historically second-person plural forms (i.e., the subject pronoun *Vos* and/or a second-person plural verb) expressed deference or distance, while historically second-person singular forms (i.e., the subject pronoun *Tú* and/or a second-person singular verb) expressed solidarity or closeness of speaker and hearer. E.g.,

Non-deferential	Deferential
Tú eres	*Vos sodes*

However, during the fifteenth century, the type *Vos sois/sos* (< *sodes*)[16] became gradually less deferential, coming to be used among equals at various social levels and therefore often becoming indistinguishable in tone from *Tú eres*. Since society continued to require modes of deferential address, for occasions when one was speaking to someone of higher rank, speakers of fifteenth-century Spanish often remedied the situation by using two-word phrases consisting of an abstract noun preceded by the hitherto deferential possessive: *vuestra excelencia, vuestra señoría, vuestra merced*, etc. Since such expressions were built upon nouns, the accompanying verb necessarily took a third-person singular form. On the eve of the discovery of America, therefore, the forms of address available in Spanish were the following:

Non-deferential	Deferential
Tú eres ~ *Vos sois/sos*	*Vuestra merced* (etc.) *es*

This was the system carried to America and is visible in the written language of all colonial centres for which we have evidence. Leaving aside the trivial changes which affected the deferential mode of address (selection of *Vuestra merced* from among the competing expressions and gradual contraction of *Vuestra merced* to *Usted*, changes which are identical for American and Peninsular Spanish), this system was adjusted differently in different parts of colonial America. On the one hand, those areas which were in closest contact with central Peninsular norms (see **5.1.2**) behaved like the latter in gradually abandoning *Vos sois/sos* and adhering exclusively to *tuteo*.[17] Thus, throughout Mexico (except for the province of Chiapas, adjacent to Guatemala), in almost all Peru, in most of Venezuela, and in the Antilles (Cuba, Dominican Republic, and Puerto Rico) *voseo* is not used.

On the other hand, those areas which were remoter from Peninsular Spanish developments during the colonial period continue to use the older system. Thus, wide areas of Spanish America use *voseo* either alone or in competition with *tuteo*. This is true of the central American republics from Guatemala (together with Chiapas in southern Mexico) to western Panama, and also of most of Colombia (except the Caribbean coast) and Ecuador. Bolivia and the countries of the Southern Cone are also characterized by use of *voseo*.[18]

Within the areas in which *voseo* is used, it finds different degrees of social acceptability and use. It is practically universal in Argentina, Uruguay, Paraguay, and Bolivia, although in all these countries there is limited use of *tuteo* at the highest sociolinguistic levels (especially in urban varieties). In these countries the appearance of *tuteo* is often defined as belonging to non-spontaneous, school-inspired speech. However, in Chile, *voseo* appears to have receded to some extent in the last century, especially among urban, educated groups, although use of historically plural verb forms, together with *Tú*, is frequent among middle-class, urban speakers (Morales 1972). In some areas of Ecuador and Colombia, *voseo* suffers strong competition from *tuteo*, and in the latter country *Usted* is used in social circumstances of closeness (between spouses, from parents to children) which in other areas would demand *Tú* or *Vos*. In the central American zone, *voseo* is strongly dominant, although in some parts of the area (e.g., El Salvador) it is possible to detect a three-level scheme of second-person address, with *Tú* reflecting an intermediate level of familiarity between *Vos* and *Usted*. Curiously, in Costa Rica, *Usted* can convey greater closeness than *Vos*, being used there by parents to children and among other close family members (Villegas 1965).

The verb forms which express *voseo* have been described above as being historically second-person plural, and this is most frequently the case, although it has to be borne in mind that such forms often present more than one pattern (as well as coexisting, in some areas of *voseo*, with verb forms which are historically singular). The morphological history of the relevant verb forms, those of the second-person plural of various tenses and moods, is described in the following paragraph.

Until the mid-fourteenth century, such verb forms (with the sole exception of the simple preterite) were marked in Spanish by the consonant /d/, and fell into three stress-pattern classes (see Penny 1991a: 138–40):

1 paroxytonic (penultimate-stressed) forms: present indicative *cantades, volvedes, salides*; present subjunctive *cantedes, volvades, salgades*; future *cantaredes, volveredes, saldredes*;

2 proparoxytonic (antepenultimate-stressed) forms: imperfect indicative *cantávades, volvíades, salíades*; conditional *cantaríades, volveríades, saldríades*; pluperfect (later imperfect subjunctive) *cantárades, volviérades, saliérades*; imperfect subjunctive *cantássedes, volviéssedes, saliéssedes*;

3 oxytonic (final-stressed) forms: imperative *cantad, volved, salid*.

From the late fourteenth century, these forms began to lose their /d/, although group (2) forms were not regularly affected until the sixteenth century, while loss of /d/ in imperatives was never categorical, and forms with and without the final consonant (*cantad/cantá*, etc.) coexisted in the Peninsula for several centuries.

Loss of /d/ in words of the first two groups gave rise to sequences of two vowels (e.g., *cantades* > *cant̲a̲e̲s, cantávades* > *cantáva̲e̲s*), sequences which were resolved in either of two ways.[19] Thus, before the discovery of America, Peninsular Spanish showed such competing pairs as *cantáis* (in which /áe/ is reduced to a single syllable through glide-formation /áe/ > [ái̯]) and *cantás* (in which /áe/ is reduced to a single syllable through assimilation /áe/ > /á/). Early in the colonial period, similar processes affected the proparoxytonic verb forms, giving rise to pairs such as *cantabais~cantabas, cantarais~cantaras*, from which it will be noted that the assimilated forms (*cantabas, cantaras*, etc.) had become identical to those that for centuries had been used in association with the subject pronoun *Tú*. This identity of verbal forms appropriate to *Tú* and *Vos* was no doubt a factor which enhanced parity between these modes of address.

All of these second-person verbal forms, it can be argued, were carried to America as part of the morphological baggage of emigrants from all over Castilian-speaking Spain, although in later centuries, in the Peninsula, the assimilated forms (*cantás, cantés, cantarés, cantabas, cantases*, etc.) were abandoned (and those that survived – *cantabais, cantaseis*, etc. – were restricted to plural addressees).

In the only tense so far not considered (the preterite), the medieval forms which accompanied (or represented) *Vos* were *cantastes*, *volvistes, salistes,* and these forms continued in use well into the sixteenth century, and longer in some varieties. Given that the preterite *Tú* forms were often identical to these *Vos* forms, since the former frequently added an /s/ which was characteristic of the *Tú* forms of all other paradigms (thus, *cantaste > cantastes*), there were added grounds for speakers to treat the *Tú* and *Vos* modes of address as equivalent, a perception further enhanced among those who deleted word-final /s/. *Cantaste* and *cantastes* both no doubt belonged to the speech of emigrants to America, both associated with either *Tú* or *Vos*. The Peninsular form *cantasteis* developed rather late (not until the seventeenth century), and was never spread to Spanish America.

The competition between the various verb forms associated with the pronoun *Vos* has never been fully resolved, and all the forms discussed in the previous paragraphs (except *cantasteis*) are to be found in areas of *voseo* in America, sometimes in active competition in the same region. A further complication is that sometimes *Vos* is found with historically second-person singular verb forms (e.g., *Vos cantas, Vos saldrás*), while *Tú* is occasionally found with verb forms which are historically second-person plural (usually limited to imperatives of the type *(Tú) cantá, salí*). Full details cannot yet be established, but the broad pattern of the verb forms used in areas of *voseo* can be stated as follows in Table **5.1**.[20]

5.1.3   Other effects of migration from the Peninsula

The features of American Spanish discussed in **5.1.1** and **5.1.2** are all ones whose pedigree can be traced to varieties spoken in Andalusia or in central Castile. However, we have emphasized that emigrants to America were drawn not only from these areas, but also from other parts of the Peninsula. Such emigrants, as we have argued (in **5.1.1**), could be expected to accommodate their speech to that of the environments in which they found themselves, in many cases adopting Andalusian features, but occasionally (if they settled in the great American administrative centres) acquiring non-Andalusian features characteristic of the central Peninsular norm. However, in a few cases, such speakers contributed northern Peninsular features to the colonial dialect mix which were accepted by others and perpetuated in American Spanish, either locally or more widely. We have already encountered the case of the velarization of word-final /-n/ (**5.1.2.4**), which arguably has its origins not only in Andalusian varieties, but also

Argentina	present indicative	V1 (but V2 in the northwest, T in Santiago del Estero)
	present subjunctive	V1 (stigmatized, so T also occurs)
	imperative	V1
	future	T
Uruguay	present indicative	V1 (also *Tú* + V1)
	present subjunctive	V1 and T
	imperative	V1
	future	T
Paraguay	present indicative	V1
	present subjunctive	T
	imperative	V1
	future	T
Chile	present indicative	V1 and V2 (also *Tú* + V1 and V2)
	present subjunctive	V1 and T
	imperative	T
	future	T
Bolivia	present indicative	T in highlands, V1 in east, V2 in Tarija
	present subjunctive	V1 and T
	imperative	V1
	future	T (*tomarís* in Tarija)
Ecuador	present indicative	V1 on coast, V1 (occasionally V2) and T in highlands
	present subjunctive	V1 and T
	imperative	V1
	future	T (occasionally V1 *harís*)
Colombia	present indicative	V1 (V2 disappearing from north)
	present subjunctive	V1
	imperative	V1
	future	T
Western Venezuela	present indicative	V1 in Andes, V2 in Maracaibo
	present subjunctive	V1 in Andes, V2 in Maracaibo
	imperative	V1
	future	T (?)
Central America	present indicative	V1
	present subjunctive	V1
	imperative	V1
	future	T (sometimes V1)

T indicates a historically second-person singular verb form (present indicative *cantas, vuelves, sales*, present subjunctive *cantes, vuelvas, salgas*, future *cantarás*, imperative *canta, vuelve, sal*).

V indicates a historically second-person plural verb form, either without diphthong in the tonic syllable (V1 = present indicative *cantás, volvés, salís*, present subjunctive *cantés, volvás, salgás*, future *cantarés*, imperative *cantá, volvé, salí*), or with a diphthong (V2 = present indicative *cantáis, volvéis, salís*, present subjunctive *cantéis, volváis, salgáis*, future *cantaréis*).

Data are taken from Alvar 1996b, Lipski 1994 and Rona 1967.

Table 5.1   Verb-forms used in areas of *voseo*

in those from the northwest of the Peninsula, where this feature is to be heard, still today, in Galician, Asturian, Leonese, and Cantabrian varieties (*ALPI* 1962: map 11). Other features of northern origin are considered in the following sections (**5.1.3.1–2**).

5.1.3.1 **/tɾ/ and /r/**
In most Spanish American varieties, the group /tɾ/ (dental plosive + alveolar flap) and the alveolar vibrant /r/ are articulated as described, just as they are in the large majority of Peninsular varieties. However, in rural varieties spoken in Navarre and Aragon, the flap in the group /tɾ/ (and sometimes also in /dɾ/) is devoiced and frequently fricatized (acquiring a sibilant character) while the /t/ is retracted to alveolopalatal position, so that the group has an acoustic quality not unlike that of English /tɾ/: [tɾ̥] or [tɹ̊]. Similarly, the vibrant /r/ is often devoiced to [r̥], and may then cease to have repeated tongue movements, becoming a strong fricative with sibilant quality: [ɹ̊] (*ALEANR* 1979–83: maps 1465, 1473).[21]

These pronunciations are also heard in Spanish-American varieties spoken in a number of different areas, as well as a groove fricative realization of /r/ (approximately [ʒ]) which is likely to be a development of a partially devoiced variant of this phoneme. Once again, full details of the distribution of these features are lacking, but the following pattern emerges (derived mainly from Lipski's (1994) country-by-country description).[22]

Retracted/devoiced /tɾ/ is heard (in words like *tren, otro*, etc.) in an Andean area stretching from southern highland parts of Colombia, through Andean Ecuador and the Altiplano of Peru and Bolivia (but excluding the lowland east of this country), and continuing into much of Chile, Paraguay, and northern Argentina. It is also found in a central American area stretching from Chiapas (southwestern Mexico) through Guatemala and Honduras to Costa Rica. It also belongs to traditional rural varieties used in New Mexico (Espinosa 1930) and to the speech of upper- and middle-class women in Mexico City (Perissinotto 1975). In both the Andean and the central American zones, although retracted/devoiced articulations are sociolinguistically dominant, they may alternate with 'standard' [tr] at the highest social levels.

These areas of modification of /tɾ/ are enclosed within broader areas in which /r/ suffers devoicing and/or assibilation. Thus, in all the regions mentioned most speakers have abandoned the voiced vibrant realization of /r/ and use [r̥] or [ɹ̊], sometimes described as similar to the prepalatal groove fricative [ʒ], in the various words concerned (*rey*, *perro*, etc.). But these articulations of /r/ extend somewhat beyond these areas (into northern and eastern Argentina, and further north through Andean Colombia to reach western Venezuela), and are also found in the Antilles (Cuba, Dominican Republic, and Puerto Rico).[23]

In this latter area, the pronunciations of /r/ just described compete with retracted articulations (the uvular trill [ʀ] or a velar fricative, most usually voiceless [x]). These realizations are highly characteristic of the speech of Puerto Rico, and are dominant there, while [ʀ] is also heard in working-class varieties used in central and eastern Cuba.

5.1.3.2 Past tense values

Another feature in which there is similarity between American Spanish, on the one hand, and northern Peninsular varieties, on the other, consists of the aspectual values of the preterite and perfect verb forms (e.g., respectively, *canté* and *he cantado*) and of the relationship between them.

In standard Peninsular Spanish, and in the spontaneous speech of the northeast, the centre and the south of the Peninsula, the main aspectual contrast between these verb forms lies in the speaker's perception of the connection between the past situation described and the moment of speaking (see Alarcos 1947). If the speaker wishes to convey that the past situation mentioned ('situation' here covering actions and states) belonged to a period of time distinct from the one in which s/he considers that s/he is speaking, then s/he selects the preterite form. By contrast, if s/he wishes to convey that the past situation belongs to a period of time which, at the moment of speaking, is still current, then the perfect will be chosen. The matter of the currency or non-currency of the period of time concerned may be made explicit by the adverbials which appear in the clauses concerned; consider:

1 *La semana pasada la vi dos veces*
   'Last week I saw her twice'
2 *Esta semana la he visto dos veces*
   'This week I have seen her twice'

In (1), the past situation (the acts of seeing the woman concerned) is viewed as occurring in a period of time ('last week') which has terminated before the moment of the speech act. In (2), by contrast, the past situation (in the view of the speaker) belongs to a period of time which is still current at the moment in which the situation is referred to. However, the presence of adverbials is by no means obligatory, and the verb-forms alone are able to convey the two ways in which the speaker chooses to mentally divide past time. Thus, for speakers in the Peninsular areas defined, the utterances

3 *Lo hice otra vez*
'I did it again'

and

4 *Lo he hecho otra vez*
'I have done it again'

indicate that the speaker either considers, as in (3), that the situation described belongs to a past which is separated from the moment of speaking (e.g., because some other relevant event has intervened), or considers, as in (4), that the situation belongs to an extended present. In each case the verbal action is both past and perfective.

It should be noted that the recency of the past situation is not the criterion which determines the choice between preterite and perfect, since, on the one hand, a very recent past situation may be considered as occurring in a period of time separate from the moment of speaking, while, on the other hand, the period of time in which the speech act takes place may be deemed by the speaker to extend indefinitely into the past and to include situations which began long ago. This can be seen in cases such as:

5 *La vi hace un momento*
'I saw her a moment ago'

6 *Siempre la he escuchado con atención, pero nunca más*
'I have always listened to her attentively, but never again'.[24]

By contrast with the large majority of Peninsular Spanish speakers, those from the northwest use a different system of contrasts between the preterite and the perfect verb forms. It is usually said that in these areas (Galicia, Leon, Asturias, Cantabria) the 'perfect tense is most frequently replaced by the preterite', so that the perfect is rare or absent (e.g., Lapesa 1980: 476, 487; Zamora 1967: 208). Detailed descriptions of the values of these verb forms in the northwest are lacking, but from the examples typically cited and from the adverbials they often contain (e.g., Zamora (1967: 208): *hoy llovió todo el día*) it can be seen that in these areas the preterite is used to refer to past situations which occur in periods of time still current at the moment of speaking (although the situation itself – in this case the rainfall – may have ceased). On the other hand, no attention is given to the use of the perfect in these northwestern areas, no doubt because, when speakers in these regions use the perfect, they use it in a way that coincides with standard usage, even though the values concerned coincide with only part of the range of values that this verb form has in the standard. It is likely (but the data to prove this point are lacking) that the perfect in the northwest is used to indicate only those situations which remain in force at the moment of speaking or which are capable of continuing into the future (e.g., standard *Siempre me han gustado los mejillones*).

Martin Harris (1982) describes the development of the perfect in Romance in the following way. The structure HABEO FACTUM (whence *he hecho* in Spanish) successively and cumulatively expresses four sets of semantic values: (1) a present state resulting from past action; (2) current relevance of the past situation indicated by the participle (also marked for duration, repetition); (3) past action with present relevance (but unmarked for duration, repetition, etc.); (4) past situations without present relevance. Although some Romance languages (French, some varieties of Italian) have progressed to stage (4), at which stage the perfect becomes identical to the preterite, and usually replaces it, standard Peninsular Spanish has reached only stage (3), which we understand to have characteristics identical with those invoked in our initial definition of the Spanish perfect: that verb form which indicates that the past situation to which it refers belongs to a period of time which, at the moment of speaking, is still current, while not necessarily indicating that the situation is still in force nor that it may be repeated.

Northwestern varieties of Spanish (and also, as we shall shortly claim, American Spanish) have arguably progressed only to stage (2) of Harris's scheme. That is to say that the perfect in these areas obligatorily implies that the past situation continues in force at the moment of speaking and may be continued or repeated in the future. This is certainly what Juan M. Lope Blanch (1961) claims for Mexican Spanish, and this view is amplified, with extensive supporting data from educated usage in Mexico City, by José G. Moreno de Alba (1978: 43–68), while a similar perfect value is reported for Bogotá by Charles Rallides (1971).

It is likely (but, in the absence of further studies, undemonstrable) that this value of the perfect is typical of the whole of American Spanish (Rona 1973). Just as in the case of northwestern varieties of Peninsular Spanish, scholars assign to American Spanish in general the sentence-type *Hoy llovió todo el día*, where the preterite is used 'in place of the perfect' (Lapesa 1980: 587–8, Zamora 1967: 434), implicitly demonstrating that in Spanish America the preterite is normally used to report past situations which occur in a period of time still current at the moment of speaking.

The geographical link between northwestern Spain and Spanish America is provided by the Canary Islands, where the same 'amplification' of the role of the preterite is reported (Lapesa 1980: 520). Because of the absence from Andalusia of the past-tense values under discussion, it must be assumed that settlers from the Peninsular northwest (of whom we know that there was a substantial contingent) contributed this feature to the Canarian dialect mixture, from the fifteenth century onwards, and that the habitual mediating role of Canarian Spanish (see **4.1.8**), between that of Spain and that of America, was responsible for the transatlantic spread of the phenomenon.

Although, as we have seen, the Spanish perfect does not generally progress beyond stage (3) of Harris's (1982) scheme, that is to say that *he cantado* does not generally encroach upon the role of *canté*, nevertheless there are isolated cases of such a development, both in America and in Spain. Alonso Zamora Vicente (1967: 330) reports this encroachment in western Andalusia (Cádiz and Málaga), and Rafael Lapesa (1980: 588) refers to it (via Kany 1945: 162–6) as occurring in northwestern Argentina and adjacent parts of Bolivia. There is similarly some evidence of this change among younger speakers in Madrid (Barrera-Vidal 1972).

5.2 Social variation

Social variation in American Spanish has been very much less well studied than geographical variation (as is generally the case, including Spain; see **4.2**). Linguistic variation correlated with social class has been mentioned in connection with pronunciation of /tɾ/ and /r/ (**5.1.3.1**), where we saw that assibilated pronunciations of these phonemes, in Mexico City, characterizes the speech of at least some middle- and upper-class women.[25] We have also seen (**5.1.2.5**) that even in areas of intense *voseo*, the use of the pronoun *Tú* is almost never completely absent, but has at least some use at the most wealthy and best educated levels of society, as is the case in Argentina and Uruguay, and even more so in Chile and central America. Similarly, where neutralization of syllable-final /-r/ and /-l/ occurs, typically in the Caribbean and other coastal areas (**5.1.2.3**), it is most intense in rural and working-class speech and is seen to fade the higher up the social scale one observes. And even in areas where weakening of syllable-final /s/ is a strongly established feature (**5.1.2.2**), the frequency of aspirated and other weakened variants, which may approach 100 per cent at lower social levels, tends to decline in frequency at least somewhat as one examines the speech of more and more favoured social groups.[26]

These remarks scarcely scratch the surface of a complex issue, but it is interesting to note that in some cases the pattern of variants of a particular variable is similar on the two sides of the Atlantic. This seems to be so in the case of neutralization of syllable-final /-r/ and /-l/, just mentioned, which, in southern Spain as much as in the Caribbean and Chile, is associated with the least prestigious social groups, rural and urban, while in more powerful sectors of society the two phonemes are kept separate. This is also the case of the variable (h), examined in the following paragraph.

5.2.1. Social variation of /h/ (< F-)

In Spain, we saw (**3.1.3.2**) that use of the glottal fricative /h/ in words of the type *humo, hambre, ahorcado* (< FŪMU, FAMINE, FURCU) is recessive in two ways. Firstly, this feature has come to be restricted geographically, to certain areas (Cantabria and eastern Asturias, western Salamanca, Extremadura, and western Andalusia) which are peripheral to the main focus of /h/-dropping, namely Madrid. But secondly, it has become socially recessive, and is now confined to the least prestigious social groups within the geographical areas just defined. The second of these two patterns (social recessiveness), but not the first, has been carried to America.

When the settlement of America began, use of /h/ in words with the relevant history must have been normal, among all social classes, in western Andalusia (the area whose speech, as we have seen in **5.1.1**, contributed most significantly to the dialect mix which arose in the various colonies). The western Andalusian Antonio de Nebrija, when he was writing his Castilian grammar in 1492, makes it clear, without reservation, that *h* represents 'tal sonido cual pronunciamos en las primeras letras destas diciones: *hago, hecho*' (Nebrija 1980: 118). Similarly, when writing his 1517 treatise on Castilian spelling (Nebrija 1977: 139), he allocates three functions to *h*, the first of which is (unequivocally) to represent the initial sound of words like *hago, hijo, higo*.

It was only later, from the second half of the sixteenth century, that /h/-dropping begin to become fashionable (see **3.1.3.2**), and began to spread rapidly, faster among the social elite than among less prestigious groups, both in Spain and the Americas. The result in Spanish America has been that the competition between educated /h/-dropping and uneducated /h/-retention has persisted across the continent (Zamora Vicente 1967: 413–14, Lapesa 1980: 574), unlike the result in Spain, where /h/-dropping has reached all speakers in by far the larger part of the territory. Pronunciation of /h/ survives above all in rural American varieties, but sometimes also in lower-class urban speech. In all cases, the same phoneme represents both the descendant of Latin ꜰ- (as in *humo, horca, ahogar*) and the product of medieval /ʃ/ and /ʒ/ (as in *caja, mujer, junto, jugar, gente*) (see **3.1.3.1**). It therefore corresponds both to standard /Ø/ and to standard /x/, but may also correspond to standard /f/, in words like *fuego, fuente, fue*, often pronounced /huégo/, /huénte/, /hué/ in the same social environments (see **3.1.3.2**, **3.5**), as well as in words which have penetrated rural speech from more educated milieux (e.g., /dihúnto/, corresponding to *difunto*).

Cases of /h/-retention can be seen in rural speech from New Mexico (Espinosa 1930) to Argentina, where it characterizes (or once characterized) the speech of the gaucho, as can be seen repeatedly in the language of the eponymous hero of José Hernández's epic *Martín Fierro*. In territories between these extremes it may go unreported, because it is so socially recessive, but it is clearly in evidence in all rural central America (Alvar 1996b: 103), in Cuba, the Dominican Republic and Puerto Rico (Alvar 1996b: 59, Henríquez Ureña 1940), in coastal Colombia (Alvar 1996b: 136), in rural Ecuador (Lipski 1994: 248–9), in highland and Amazonian Peru (Lipski 1994: 320, 323), in the rural east and south of Bolivia (Alvar 1996b: 176), and in Paraguay (Alvar 1996b: 201). Despite centuries of stigmatization, pronunciations with /h/ intact cling on everywhere across the continent in the speech of the least powerful.

5.3 New dialects: *fronterizo*

The geographical relationship of Spanish and Portuguese in the New World is rather different from their relationship in the Peninsula. In Europe, there is an abrupt transition from one language to the other along that part of the Spanish–Portuguese frontier which stretches south between the River Douro/Duero and the mouth of the Guadiana (see **4.1.3**), although the varieties spoken in Portugal are connected to those spoken in Spain through the dialect continuum which extends up through northern Portugal and Galicia into Leon and Castile (**4.1.2**). However, because Spanish and Portuguese were extended overseas as the result of separate colonizing enterprises, after the process of standardization had begun in both cases – at a time when the two languages consequently already enjoyed distinct identities – they never formed part of a dialect continuum in the Americas.

In most frontier areas where Brazil adjoins its Spanish-speaking neighbours, the transition between the two languages takes place in sparsely populated regions of the Amazon basin, where there are few speakers of either language and communications across the frontiers are poor. The frontiers themselves sometimes remain undefined, and many of the scattered groups who inhabit these areas do not speak either Spanish or Portuguese as a first language, and often do not know them at all. Only in northern Uruguay, it seems, have communications across the frontier allowed Spanish and Portuguese to come into contact, producing communities in which both languages are used. As a result of this contact, a number of compromise dialects have arisen, displaying varying mixtures of Spanish and Portuguese features, and referred to by linguists as *fronterizo* or *fronteiriço* speech.

The territory concerned is a broad swathe of northern Uruguay, adjacent to Brazil, where sovereignty was disputed both by the colonial powers and by their independent successors (see Rona 1963, 1965, and the map in Canfield 1981: 89). Not only were there some Portuguese speakers established south of the frontier, but Spanish speakers were until recently in closer contact with Brazil, for markets and education, than with the rest of Uruguay. No doubt because of the very high degree of mutual intelligibility between the two languages, speakers of Spanish accommodated to the local Brazilian Portuguese, adopting large numbers of phonological, morphological, and lexical features. The result has been a series of interlocking varieties, which, as one moves from central Uruguay towards the Brazilian frontier, might be described successively as 'Spanish', 'Spanish-based *fronterizo*' (i.e., Spanish with a strong admixture of Portuguese features), 'Portuguese-based *fronterizo*' (i.e., Portuguese with some Spanish features), and more or less normal Southern Brazilian Portuguese.

Elaborating on the features listed by Lipski (1994: 342–5), it is possible to describe this transition from Spanish to Portuguese in the following terms, where the frequency of the Spanish feature decreases and the frequency of the Portuguese feature rises as one moves from central Uruguay to the Brazilian frontier:

1   At the Spanish end of the spectrum, the vowel system comprises the usual five vowels, with little variation between stressed and

unstressed realizations, while at the Portuguese end (within Uruguay) there are seven oral and five nasal vowels, some with sharply different realizations in unstressed syllables (e.g., /e/ and /ɛ/ raised to [i], /o/ and /ɔ/ raised to [u], /a/ raised to [ɐ]). At intermediate points within the transition area, the number of vowel phonemes in use, and the degree of atonic vowel reduction, rise as one approaches the frontier.

2 Central Uruguayan Spanish, like all varieties of American Spanish, has inherited only one sibilant phoneme (/s/; see **5.1.1.1**), although it has also acquired /ʒ/ (the local outcome of the merger between /ʎ/ and /ĵ/; see **5.1.2.1**), while Portuguese has four: /s/, /z/, /ʃ/, /ʒ/. Different *fronterizo* dialects display two, three, or four sibilants.

3 The Spanish system of definite articles, *el, la, los, las* gives way to the Portuguese system, *o, a, os, as,* so that intermediate dialects often combine a Portuguese article with the Spanish nominal (*todo o día* rather than *todo el día* or Brazilian Portuguese [túðu u dʲía], or vice versa (*la importação* rather than Portuguese *a importação* or Spanish *la importación*).

4 Unlike the speech of most of Uruguay (see **5.1.2.5**), *fronterizo* varieties prefer *tuteo* as the style of second-person singular informal address. This feature no doubt reflects a transition towards the Brazilian Portuguese spoken beyond the frontier, which (unlike most other varieties of Brazilian Portuguese) makes frequent use of *Tu* (rather than more general *Você*) (Lipski 1994: 343).

5 Because local Brazilian Portuguese frequently reduces verbal endings to that of the third-person singular of the paradigm concerned, similar effects may be seen in Uruguayan *fronterizo* varieties (e.g., *nos tinha* 'we had', beside Spanish *(nosotros) teníamos*; cf. standard Portuguese *(nós) tínhamos*) (Rona 1965: 12, Lipski 1994: 344).

6 Local Brazilian Portuguese frequently marks plurality only once in a given noun phrase, usually on the first element capable of expressing number, a pattern also to be seen in the varieties under discussion (e.g., *unos tío* 'aunts and uncles', *trinta y sei gol* 'thirty-six goals'; examples from Lipski 1994: 344).

7 The vocabulary of these varieties frequently intermixes Portuguese and Spanish elements, so that amid a predominantly Spanish lexical system (although containing many items which

belong to both Spanish and Portuguese), there are many individual Portuguese words in use (e.g., *fechar* 'to close', beside *cerrar*, *janela* 'window', beside *ventana*).

Some of these mixed varieties, mostly spoken by people of humble background, are described as fairly stable (meaning that they have been transmitted from parents to children without major modification, and that they are the only or the main means of communication of the social groups concerned). In the terms that Trudgill uses to describe these varieties (1986: 83–6, following Le Page and Tabouret-Keller 1985), some of them have become relatively *focused* dialects. That is, speakers of some varieties of *fronterizo* are aware of the linguistic code they use as a distinct entity, by contrast with speakers who find themselves in a *diffuse* linguistic situation, in which they mix elements from a variety of overlapping and competing linguistic systems. Now that better communications make them subject to increasing standardizing pressure from Montevideo, it remains to be seen whether these varieties will survive as separate entities.

5.4 Creoles and creolization

The introduction of large numbers of west African slaves into the Spanish American colonies, which began in the early sixteenth century, created conditions under which pidgins were very likely to arise. Any shipment of slaves typically consisted of individuals speaking a wide variety of different languages, usually lacking any medium with which to communicate among themselves or with their owners. Such conditions led to the creation of pidgins, forms of language with dramatically simple grammar and a vocabulary restricted solely to the limited topics required for inter-group communication. Such pidgins, by definition, were always acquired in addition to one or more native languages, and had no native speakers of their own.

Creoles, by contrast, are full languages which typically come into existence when the children of slave parents, learning to speak in a community which only has a pidgin for communication among its adults, construct an elaborated grammar from the pidgin they hear and extend the vocabulary of this language by massive borrowing from all available sources (Romaine 1988, 1994: ch. 6).

Since the Atlantic slave-trade was for two or more centuries principally in the hands of the Portuguese, and since many slaves were first brought to Lisbon before being transferred to Spain and its colonies, Portuguese was often the first non-African language to which many of these slaves were exposed, and it is likely that the first pidgins contained Portuguese elements, especially vocabulary.[27] However, in the case of slaves sold to Spanish colonial masters, it is likely that, as creoles developed, such elements were overlaid with borrowings from Spanish (in those cases where Spanish differed from Portuguese), just as, in other colonial territories, creoles arose which drew their vocabulary and other features from English or French.

When a creole remained in contact with the language from which most of its vocabulary has been borrowed, it was subject to decreolization, a process of gradual adjustment to that language. In slave societies, this process typically led to a spectrum of linguistic varieties, ranging from some form of the prestige language, used by the most powerful, to unmodified creole speech, used by the least powerful, and with intermediate varieties of every degree. Decreolization would have been slow in communities where there were few speakers of the prestige language, or where social conditions made it difficult for creole-speakers to come in contact with them.

In the case of Spain's American Empire, slaves were shipped in large numbers from Seville to authorized points of sale in the Caribbean, at first only three: Veracruz (Mexico), Cartagena de Indias (Colombia), and Portobelo (Panama). This trade must frequently have led to the creation of creoles, but decreolization appears to have taken place more easily and quickly in the Spanish colonies, and their successor states, than in British or French colonies, so that few Spanish creoles have survived into the twentieth century and only two are spoken today: Papiamentu and Palenquero.

5.4.1   Papiamentu

This Spanish creole is spoken in the islands of Curaçao, Aruba and Bonaire (also known as the ABC Islands), which are located off the coast of Venezuela and which became part of the Spanish Crown from 1527. After alternating between Dutch, French and British control, they became definitively Dutch and now comprise the Netherlands Antilles. After these territories passed from Spanish control in 1634, decreolization (at least, decreolization towards Spanish) became impossible, and Papiamentu remains the language of the large majority, being used alongside Dutch (the official language), Spanish and English. As well as

	Front		Central		Back
	Unrounded	Rounded	Unrounded	Rounded	Rounded
High	/i/ *iglesia*	/y/ *minüt*			/u/ *mundu*
Mid high	/e/ *pechu*		/ə/ *pober*	/ɵ/ *bùs*	/o/ *loko*
Mid low	/ɛ/ *skèr*				/ɔ/ *òmelet*
Low			/a/ *akabado*		

Table 5.2   Papiamentu vowel phonemes

large numbers of west African slaves, the ABC Islands received substantial numbers of Spanish- and Portuguese-speaking Sephardic Jews (see Chapter 6), from Amsterdam and Brazil, beginning in the mid-seventeenth century (Alvar 1996b: 68–78; Munteanu 1996).

Papiamentu is not mutually intelligible with other varieties of Spanish (an observation which begs the question of whether we should consider it a variety of Spanish), and although it shares a good many features with other types of Spanish (*yeísmo* (**5.1.2.1**), *seseo* (**5.1.1.1**), neutralization of /-r/ and /-l/ leading to their loss (**5.1.2.3**), /h/-retention (**5.2.1**), velarization of word-final /n/ (**5.1.2.4**), etc.), it displays a certain number of characteristics found nowhere else in the Spanish-speaking world. Among the latter are the following (drawn from Alvar 1996b: 68–78, Munteanu 1996: 191–226):

1   It has a phonemic contrast between rising and falling tones, so that /tápaˊ/ (with rising tone) 'to cover' is in opposition to /tápaˋ/ (with falling tone) 'cover (noun)'.

2   It has a vowel system of ten phonemes (see Table **5.2**).

3   The Papiamentu consonant system comprises as many as twenty-one phonemes (Munteanu 1996: 227–62; see Table **5.3**).[28]

4   Modification of nasal consonants (possibly as a result of features taken from African languages): *kabaron* (cf. Sp. *camarón* 'shrimp'), *kaminda* (cf. Sp. *camino* 'road'), *hunga* (cf. Sp. *jugar* 'to play').

5   Intervocalic /x/ is often lost: *abou* (cf. Sp. *abajo* 'down below'), *orea* (cf. Sp. *oreja* 'ear').

6   There is no grammatical gender.

7   Use of the plural marker *nan* (which is also the third-person plural subject pronoun): sg. *kas*, pl. *kasnan* (cf. Sp. *casa, -s* 'house(s)'), sg. *buki*, pl. *bukinan* (cf. Sp. *libro, -s* 'book(s)').

Table 5.3 Papiamentu consonant phonemes

	Bilabial	Labiodental	Dental/Alveolar	Palato-alveolar	Palatal	Velar	Glottal
Plosive	/p/ *pober* 'poor' /b/ *bunita* 'pretty'		/t/ *tapa* 'lid' /d/ *duru* 'hard'			/k/ *kustia* 'rib' /g/ *amigu* 'friend'	
Fricative		/f/ *fòrki* 'fork' /v/ *alavez* 'also'	/s/ *sombré* 'hat' /z/ *abuzá* 'to abuse'	/ʃ/ *ofishi* 'job' /ʒ/ *zjonzjoli* 'sesame'		/x/ *joya* 'jewel'	/h/ *humá* 'to smoke'
Affricate				/tʃ/ *lechi* 'milk' /dʒ/ *djaluna* 'Monday'			
Lateral			/l/ *laba* 'to wash'				
Vibrant			/r/ *tera* 'earth'				
Nasal	/m/ *machu* 'male'		/n/ *nochi* 'night'		/ɲ/ *kaña* 'cane'		

	Singular	Plural
First person	*mi, ami*	*nos, anos*
Second person	*bo, abo*	*boso(nan), aboso*
Third person	*e(l)(e)*	*nan, anan*

Table 5.4   Papiamentu personal pronouns

8   Number is marked only once in the noun phrase, either by a modifier with plural sense or by the ending *nan*, applied either to the noun or to an adjective: *tur stul* (cf. Sp. *todas las sillas* 'all the chairs'), *e kasnan bunita* or *e kas bunitanan* (cf. Sp. *las casas bonitas* 'the pretty houses').

9   Papiamentu personal pronouns are as listed in Table 5.4. These forms function both as subject and as object pronouns, although the first-cited forms appear to be preferred for subject use. Together with *di*, these pronouns express possession: *e di mi* (cf. Sp. *el mío, la mía* 'mine').

10   The forms of the demonstratives are: *esaki* (cf. Sp. *este, esta*), *esei* (cf. Sp. *ese, esa*), *esaya* (cf. Sp. *aquel, aquella*).

11   Tense and aspect in the verb are marked by a series of particles which precede an invariable verb form (inherited from the third-person singular form of the Spanish present indicative). Duration/repetition is expressed by *ta* (probably from Sp. *está*): *(mi) ta kanta* 'I sing, I am singing'; past time by *a* (probably from Sp. *ha*): *(mi) a kanta* 'I sang, I have sung'; futurity by *lo* (probably from Ptg. *lôgo* or Sp. *luego*): *lo (mi) kanta* 'I shall sing'. These particles may be combined in a variety of ways: *(mi) ta'a* (or *tabata*) *kanta* 'I was singing'; *lo (mi) ta kanta/kantando* 'I shall be singing'; *lo (mi) tabata kanta/kantando* 'I would be singing'; *lo (mi) a kanta* 'I shall have sung'.

12   Papiamentu makes use of so-called serial verbs, comprising two or more verbs in their (normal) invariable form, with a variety of meanings. Munteanu (in Alvar 1996b: 77) cites: *el a para mira e barkonan* 'he stopped to look at the boats = he is looking at the boats'; *el a bula bisa*, lit. 'he spoke flying', i.e., 'he suddenly spoke'.

13   Although the basic vocabulary of Papiamentu is substantially drawn from Spanish and/or Portuguese (about two-thirds on one

count, reported by Munteanu (in Alvar 1996b: 77)), there is a large Dutch component (28 per cent), as well as words borrowed from other sources, including English. Not all borrowings are drawn from non-Hispanic sources; many are drawn from Spanish, because this language has had continuous minority use in the ABC Islands, and because of contacts with the wider Spanish-speaking world.

Papiamentu appears to be firmly established in the areas where it is spoken, being used by the majority and the object of considerable pride. It is increasingly standardized and is used for a wide variety of published material, newspapers, magazines, and books.

5.4.2 Palenquero

Cartagena de Indias was one of the earliest Spanish settlements in the New World, and, as we have noted (**5.4**), became one of the three largest entrepôts of the American slave trade. As early as 1540, there were cases of groups of slaves escaping from Cartagena and setting up fortified villages or *palenques* in the Colombian interior, and further mass escapes are known during the sixteenth, seventeenth, and eighteenth centuries. Despite attempts to suppress these communities, some maintained their effective independence into the twentieth century.

These escaped slaves no doubt spoke Spanish creoles, and in a few cases their descendants continued to do so centuries later, although realization of this fact only came a few decades ago. The most famous instance is that of San Basilio de Palenque, some 70 km south of Cartagena, where creole continues to be spoken, now in competition with non-creole varieties of Spanish (Bickerton and Escalante 1970, Megenney 1986, Montes 1996).

The phonology of Palenquero shows, in extreme degree, all of the features of rural lowland American Spanish: *seseo* (**5.1.1.1**), *yeísmo* (**5.1.2.1**), neutralization of atonic /i/ and /e/, and of /u/ and /o/ (e.g., *vitilo, kumé*, cf. standard *vestido, comer*) (**4.2.4**), weakening of syllable-final /-s/ (e.g., *dehpwé, kateyáno*, cf. standard *después, castellano*) (**5.1.2.2**), merger and loss of syllable-final /-r/ and /-l/ (e.g., *ákko, kál·lo, kumé*, cf. standard *arco, Carlos, comer*) (**5.1.2.3**), as well as other features which occur sporadically in such varieties of Spanish: confusion of /d/ and /ɾ/ (e.g., *poré, rebé*, cf. standard *poder, deber*), confusion

		Singular	Plural
First person	subject	*i*	*suto*
	object	*mi*	*suto*
Second person	subject	*bo*	*enú/utere*
	object	*bo*	*enú/utere*
Third person	subject	*ele*	*ané*
	object	*lo/ele*	*ané/lo*

Table 5.5   Palenquero personal pronouns

of syllable-initial /ɾ/ and /l/ (e.g., *kolasó*, cf. standard *corazón*). More strikingly, Palenquero displays pre-nasal oral plosives, a feature probably transferred from a west African language or languages: *ndejá*, *nganá*, cf. standard *dejar*, *ganar*).

It is in its morpho-syntax, as is to be expected, that Palenquero reveals its creole nature. The major relevant features are the following:

1   The personal pronoun system rarely contrasts subject forms with object forms, which are simply postposed to the verb. In the first-person singular, however, there is such a contrast, which also operates optionally in the third person (see Table **5.5**).

2   Among the pronouns listed in Table **5.5**, the forms *mi, ele, suto, utere* and *ané* also function as possessives, postposed to the head noun, while the second-person singular possessive form is *si*.

3   Grammatical gender is lacking.

4   In the noun phrase, plurality is marked only by the particle *ma*, usually placed before the head noun.

5   Verbal inflexion is almost entirely absent (a gerund sporadically occurs, as does a past imperfective suffix *-ba*); tense and aspect are marked by particles which precede an invariable verb form, derived from the infinitive. Perfective aspect is marked by *a* (e.g., *i a semblá un mata maí* = '(yo) sembré una mata de maíz'), durative or habitual aspect by *ta* or *se* (e.g., *pueblo mi ta pelé lengua ané* = 'mi pueblo está perdiendo su lengua'), future time by *tan* (e.g., *eso fue Juan tan asé* = 'eso fue lo que Juan hará'). These particles may be combined in a number of ways: past habitual situations are marked by *a se* (also *a sebá*) (e.g., *a ten maní a sebá limpiá nu* = 'hay maní que no se limpiaba').

6 In the Palenquero vocabulary, a fair number of words of African origin have been recognized, although the very large majority of words have Hispanic roots.[29]

Palenquero has existed in a situation of diglossia (see **2.5.4**) with Spanish for a century or more. Rather than becoming decreolized, it seems that it is being abandoned by younger generations and is therefore threatened with language death.

6   Variation in Judeo-Spanish

Judeo-Spanish (in Spanish, *judeoespañol*) is the name given by many scholars to those varieties of Spanish spoken by descendants of the Jews who were expelled from Spain in 1492. There is no universal name by which these varieties are known to their speakers, although both *judezmo* and the simple *español* are used by some of the relevant communities, as is *ladino*. However, this last term is reserved by some scholars for written varieties of Judeo-Spanish, especially renderings of the Old Testament which closely follow the syntax of the Hebrew while using Spanish morphemes. The term *Sephardic Spanish* (*español sefardí* or *español sefardita*) has the same broad meaning as Judeo-Spanish, but is only used in academic and similar writing.

Before the expulsion from Spain, Jews wrote Spanish using Hebrew characters (on the basis of transliteration of each Latin character into a Hebrew letter), and notable literary and non-literary examples of this writing survive from medieval Spain. This style of writing continued after 1492, in various parts of the Balkan and Mediterranean world, and has provided many surviving examples, but lack of contact with Peninsular Spanish meant that Judeo-Spanish spelling acquired independence from its Peninsular model.[1] Later, in the nineteenth century, there grew up the practice of writing Judeo-Spanish in the Latin alphabet, a system now consisting of correspondences between Latin letters and Judeo-Spanish phonemes, but with spellings based on French orthographical rules. There were many further locally inspired modifications to this system, such as those based upon the Roman-alphabet spelling of Turkish, introduced as a result of Mustafa Kemal Atatürk's reforms in 1926, and there continues to be no single way of writing Judeo-Spanish (see Hassán 1988). Alongside this written language, there was until recently a flourishing oral literature of songs, ballads, and stories.[2]

6.1 The language of the medieval Jewish communities

There were Jewish communities in the Peninsula from Roman times, especially in the southern province of Baetica, and there were further immigrants who arrived at the time of the Islamic invasions in the eighth century and later. Hebrew and Aramaic did not survive as vernacular languages, although Hebrew was used in the synagogue and was written by some educated Jews.

Those Jews who lived in Islamic Spain were, like all others there, members of a bilingual society, in which Arabic was used for almost all official and literary purposes and local varieties of Romance (i.e., Mozarabic, see **4.1.1**) were the everyday medium of communication, whether the speaker was Muslim, Christian or Jewish. A small amount of bilingual poetry, Hebrew–Mozarabic (perhaps an imitation of Arabic–Mozarabic poetry), has survived, and it is known that educated Jews played a vital role in the translation of Arabic texts into Spanish, when this activity came to be officially sponsored from the thirteenth century.

Following the late-eleventh-century conquest of Islamic Spain by fundamentalist groups from north Africa (the Almoravids, followed by the Almohads from the mid-twelfth century), persecution of non-Muslims caused the emigration of many Jews (and Christians) into the northern, Christian, states. It will be recalled (from **4.1.4**) that three of these states were in the process of significantly expanding their territory, at the expense of Islamic Spain, incorporating such cities as Toledo (1085), Lisbon (1147), and Valencia (1238), centres which became important targets of Jewish immigration. Similarly, following the Castilian reconquest of northern and western Andalusia, from 1212, Jewish communities were re-established in the main Andalusian cities, such as Córdoba and Seville. As a result of these movements, and of the persistence of other Jewish communities, almost all sizeable Peninsular towns and cities had a Jewish quarter in the later Middle Ages.

The question of how Jews spoke in the centuries before their expulsion (and, consequently, of what kind of Spanish they carried with them) has been much debated (see, for example, Marcus 1962). Some have held that Jewish speech was already distinctive, differing from that of Christians (and Muslims), but careful examination of literary, religious, and other texts written by Jews in the fourteenth and fifteenth centuries (Alarcos 1951, Vàrvaro 1987, Minervini 1992) reveals that, except in the technical vocabulary of religion, there was little if any difference between the language of Jews and the language of non-Jews who lived in the same place at the same time (see Lleal 1992: 5–15). This implies that varieties of Jewish speech in the Peninsula (like all other speech) occupied a series of points along the northern Peninsular dialect continuum (**4.1.2**), or along the three dialect continua which extended down the Peninsula as a result of the expansion of the northern Christian states during the reconquest of central and southern Spain and Portugal (**4.1.7**).

6.2 The expulsion and its linguistic effects

The Catholic Monarchs, Isabella I of Castile and Ferdinand II of Aragon, decreed in March 1492 that all Jews who had not been converted to Christianity had to leave Spain by the end of July of that year. Although some Spanish Jews fled to Portugal and Navarre, they were similarly expelled from Portugal in 1497 (together with Portuguese Jews), and then from Navarre when that kingdom was incorporated in the Spanish Crown in 1512.

The routes taken by groups of Jews from particular Peninsular localities are not known, although their destinations were varied. Considerable numbers emigrated to Flanders, where they established flourishing communities and maintained contact with the Peninsula, and from where some moved on to Brazil and Spanish America when they saw the opportunity, although this was illegal.[3] Many others crossed from Spain to north Africa and to Italy. Although common sense suggests that there may have been a preponderance of Jews from northern Spain among those established in the Low Countries, of those from eastern Spain in Italy, and of those from southern Spain in north Africa, what evidence we have shows that Jews from all parts of the Peninsula reached all these destinations. This continues to be the case when, a little later, Sephardic Jews were invited by the Turkish Sultan Bayazid II to settle in the Ottoman Empire, an invitation accepted by many of those who in the meantime had reached Italy and north Africa. The conditions they found there were ones of linguistic and religious tolerance, and many Sephardic Jews achieved high professional and social standing in the Ottoman world.

Sephardic communities were established in the main cities of the Empire, among them Constantinople, Smyrna, Salonica, Bucharest, Sofia, Sarajevo, and in other towns in Bosnia, Serbia, Macedonia, Greece and Rhodes. In some of these cities, it is known that during the first part of the sixteenth century there were separate synagogues established by Jews from particular regions of the Peninsula (Castilians, Aragonese, Catalans, Portuguese) or even by those from specific cities (Lisbon, Barcelona, Córdoba). This indicates that Jews from various parts of Spain reached the same destination cities, and that Jews from the same Peninsular region reached a variety of destinations. Although family groups no doubt remained together during these complex migrations, there is no evidence that groups much larger than the family set out from the same place and reached the same destination, and indeed common sense argues against such an outcome.

These patterns of emigration imply far-reaching changes of social structure, and clearly gave rise to dialect contact and mixing, both of which features bring important linguistic consequences. Firstly, modern studies have shown (Milroy and Milroy 1985) that emigration leads to a predominance of weak social ties in the networks linking individuals (see **3.3**), a situation which encourages linguistic change. In accordance with this principle, we shall see (in **6.3.1**) that Judeo-Spanish shows a considerable degree of innovation, especially in phonology and lexis. This view contradicts the conventional opinion (e.g., Lapesa 1980: 526) that Judeo-Spanish is intensely conservative in nature, although it does not deny that Judeo-Spanish preserves some features of fifteenth-century Spanish which have disappeared everywhere else (**6.3.2**).

Secondly, we have also seen (**3.1**) that dialect mixing predictably leads to linguistic simplification (**3.1.4**) and to the levelling of differences between competing varieties (**3.1.3**). Once again, we shall see ample evidence of these effects in the development of Judeo-Spanish. On the one hand, simplification in phonology is evident, and can also be claimed for morphology and syntax (**6.3.3**). On the other hand, the appearance in Judeo-Spanish of features which belong to regions other than Castile (see **6.3.4**) is entirely in keeping with the view that each new Jewish settlement comprised people from all over the Peninsula, a situation which led to a multiplicity of competing linguistic variants in the speech of these communities. This competition was by no means always resolved in favour of the Castilian variants, especially if the non-Castilian variants offered the advantage of greater simplicity. An instructive contrast can be made, in this regard, between the linguistic development of the Judeo-Spanish communities in the Mediterranean and that of the Spanish settlements in America: whereas the role of Seville was overwhelmingly powerful in the initial settlement and later development of the American colonies (see **5.1.1**), an influence only partly challenged by that coming from Madrid (**5.1.2**), in the case of the Sephardic settlements there was no overall dominance of the process exerted by any single Peninsular region. The result was that the Judeo-Spanish dialect mixture was not dominated by variants from one or two regions, and in the subsequent reduction of variation it was by no means always the case that Castilian variants were selected. It is true that Castilian features were selected rather more frequently than non-Castilian, perhaps reflecting the already higher prestige associated with Castilian variants in the late fifteenth century, but selection of features typical of other Peninsular regions was much more frequent than in the case of American Spanish (see **5.1.3**), where Andalusian (and sometimes central Castilian) features dominate to the almost total exclusion of features from other regions.

A further difference between Judeo-Spanish, on the one hand, and Peninsular and American Spanish on the other, is the almost total lack of standardizing pressure in the former case. Whereas in Spain and America, from the sixteenth century onwards, literary, academic and social developments led to selection of variants associated with powerful urban groups (**7.1.1**), with the consequent exclusion from the norm of other variants and their confinement to the geographical and social periphery, this selection process was effectively absent from Judeo-Spanish (Lleal 1992: 17–45, Minervini 1997–8), and features which in Spain became marked as rustic or uneducated continued in use in all varieties of Judeo-Spanish and never came to be excluded from written use (**6.3.5**).[4]

This lack of standardizing pressure also allowed much greater geographical variation to persist within Judeo-Spanish than within Peninsular Spanish (at least among urban varieties of Peninsular Spanish). Not only were the north African communities out of contact with those of the Ottoman Empire, but Judeo-Spanish everywhere was spoken in geographically separate urban ghettos. Although contacts were frequent and lasting among speakers living in the various Ottoman cities, these contacts were insufficient to prevent a different selection of variants (from the mixture produced by dialect contact) in each city (**6.3.6**). And when the Ottoman Empire later dissolved into a series of competing nationalistic states, these contacts were weakened, so that linguistic diversity was allowed to continue and (especially at the lexical level) to increase.

6.3 Features of Judeo-Spanish

6.3.1 Innovations

Despite the repeated characterization of Judeo-Spanish as archaic and conservative (see **6.2**), it shows a substantial number of innovations not seen elsewhere in the Spanish-speaking world (see Sala 1976, Penny 1992, 1992–3a, and Lleal 1992: 43–4).

1 No variety of Judeo-Spanish distinguishes the vibrant /r/ from the flap /ɾ/, phonemes which are contrasted in all other varieties of Spanish (except creole varieties: **5.4.1(3)**, **5.4.2**). This merger (in /ɾ/) also simplifies the phonology of Judeo-Spanish, in keeping with what is predicted by dialect-contact theory (see **3.1**).

2 The word-initial sequence /nue/ is regularly modified to /mue/: *muevo, mueve, muestro* (cf. standard *nuevo, nueve, nuestro*). This process may be an extension of a Peninsular process, now confined to recessive rural use (see **6.3.5**), by which the first-person plural pronoun *nos* was modified to *mos* under the double influence of the corresponding singular pronoun *me* and of the first-person plural verbal ending *-mos*.[5] From *mos*, the change was no doubt first extended to the related possessive *nuestro*, whence JSp. *muestro*, and thence to all similarly structured words.

3 The diphthong /ue/ is reinforced, not only when it is syllable-initial (as in non-standard Peninsular and American Spanish; see **4.2.5**, **6.3.5**), but also when preceded by a consonant in the same syllable. Thus, *luego* > *[lɣwé-ɣo], a process which has the imme-diate effect of enforcing a resyllabification and the addition of a vowel before the consonant: [el-ɣwéɣo]. Where the consonant concerned is voiceless, the reinforcing element is also realized as voiceless [ʍ]: [swéɲo] > *[sʍwéɲo] > [esʍwéɲo] (cf. standard *sueño*), sometimes written *esfueño*.

4 After labials and velars (i.e., segments which are [+grave]), a labio-velar on-glide is generated in some varieties, so that *padre* is real-ized as [pwáðɾe] and *gato* as [ɣwáto], the latter series of words there having the same sequence as words of the type *huerta* and *agua*, all with [ɣw] or [ɣw].

5   Almost all varieties of Judeo-Spanish merge [ɲ] and [nj] (cf. standard *huraño* vs *uranio*) in [nj]: *espaniol*.[6] It will be noted that this change has the effect of simplifying the phonology of Judeo-Spanish, by removing one phoneme from its inventory (see also **6.3.3**). Similarly, [lj] was merged with [ʎ] before the latter was involved in *yeísmo* (**6.3.3(2)**), so that *caliente, lienzo, familia*, etc., received the same treatment as *callar, llamar, cuchillo*, etc., resulting in JSp. *kayenti, yensu, famia*.

6   The sequence /ɾd/ is regularly and universally modified to /dɾ/: *vedri, godru, akodrarsi, guadrar* (cf. standard *verde, gordo, acordarse, guardar*).

7   Syllable-final /s/ is palatalized to [ʃ] before velar /k/: /móʃka/, /buʃkár/, /piʃkádu/ (cf. standard *mosca, buscar, pescado*).

8   No doubt as a result of incorporating loans, especially from Turkish and French, the Judeo-Spanish phoneme inventory has been enriched by the phonologization of the sounds [ʒ] and [dʒ]: /ʒuɾnál/ 'newspaper' vs /dʒugár/ 'to play'. Before this change, it is likely that [ʒ] and [dʒ] were merely positional variants of a single phoneme /ʒ/, as was the case in medieval Spanish.

9   The first- and second-person plural object pronouns *nos* and *vos* lose their final consonant when followed by another clitic pronoun: *no lo dexó, vo lo digo* (cf. standard *nos lo dejó, os lo digo*). This loss is unrelated to the widespread weakening of syllable-final /s/ in Southern Peninsular Spanish (**4.1.7.2.4**) and in many varieties of American Spanish (**5.1.2.2**), since weakening or loss of /-s/ is otherwise unknown in Judeo-Spanish.

10 The reflexive clitic *se*, which is elsewhere unmarked for number, has a separate form *sen* in Judeo-Spanish when its referent is plural: *en biéndosen, kozersen* (cf. standard *al verse, cocerse*).

11 The third-person possessive *su*, in some varieties of Judeo-Spanish, is marked for the number of the possessor, rather than for the number of the thing or person possessed: *sus kaza* 'their house' (cf. standard *su casa (de ellos)*).

12 Second-person plural endings in the verb have come to be marked by /ʃ/, as a result of an assimilation between earlier final /s/ and the preceding off-glide [i̯] (as also seen in *seis* > *sex/sech/sesh*): /kantáis/ > /kantáʃ/. This marker was then extended to verbal endings where there had been no off-glide: /kantáteʃ/.[7] (For forms of address in Judeo-Spanish, see **6.3.2(7)**.)

13 First-person preterite forms of *-ar* verbs have adopted the endings /-í/, /-imos/: *kantí, kantimos* (cf. standard *canté, cantamos*). This change has the simplifying effect of merging the endings of all classes of verbs in this part of their paradigms.

14 The second-person preterite forms of all verbs show the analogical addition of a final /-s/ to the singular (as in the majority of non-standard varieties of Spanish throughout the world), but then deletion (perhaps by dissimilation) of the internal /s/ from both singular and plural forms: sing. /topátes/, /izítes/, plur. /topáteʃ/, /izíteʃ/ (cf. standard *hallaste, hiciste, hallasteis, hicisteis*).

15 Among syntactical innovations, the gerund *siendo* has been converted into a causal conjunction ('since, seeing that'): *y siendo no topó, tomó él un papel.*

6.3.2 Retentions

Traditional accounts of Judeo-Spanish emphasize the way in which it has retained features of medieval Spanish which have disappeared from Peninsular and American varieties. Some scholars have even discussed Judeo-Spanish as if it were medieval Spanish preserved unchanged for five centuries. It is indeed true that, because of the lack of contact between the Sephardic Jews settled in the Ottoman Empire and Peninsular Spanish speakers, and the little contact between the latter and the Jews who emigrated to north Africa, post-1492 innovations which arose in Spain could not reach Judeo-Spanish. Sephardic Spanish therefore shows a number of features which, from a Peninsular viewpoint, can be regarded as 'archaic', but it should be remembered that this is a relative term, and that the number of such features is not particularly great, compared with innovations discussed in **6.3.1**. The principal features which represent this kind of retention are the following:

1 The development of the medieval system of sibilant phonemes differs from that of the rest of the Spanish-speaking world in the retention of the contrast between voiceless and voiced units. It will be recalled (from **3.1.3.1**) that the six late-medieval sibilants (leaving /tʃ/ aside) were as in Table **6.1**. This system underwent, in mainstream Castilian, two further sets of changes, of which the first was a merger of the three voiced phonemes with the corresponding voiceless phonemes, leaving /ʃ/, /s/ and /s̺/ as the outcome. This change came too late to affect Judeo-Spanish, so

	Voiceless	Voiced
Pre-palatal fricative	/ʃ/ *caxa* 'box'	/ʒ/ *muger* 'woman'
Apico-alveolar fricative	/s/ *passo* 'step'	/z/ *casa* 'house'
Dental fricative	/ṣ/ *alçar* 'raise'	/ẓ/ *dezir* 'say'

Table 6.1 Late-medieval sibilants in Spanish

	Voiceless	Voiced
Pre-palatal fricative	/ʃ/ *casha* 'box'	/ʒ/ *mujer* 'woman'
Dental fricative	/ṣ/ *paso* 'step' *alsar* 'raise'	/ẓ/ *kaza* 'house' *dezir* 'say'

Table 6.2 Judeo-Spanish fricative sibilants

that the voiced phonemes remained unmerged with their voice-less counterparts, although (as we shall see in **6.3.3**) a different merger, between the dentals and apico-alveolars, did take place, reducing the six medieval phonemes to four in Judeo-Spanish. Using spellings frequently employed for twentieth-century Judeo-Spanish, this outcome can be expressed as in Table **6.2**.[8] It should be noted that this outcome is identical to that of the same phonemes in modern Portuguese (e.g., /ʃ/ *caixa*, /ʒ/ *ajudar*, /ṣ/ *passo, alçar*, /ẓ/ *casa, dizer*), and that this result may be one of many manifestations of the non-Castilian contribution to the dialect mixture which arose in Sephardic communities after the expulsion (see **6.3.4**). A further similarity with Portuguese, and with Catalan, is the treatment of word-final sibilants before a word-initial vowel; under these circumstances, /ṣ/ and /ẓ/ are neutralized and pronounced as (voiced) [ẓ]: *maz o menos* 'more or less', *doz o tres* 'two or three'.

2   As we have just seen, Judeo-Spanish retains the palatal sibilants of medieval Spanish, unlike all other varieties of Spanish, where they are velarized and may become further retracted to glottal position (**3.1.3.1, 4.1.7.2.3**). Again, the Judeo-Spanish retention of the medieval palatal sibilants is identical to the treatment

by which modern Portuguese retains its medieval palatal phonemes.

3   Although the merger of medieval Castilian /b/ and /β/ had begun before the expulsion of the Spanish Jews (see **3.1.3.3**), it was far from complete, and many varieties of Judeo-Spanish have retained this contrast, at least in part. In word-initial position the two labials have usually merged into one, generally /b/, so that no distinction is made between the initial consonants in *boka* 'mouth' (< medieval *boca*) and *baka* 'cow' (< medieval *vaca*). However, in intervocalic position most ex-Ottoman Judeo-Spanish varieties maintain a contrast, most usually between bilabial /b/ and labiodental /v/, so that *alaba* 'he praises' does not rhyme with *kantava* 'I sang' (< medieval *cantava*). It can be seen that Sephardic Spanish has inherited the southern Peninsular system of voiced labials, today only preserved in central and southern Portuguese and some varieties of southern Catalan.

4   Loss of medieval /h/ had probably begun in parts of rural Old Castile before the expulsion of the Jews, but it only became socially and geographically widespread after that event (see **3.1.3.2**). Consequently, /h/-retention was typical of at least some of the Jews who emigrated. However, other Jews contributed /h/-dropping to the various dialect mixtures which formed in the different destination cities, while still others contributed the /f/ which typified the lateral zones of the Peninsula (much of Asturias and Leon, Galicia and Portugal; Aragon, Catalonia and Valencia), and is still to be heard in most of these regions. The outcome of this competition between /Ø/, /h/ and /f/ (e.g., /úmo/, /húmo/, /fúmo/, all ultimately from Lat. FŪMU) is complex: north African varieties appear always to have preferred /Ø/, while /f/ dominates in Bosnia, Macedonia, Salonica (Lapesa 1980: 527), and in other Balkan and Turkish regions /h/ alternates with /Ø/, and /f/ is found only in a few words.

5   Syllable-final /b/ (in words like *çibdad* 'city', *vibda* 'widow', *debda* 'debt') was in the process of vocalizing to [u̯] in late medieval Spanish (Penny 1991a: 78), a development which implied merger with pre-existing [u̯] (in words like *causa* 'cause', *autoridad* 'authority') and which is manifested in interchange of *b* and *u* in both sets of words (*çibdad/çiudad, vibda/viuda, debda/deuda, cabsa/causa, abtoridad/autoridad*). This vocalization has not been carried through in Judeo-Spanish, but the alternation between [β] and [u̯]

	Singular	Plural
Non-deferential	*tu* (+ 2 sing.)	*vozotros* (+ 2 plur.)
Deferential	*vos* (+ 2 plur.) *el/e(y)a* (+ 3 sing.)	*e(y)os/e(y)as* (+ 3 plur.)

The (historical) form of the verb which accompanies or represents these pronouns is indicated in parentheses (e.g., *tu sos/eres, vozotros/vos sox, el/e(y)a es, e(y)os/e(y)as son*).

Table 6.3   Modes of address in Judeo-Spanish

must have been part of the speech of many Sephardic Jews, later resolved as [β] or [v], since not only *sivdat, bivda, devda* retain a labial consonant, but it also appears in *avtoridad, evnuko, kavsa*, etc.

6   The first-person singular present indicative of the verbs *estar, ser, dar, ir* in late Old Spanish showed hesitation between traditional *estó, so, do, vo* and innovatory *estoy, soy, doy, voy* (Penny 1991a: 162). No doubt the older forms were more prevalent in non-metropolitan varieties than in the urban speech which forms the basis of the Peninsular standard, so that the retention of *estó, so, do, vo* in Judeo-Spanish is not only a conservative feature, but one which links Judeo-Spanish to non-standard Peninsular speech (see **6.3.4**).

7   Modes of second-person address in Judeo-Spanish are conservative even for fifteenth-century Spanish. Already at that time (see **5.1.2.5**), *Vos* (with second-person plural verb) had become distinctly non-deferential in many varieties of Spanish, yet this usage continues in Judeo-Spanish as a form of polite address, regularly in north Africa and as one possibility in the East. Arlene Malinowski (1983–4) reports that in present-day Israel some speakers use *Vos* to strangers, although the majority prefer *el/e(y)a*, and some use both forms. The type *él/ella* is well known from Golden-Age Spanish (Hodcroft 1993–4), while a further form of deferential address, namely *su mersed* (related to *vuestra merced*, whence *usted*), formerly used in the Ottoman Empire, is now defunct. We can therefore summarize the forms of address in eastern Judeo-Spanish as in Table **6.3**.

8   The object and reflexive pronoun *vos* retains its initial consonant: *benívos* (cf. standard *veníos* 'come!').

9   The *-ra* verbal form continues to have conditional value: *izo saver a los payizes arabos komo el kontinuara a dezvelopar...* (cf. standard *continuaría*).

10 The preferred (perhaps the unique) affectionate diminutive in eastern Judeo-Spanish is formed with the suffix *-iko* (e.g., *pexkadiko, kazika*), while *-ito* and *-eto* are preferred in north Africa. In Peninsular Spanish, *-ico* was a strong competitor of *-ito* until the Golden Age, although since then it has come to be restricted (except in a few words) to Navarre, Aragon, Murcia and eastern Andalusia, and some regions of Spanish America.

11 Certain lexical items which were common in medieval and Golden-Age Spanish have only survived in Judeo-Spanish, e.g., *amatar* 'to extinguish', *conducho* 'provisions', *güerko* (cf. OSp. *huerco*) 'Devil', *mansevo* 'young man'.

6.3.3 Simplifications

The expected outcome of competition among variants in a situation of dialect mixing is preference for the simpler or simplest variant (**3.1.4**). This principle implies that mergers will be frequent under these conditions, and this is observably the case in the dialect mixing which comprises the early history of Judeo-Spanish. Sometimes the merger is unique to Judeo-Spanish (as in the case of the mergers of /ɲ/ with [nj], and of /ʎ/ with [lj] already discussed at **6.3.1(5)**, or the merger of first-person preterite endings, so that *kantí, kantimos* have come to share the same morphemes as *vendí, vendimos, salí, salimos* (**6.3.1(13)**)); in other cases, the mergers concerned are shared with varieties of Spanish other than those of the central Peninsula.

1 Many Sephardic emigrants came from regions of the Peninsula where the apico-alveolar and the dental sibilants had merged or were in the process of merging (**4.1.7.2.1, 5.1.1.1, 6.3.2(1)**). That is, they came from areas where /s/ was merging with /ṣ/ (as in *passo* and *alçar*, respectively), and /z/ was merging with /ẓ/ (as in *casa* and *dezir*). This is the familiar process of *seseo*, identical to that of many Andalusian varieties and all American varieties of Spanish. However, we have to take into account the fact that in those varieties where voiced sibilants persisted (as they did in Judeo-Spanish, in Portuguese, and in Catalan, not to mention Occitan and French) there was a parallel merger among these phonemes which we can call *zezeo*. The outcome of *seseo* and *zezeo* in Judeo-Spanish was a pair of dental fricatives, /ṣ/ and /ẓ/ (e.g., *paso, alsar; kaza, dezir*, see Table **6.2**), just as in Portuguese, Occitan and French, although slightly differently from Catalan,

	Voiceless		Voiced	
Pre-palatal fricative	/ʃ/	*casha* 'box'	/ʒ/	*mujer* 'woman'
Pre-palatal affricate	/tʃ/	*nochi* 'night'	/dʒ/	*djugar* 'to play'
Dental fricative	/ş/	*paso* 'step' *alsar* 'raise'	/z̧/	*kaza* 'house' *dezir* 'say'
Dental affricate			/d̯ᶻ/	*dodze* 'twelve'

Table 6.4   Judeo-Spanish sibilants

where the outcome of these mergers is a pair of apico-alveolar sibilants.

A further difference between Judeo-Spanish and all other varieties of Spanish is that Judeo-Spanish has created a contrast between the voiced dental fricative (in *kaza, dezir*) and a voiced dental affricate /dᶻ/ (in a few words like *dodze, dodzena, tredze*, where the plosive element of /dᶻ/ may reflect the -D- of the Latin antecedents of these words, DUŌDECIM, TRĒDECIM, etc.). Taken together with the later introduction of the affricate /dʒ/ beside fricative /ʒ/ (see **6.3.1(8)**), and the retention of the affricate /tʃ/ (in *nochi*, etc.), the full sibilant system of Judeo-Spanish is as in Table **6.4**.[9]

2 Although in 1492 only a minority of (mainly Andalusian) Peninsular varieties are thought to have merged /ʎ/ and /ĵ/, this process (*yeísmo*) has become universal in Judeo-Spanish, usually with a weak mid-palatal fricative outcome (compare **4.1.7.2.2** and **5.1.2.1**). As in the case of comparable dialect mixing, in Andalusia and America, there would have been little resistance to this simplification, since it would have been almost cost-free, in the sense that there were very few minimal pairs whose members were distinguished by the /ʎ/–/ĵ/ contrast (e.g., *mallo* 'mallet' vs *mayo* 'May'). It will also be seen (in **6.3.4(5)**) that the output of this merger was regularly deleted after front vowels.

3 Some varieties of Judeo-Spanish have moved towards simplification of verbal stems by extending the preterite stem to other parts of the verb: *tuvido, ovido* (cf. standard *tenido, habido*). This kind of merger is not unknown in the Peninsula, but is highly recessive,

being confined to a few rural varieties (see, for example, Penny 1970a: 132–7, 1978: 98).

4 The present contrast (in Peninsular and American Spanish) between personal direct objects, marked by the preposition *a*, and non-personal direct objects, marked by absence of preposition, was far from being established in the late fifteenth century. At the time of the expulsion, *a* was not obligatory with personal direct objects, but was used to disambiguate sentences where a direct-object noun phrase without *a* might be construed as the subject phrase (e.g., *mataron los reyes a sus enemigos*). Many varieties of Judeo-Spanish have simplified this structure by imposing *a* on all direct-object noun phrases: *mantenia a sus kazas* (cf. standard *mantenía sus casas*) (Lleal 1992: 36).

6.3.4 Non-Castilian features

Judeo-Spanish provides abundant evidence that Castilian features were by no means the only ones which were fed into the dialect mixture which arose in Sephardic communities in north Africa and the Ottoman Empire and by no means always the ones which were adopted by these communities (see **6.2**). We have already seen non-Castilian outcomes in the treatment of voiced sibilants (**6.3.2(1)**, **6.3.3(1)**), in the treatment of palatal consonants (**6.3.3(2)**), the adoption of *seseo* (**6.3.3(1)**), the retention of the /b/-/β/ or /b/-/v/ contrast (**6.3.2(3)**), and in the use of /f/ and /h/ as competitors of /Ø/ in words which in Old Castilian displayed /h/ (**6.3.2(4)**). Other non-Castilian features of Judeo-Spanish include the following:

1 In those varieties of Judeo-Spanish spoken in the western Balkans (Bosnia, Serbia, Macedonia) and elsewhere, the three vowels found in final syllables are the maximally differentiated /i/, /a/ and /u/, as is also the case in most Portuguese, Asturian, and Cantabrian varieties (e.g., *vedri, kaza, filu*). Other varieties of Judeo-Spanish have inherited the Castilian system (e.g., *vedre, kaza, (h)ilo*).

2 The labio-dental /f/, which (except in learned words and a few others patterned like *fuente, fuerte, fue*) was absent from fifteenth-century Castilian (**3.1.3.2**), has been inherited by some varieties of Judeo-Spanish, no doubt from Peninsular varieties which then maintained, and in most cases still maintain, /f/ (Catalonia,

Valencia and Aragon; much of Asturias, Leon, Galicia and Portugal). However, where it is retained, Judeo-Spanish /f/ is limited to only part of the vocabulary (e.g., *filo* 'thread', *fogera* 'bonfire', *forno* 'oven').

3 In the fifteenth century, as now (see **4.1.5(6)**), the Peninsula was divided between those varieties which preserved the group /mb/ (the northwest and west, e.g., *pomba*, *palomba* 'dove'), and those, including Castilian, which reduced /mb/ to /m/ (e.g., *paloma* 'dove'). Judeo-Spanish most frequently inherits the former result: *lombo* 'back (of the body)', *palombika* 'little dove', *lamber* 'to lick'.

4 As in Leon (Zamora 1967: 136, 148), /ʎ/ was depalatalized to /l/ when another palatal consonant occurred later in the word. Consequently, such words avoided *yeísmo* (**6.3.3(2)**) and appear with /l/ in Judeo-Spanish: *kaleja* 'alley', *luvia* 'rain', *pileyu* 'skin, hide', *pelixku/pelixkar* '(to) pinch' (cf. Cast. *calleja*, *lluvia*, *pellejo*, *pellizco/pellizcar*).

5 In some parts of the north of the Peninsula, the consonant /ǰ/ is deleted after tonic /e/ or /i/, either in the case of /ǰ/ resulting from Latin -LL-, as happens in Cantabria (Penny 1970a: 55–6), or in the case of /ǰ/ from -C'L-, -G'L-, -LJ-, as occurs in Asturias, Leon and Zamora (Zamora 1967: 148–9). This deletion has become general in Judeo-Spanish (where /ǰ/ descends only from -LL-): *kastío*, *bolsío*, *amaría*, *ea* (cf. standard *castillo* 'castle', *bolsillo* 'pocket', *amarilla* 'yellow', *ella* 'she'), and has been extended to cases where original /ǰ/ preceded tonic /í/: *aí*, *gaína* (cf. standard *allí* 'there', *gallina* 'hen').

6 At the time of the expulsion, the Peninsula was divided (as it is now) between central areas where Latin tonic /ɛ/ and /ɔ/ had given rise to diphthongs (typically [je] and [we]), and lateral areas where /ɛ/ and /ɔ/ remained undiphthongized (typically [ɛ] and [ɔ]) (see **4.1.3**). In the new Sephardic communities, therefore, there were no doubt competing variants of many words, with and without the relevant diphthong, and the variant eventually selected did not always conform to the Castilian diphthongized pattern. Thus we find *preto* 'black', *ponte* 'bridge', *sorte* 'fate' in Istanbul, *kenker* 'anyone', *kualker* 'whatever', *portu* 'port' in Bosnia, and similar forms in Bucharest and elsewhere (cf. Castilian *prieto*, *puente*, *suerte*, *quienquiera*, *cualquier*, *puerto*). This uncertainty occasionally led to the introduction of a diphthong

where one was not found in Castilian, as in *adientro* 'inside', a
form also found in Asturias. But the greatest uncertainty of
outcome lies in the verb, where the added factor of analogy
between diphthongized and undiphthongized forms of the same
verb has often led in Judeo-Spanish to patterns which differ from
those of Peninsular and American Spanish: *rogo/rogar* 'to beg',
kero/kerer 'to wish', *puedo/pueder* 'to be able', *muestro/muestrar* 'to
show', etc. (Zamora 1967: 353, Penny 1991a: 156–7).

7   Although hypercharacterization of gender in nouns, adjectives
and pronouns occurs in the history of Castilian (Penny 1991a:
112, 115), this process of overtly marking the gender of such
words was more frequent in the east of the Peninsula, especially
in Catalan, than in the centre. Judeo-Spanish has inherited, probably from these eastern varieties, a greater number of such cases
than can be seen in Castilian. Hypercharacterization of gender is
frequent in the case of Judeo-Spanish adjectives (e.g., *grande/-a,*
firme/-a, libro/-a, inferior/-ra, cf. invariable standard *grande, firme,*
libre, inferior), but less frequent in nouns (*vozas, fuentas*, cf. standard *voces, fuentes*), although it also regularly affects the relative/
interrogative *kualo/kuala* (cf. standard *cual, cuál*).

8   Third-person clitic pronouns are often used in a way that differs
from standard Peninsular or American usage, but which broadly
accords with the semantically based system of pronoun reference
observable in much of Old Castile, Cantabria, Leon, and Asturias
(**4.1.2.3**). Coloma Lleal reports (1992: 41) that in north Africa no
distinction is made between direct and indirect objects (masculine
or feminine), but that within the masculine a distinction is made
between definite and indefinite referents: *a él* **le** *amas, a él* **le** *dates el*
libro, el libro **le** *komprates, algún libro* **lo** *komprates, a ella* **la** *exkrivites.*
This *laísmo* and this extreme *leísmo* were no doubt due to input
into the early Judeo-Spanish dialect-mixing provided by speakers
from the north of the Peninsula, and cause Judeo-Spanish to differ
sharply not only from standard Castilian, but from the varieties of
Spanish (namely, Andalusian) spoken in that part of the Peninsula
which is closest to north Africa (see **4.1.7.2.7**).

9   Although data are less than complete, it seems that many if not all
varieties of Judeo-Spanish distinguish the preterite from the
perfect in the same way as Portuguese and northwestern
Peninsular varieties do, restricting the perfect to situations which

are still current at the moment of speaking and which may continue or be repeated in the future (a contrast which was also inherited by American Spanish; **5.1.3.2**).[10]

10   Although most of the vocabulary inherited by Judeo-Spanish is of
Castilian origin, there are numerous contributions from non-
Castilian Peninsular sources (Lapesa 1980: 528), e.g., *aínda* 'still'
(from Galician–Portuguese), /ʃamaráda/ 'fire' (from Leonese or
Portuguese), *anojar* 'to annoy', *embirrarse* 'to get angry', *froña*
'cover' (all from Portuguese), *lonso* 'bear' (from Aragonese) (cf.
Castilian *todavía, llamarada, enojar, enfurecerse, funda, oso*).

6.3.5   Features retained in Judeo-Spanish but rejected by the Peninsular standard

In the late fifteenth century, standardization of Spanish had begun but
was far from complete (Chapter 7). Consequently, there was still much
competition, even among urban, educated speakers, between different
forms which carried the same meaning. Subsequently, selection of
certain variants for use in writing and in the speech of the educated
classes increasingly relegated competing variants to rural and uneducated speech, in both Spain and America. However, in Judeo-Spanish,
the selection of variants was carried out in isolation from what
occurred in Spain and on a different basis: the prestige later associated
with certain Castilian variants, and the loss of prestige of others, could
not be felt in the new Sephardic communities, which not only inherited
competing variants from mainstream Castilian, but (as we have seen) a
host of further competing forms from other Peninsular varieties.
Consequently, variant reduction in Sephardic Spanish often favoured
forms which in Spain came to be excluded from the standard and
socially stigmatized, and such forms were then able to continue to be
used by all Judeo-Spanish speakers, whatever their social background,
without stigma. Since we know that variant reduction, in situations of
dialect contact, is dominated by simplification processes (**3.1**), we
should not be surprised to find that, where Judeo-Spanish forms coincide with rural Peninsular and American forms, these forms represent
a simpler outcome than that observed in the Peninsular and American
standard.

1   Merger of atonic /i/ with /e/ and /u/ with /o/, with realizations
varying between high ([i] and [u]) and mid ([e] and [o]), was

common in medieval Spanish, giving rise to variation such as that between *vestido/vistido, le(c)ción/lición, señor/siñor, coidar/cuidar, logar/lugar, sobir/subir*. Later standardization led to the confinement of all but one member of each of such sets to non-standard usage (see **4.2.4**), often on etymological grounds (e.g., preference for *vestido, lección, señor* was based on the Latin spellings VESTITUM, LECTIO(NEM), SENIOR(EM)). However, forms excluded from polite Peninsular and American use continue to typify Judeo-Spanish: *siñor, fiñir, sigundo, sigir, asigurar, rencón, coidar, logar, pudía* (cf. standard *señor, heñir, segundo, seguir, asegurar, rincón, cuidar, lugar, podía*), etc.

2   As /h/-dropping became the norm in Spain and America from the sixteenth century, retention of this phoneme was increasingly restricted to uneducated usage in certain regions (**3.1.3.2, 4.1.7.2.3, 5.2.1**). However, many varieties of Judeo-Spanish, especially those of the western Balkans, have maintained /h/ in the relevant lexical items (/húmo/, /hazér/, /haragán/, etc.).

3   The reinforcement of morpheme-initial [ʸwe] and [ᵝwe] to [ɣwe], which we saw came to be restricted to rural use in Spain and America (**4.2.5**), resisted the stigma attached to it in those areas and became normal in Judeo-Spanish. Thus, words which in the standard have minimal initial friction (e.g., *huerta, huele, deshuesar, ahuecar*), and words which in the standard may now only show [ᵝwe] (e.g., *bueno, vuelta, abuelo*) have become regularized in Judeo-Spanish with [ɣwe]: *güerta, güele, dezgüesar, agüekar, güeno, güelta, agüelo*, etc.

4   The second-person plural imperative in late-medieval and Golden-Age Spanish could appear with or without final /d/: *cantá/cantad, volvé/volved, salí, salid* (Penny 1991a: 139). While the forms without /d/ have been abandoned by the standard (except when a reflexive pronoun follows: *sentaos*), Judeo-Spanish has maintained what are now non-standard forms in the Peninsula: *kantá, bolbé, bení*, just as many American *voseante* varieties do (**5.1.2.5** and Table **5.1**).

5   Whereas the appearance of a final /s/ in the second-person singular of preterite verb forms is now stigmatized (but extremely widespread in Spain and America), this ancient feature (Penny 1991a: 183) has become normal in Judeo-Spanish: *(tú) kantates, bolbites, salites*, etc.

6   Although rather scantily reflected in writing, it is likely that there was variation in late-medieval Spanish usage of existential *haber*, between an invariably third-person singular verb (e.g., *hubo un muchacho/hubo varios muchachos*) and number agreement between verb and complement, which is then construed as the verbal subject (e.g., *hubo un muchacho/hubieron varios muchachos*). The latter usage has been excluded from the standard in Spain and America in favour of the former, but continues to be very widely used, even occasionally by educated speakers. In Judeo-Spanish, isolation from this standardizing pressure has allowed the number-agreement type to become universal, e.g., *hubieron tres antorchas*.

7   A good number of lexical variants which have been excluded from the Peninsular standard, while continuing to exist as rural, stigmatized forms in Spain and America, are normal in Judeo-Spanish. Among these forms are the following: *onde* 'where', *agora* 'now', *ansí* 'thus' (cf. standard *(a)donde, ahora, así*).

6.3.6   Variation within Judeo-Spanish

Although, as we have seen (**6.2**), contacts between communities of Judeo-Spanish speakers in the various cities of the Ottoman Empire were maintained for centuries, the conditions under which Judeo-Spanish was established and then continued to be used across the Mediterranean and Balkan world, in well-scattered urban ghettos, could scarcely prevent local differentiation. We have had reason to draw attention to geographical variation in respect of the descendants of Latin F- (namely /f/, /h/ and /Ø/) (**6.3.2(4)**), of merger and distinction between /b/ and /β/ or /v/, and the distribution of bilabial /β/ and labiodental /v/ (**6.3.2(3)**). Many more such cases might be cited.

Of particular importance in this regard is the fact that, following the Spanish involvement in Morocco, from the middle of the nineteenth century, and the rediscovery by Spaniards of Sephardic communities there, north African Judeo-Spanish came into contact with Peninsular Spanish and began to adopt certain of its features, especially those used in that part of Spain closest to Africa, namely Andalusia. For these reasons, Moroccan Judeo-Spanish replaced its traditional phonemes /ʃ/ and /ʒ/ by /h/, thus 'modernizing' such words as /deʃár/ *dexar* 'to leave', and *ojo* /óʒo/ 'eye' to /dehár/ and /óho/ (see

4.1.7.2.3). Similarly, syllable-final /s/ and /ʃ/ underwent weakening there to [h], etc., and word-final /-n/ became generally velarized, in the Andalusian manner (see 4.1.7.2.4, 5.1.2.4).

6.4 Death of Judeo-Spanish

After surviving for more than five centuries, Judeo-Spanish is on the point of extinction (Harris 1994). North African Judeo-Spanish survives today only in a traditional repertoire of ballads, wedding-songs, etc., and already in the nineteenth century the Judeo-Spanish of the ex-Ottoman Empire began to be ousted under pressure from the national languages of the states that emerged from the Ottoman world, Serbo-Croatian, Romanian, Bulgarian, etc. In the twentieth century, large numbers of speakers were still to be found in Salonica, Istanbul, and Izmir (Smyrna), but the events of the Second World War caused the near-destruction of these communities; those not killed mostly emigrated to Israel, New York, San Francisco, and other cities, where the Judeo-Spanish of the emigrants is not being passed on to the younger generations of these families.

7 Standardization

Most of the discussion in this book has been concerned with non-standard varieties of Spanish, since it is there that most cases of variation and change are to be observed. However, account must also be taken of the standard varieties, which are perhaps best regarded as highly unusual forms of language, in the sense that they are rare (all humans use language, but only a minority use a standard language) and recent (they arose only in the last few thousand years of the multi-millennial history of human language). The reason why the process of standardization has an important place in any treatment of linguistic variation and change, in Spanish and other languages, is that an essential aspect of this process is reduction in variation within certain high-prestige varieties (see **7.2**). However, paradoxically, we should not ignore the fact that for speakers of low-prestige varieties, the establishment of a standard may imply an increase in the range of variation available, since variants from the standard may enter the speech of non-elite groups and be added to the competition among pre-existing variants (see **7.3**).

Although we have seen (**1.1–2**) that variation is inherent in language, the process of standardization may, in principle, reduce variation to zero in the variety which is subject to it. This elimination of variants, naturally, applies to instances of variation which are due to the normal effect of changes which are working their way through society (**3.4**), as well as to instances of variation which are more stable and long-established.[1]

Standardization is a process which takes place within written language, and which is indeed inconceivable in the absence of writing. However, the variants selected for use in writing may then oust their competitors from those varieties of spoken language which have most in common with written language (those based on written language and used on formal social occasions), and may go on to be similarly selected in other spoken varieties, owing to the prestige associated with written forms of language. But because standardization belongs essentially to written language, it cannot, in principle, directly affect the phonetic and phonological levels of language. That is to say that those who use a given standard may do so while differing from one another in their pronunciation. Nevertheless, the speech of those who are responsible for the development of a linguistic standard (generally, members of powerful urban groups) is likely to be invested with the prestige which derives from their association with (including control of) the written language, so that the pronunciation features used by such groups may come to constitute an effective phonetic standard, and over time there is likely to be reduction of phonetic and phonological variation in the society concerned.

Nor should we overlook the fact that the spelling system which is used to write a language can have an effect on the phonology of spoken varieties. Although orthographical systems, when they are first applied to a language, typically match the phonological structure of (some high-prestige variety of) that language, this one-to-one relationship between letter and phoneme may be disrupted (by phonological change, etymological preconceptions, etc.), so that mismatches occur. Given the prestige that is associated with writing, users of the language may come to believe that distinctions made in spelling ought to be reflected in phonological distinctions, and may then make changes in their pronunciation. Thus, it may have been an awareness of spelling (in this case the Latin spellings CRUDUS, NIDUS, NUDUS, VADUM) which resolved the variation in early medieval Spanish between *crudo, nido, desnudo, vado,* etc. and *crúo, nío, desnúo, vao,* etc., in favour of the forms with /d/ (see **1.2**). Similarly, the early modern resolution of variation between such pairs as *escrebir~escribir, recebir~recibir, vevir~vivir* (in favour of the forms spelt with <i> and pronounced with atonic /i/, despite the strong dissimilatory pressure which led to preference for *decir, sentir,* etc., from earlier *dezir~dizir, sentir~sintir,* etc.) may be due to spelling influence from Latin SCRĪBERE, RECIPERE, VĪVERE (Penny 1991a: 159–60). Again, although unsuccessful in the long run, an attempt has frequently been made by schoolteachers, especially in Spanish America, to introduce a labiodental /v/ in words spelt <v> (e.g., *vivir*), in order to make a contrast with bilabial /b/, which should supposedly be reserved for words with <b> (e.g., *beber*); this, despite the fact that there has been only one non-nasal voiced bilabial phoneme in Spanish since the sixteenth century (see **3.1.3.3**).

In the case of the standardization of Spanish, the processes concerned almost all occurred in Spain, with the prescriptive results being exported to the rest of the Spanish-using world.[2] Only since the middle of the twentieth century has American Spanish been taken into account in establishing prescriptive grammars and dictionaries of the language, a change of vision which has accompanied increasing worries about the unity of the language and which has perhaps been spurred by a perceived threat of its fragmentation into mutually unintelligible varieties.[3]

In discussing standardization it is useful to distinguish between two contrasting but interlinked aspects of the process. On the one hand, there are the more purely social, strictly extra-linguistic, aspects; these are concerned with the way in which society selects a variety to serve as a basis for the standard, codifies and promotes it, and seeks acceptance for it. These aspects are sometimes encapsulated in the term *status planning*.[4] On the other hand, there are the intra-linguistic aspects of the process, concerned with which variants are selected and which abandoned, and with such matters as the sources of elaboration of syntax and vocabulary. Although these aspects of standardization are often less conscious, an element of planning may be involved here, and the label *corpus planning* is sometimes applied to this part of the process. We shall consider status planning (**7.1**) and corpus planning (**7.2**) in turn.

7.1 Status planning

The processes which make up status planning (selection, codification, elaboration of function, and acceptance; see Haugen 1972; Hudson 1996: 32–4) reflect the different degrees of power exercised by different social groups. Only varieties spoken by politically and economically powerful groups are likely to be selected as the basis of a standard language. Similarly, only such groups (or individuals) are capable of imposing particular codifications of the language and of ensuring it will be used in an increasing number of domains. Likewise, only the powerful can bring about acceptance of the emerging norm, since only they enjoy sufficient social prestige to cause other groups to follow their linguistic preferences.

7.1.1 Selection

Every standard language grows out of some spoken variety or varieties, which are in competition with a much larger number of other varieties, which are not so selected. Since the creation of a standard cannot be achieved without the devotion to it of great resources (required for writing, making, and copying books, etc.), it follows that the varieties which underpin standards are always those spoken by the wealthiest and most powerful groups. The development of standard Spanish is no exception to this rule.

A number of the features which later help to characterize standard Spanish are seen to occupy areas which, in the tenth and eleventh centuries, overlap in a small segment of the northern Peninsular dialect continuum (**4.1.2**), an area comprising the city of Burgos and a number of surrounding towns in northern Old Castile (Menéndez Pidal 1964: 485–6). Among the most geographically restricted of these features are:[5]

1   Use of glottal /h/ as a reflex of Latin F-, while surrounding districts maintained labiodental /f/ (e.g., /húmo/ vs /fumo/ < FŪMU 'smoke'; **3.1.3.2**).

2   Use of prepalatal /ʒ/ as the reflex of the Latin groups -C'L-, -G'L-, -L- + [j], while adjacent districts showed /ʎ/ (e.g., /abéʒa/ vs /abéʎa/ < APIC(U)LA 'bee'; **3.1.3.1**).

3   Loss of the initial palatal consonant (probably /ǰ/ in spoken Latin) when followed by an atonic front vowel, while other areas maintained a palatal of some description (e.g., /enéro/ vs /ǰenéro/, /ʒenéro/, etc. < *JENUĀRIU 'January').

4   Use of the prepalatal affricate /tʃ/ as a reflex of Latin -CT-, while further afield the Latin /t/ was maintained, sometimes preceded by a palatal glide (e.g., /estrétʃo/ vs /estréito/, etc. < STRICTU 'narrow').

5   Use of the dental affricate /tˢ/ as a reflex of the Latin groups -SC- (followed by a palatal vowel), -SC + [j], and -ST + [j], etc., while surrounding districts showed the prepalatal fricative /ʃ/ (e.g., /kretˢér/ vs /kreʃér/ < CRESCERE 'to grow', /atˢuéla/ vs /aʃuéla/, etc. < ASCIOLA 'hoe').

6   Retention of undiphthongized /o/ as a reflex of Latin tonic ŏ in the vicinity of a palatal glide, while surrounding varieties show a diphthongized result (e.g., /óʒo/ vs /uéʎo/, etc. < OCULU 'eye').

Since, at this time, no spelling system was in use in Spain which was capable of specifying contemporary phonology (by contrast with the traditional writing-system usually referred to as 'Latin'; see Wright 1982), there was no possibility of the development of a standard language based on the speech of Burgos. However, many of the features of Burgos speech were extended outwards from this core district, from the eleventh century onwards. This happened partly as a result of resettlement of people from Burgos to other areas, in the wake of the military success of Castile during the early Reconquest (**4.1.7**), and partly as a result of accommodation processes (**3.1.1**) which led speakers in a wider and wider area to imitate the speech of the politically and culturally prestigious city of Burgos. Crucially, groups of speakers who used varieties which had developed in the Burgos area achieved political and social power in Toledo, following its recapture in AD 1085, and, in the dialect mixture which consequently arose in the new Castilian capital, features of Burgos speech more often found favour than those of the local Toledan varieties (**4.1.1**) or those brought by other immigrants (see **3.1**). Consequently, when the speech of upper-class Toledo was selected as the basis of the Castilian standard, it was characterized by a significant number of features imported from Burgos.

The selection of the speech of Toledo as the foundation of the standard followed from the political and religious importance of the city (it was the headquarters of the Castilian Church, and the most usual seat of the Castilian Court), and from its cultural prestige (it was there that the major scientific and literary enterprises of the twelfth and thirteenth centuries took place). When new systems of writing Romance were introduced from France (applied sporadically from the late eleventh centuries, and regularly from the early thirteenth; see Wright 1982), these were employed to write literary and non-literary texts using varieties of Romance from a wide range of localities. But, within Castile (and Leon following the definitive merger of the Crowns in 1230), it was the features of educated Toledan Spanish which soon became pre-eminent in writing. Because of the overwhelming use of this variety in the literary, legal, and scientific output of the scriptorium of Alfonso X the Learned (1252–84), it became the model for all writing, including that of government documents, throughout the kingdom.

This state of affairs continued until the mid-sixteenth century, despite competition from the great mercantile and cultural centre of Seville (**4.1.7.2**). Juan de Valdés, the great arbiter of linguistic taste, writing his *Diálogo de la lengua* in about 1535, derives his self-assigned authority from the fact that he is an 'hombre criado en el reino de Toledo y en la corte de España'.[6] Others evidently shared his perception of the prestige of Toledan Court usage, since the forms he selected for recommendation were most frequently, if not quite always, those that came to be preferred in the written standard. His often unreasonable objections to the prescriptions of Antonio de Nebrija (see (**7.1.2**) were based on the fact that Nebrija was from Andalusia.

The situation only changed in 1561, with the creation of Madrid as the capital of Spain (see **3.1.3.1–3**). The new dialect mixture that this event inspired, through influx of speakers from Old Castile, gave rise to a selection of features that differed to some extent from those used in Toledo. Thereafter, whatever might be claimed by other centres, such as Valladolid, it was educated varieties of Madrid Spanish that were mostly regularly reflected in the written standard.

What happened in Castile was paralleled by the selections made in other parts of the Peninsula. In the west, the early importance of Santiago de Compostela as a religious and cultural centre implied that, when characteristically Romance writing emerged in the northwest, it would be based on the speech of that city. Galician writing of this kind continued until it was replaced by the Castilian standard in the early modern period. However, although the features of northwestern speech, extended southwards during the Reconquest (**4.1.7.1**), contributed substantially to the dialect mixture which arose in the major cities of Portugal (independent of Castile–Leon from 1143), the Portuguese standard which later emerged, based upon the speech first of Coimbra and then of Lisbon, differed in minor ways from the norm applied in Santiago (which remained part of Castile–Leon).

Some texts written in the early thirteenth century in Castile–Leon show certain features characteristic of the speech of regions other than Toledo. Thus a number of Leonese features appear in one version of the *Libro de Alexandre*, northern Castilian features are visible in the *Disputa del alma y el cuerpo*, the poetry of Gonzalo de Berceo has some features characteristic of La Rioja, and the language of the *Poema de mio Cid* has been identified as belonging to the east of Old Castile (Lapesa 1980: 203–5). Similarly, the language of the *Auto de los reyes magos*, the subject of much dispute, most probably reflects varieties of Toledo speech distant from that of the most cultured classes, and preserving certain features of Mozarabic origin.

Aragon remained a separate kingdom until the union with Castile–Leon in 1474, and was a territory where two standards emerged. The Catalan standard was based upon the speech of the main northeastern cities, principally that of Barcelona, because of its political and mercantile importance, but came to be used throughout Catalonia, Valencia, and the Balearic Islands, as a result of the Reconquest of these areas, during the thirteenth and fourteenth centuries. From the beginning of the sixteenth century, the Castilian standard became the normal vehicle of writing, and Catalan writing was restricted to documents of purely local significance, until the nineteenth-century recreation of a Catalan standard, which continues in use beside Castilian.

In the inland regions of the Crown of Aragon, it was the city of Saragossa that played the major linguistic role. A flourishing centre of Islamic commerce and culture, it was recaptured in 1118 by the then tiny kingdom of Aragon and immediately became the new capital, retaining this role after the merger of Aragon with Catalonia in 1137. The development of writing there seems never to have been based simply upon the speech of the city, which, in the century following its reconquest, no doubt consisted of a dialect mixture comprising varieties transferred there from the central Pyrenean valleys (the core territory of the kingdom), together with Mozarabic varieties spoken by the existing population, and other forms of speech contributed by immigrants from other Peninsular and trans-Pyrenean areas. Even the earliest Romance writing produced in the expanded Aragon shows a preponderance of Castilian features, and the same continues to be true even during the fourteenth-century expansion of Aragonese writing sponsored by Juan Fernández de Heredia. Although this Aragonese standard had developed in a state which was politically independent of Castile, it was not independent of the Castilian linguistic standard which had emerged in thirteenth-century Toledo, and scarcely survived the union of the Crowns in 1474.

7.1.2 Codification

Following selection of a base-variety for the purposes of writing, a further important stage in the process leading to standardization is the codification of this variety. The goal of this mechanism (utterly unachievable in the case of spoken language) is 'minimal variation in form' (Haugen 1972: 107). In the case of written language, it consists of the prescription of a set of unvarying orthographical, grammatical, lexical, and other rules to which writers should conform, if their writing is to carry the highest prestige.

Although explicit codification of Spanish did not begin until the late fifteenth century, the linguistic preoccupations manifested by Alfonso X in the works he sponsored (7.1.1) had the effect of producing a linguistic model which could be and was imitated by other writers.

Whereas at the beginning of his reign, in the mid-thirteenth century, there was much variation between the language of one text and that of another (see **7.1.1**), only half a century later this variation has significantly declined. By the end of the thirteenth century, as a direct result of the linguistic efforts that went into producing the vast Alfonsine literary and scientific output, it is no longer possible to recognize the regional origins of the writer, and other types of variation have been very much reduced.

Another, even more effective, type of informal codification of Spanish is that carried out by the early printers. Ray Harris-Northall (1996–7), by comparing the manuscripts of the *Gran conquista de ultramar* with the early-sixteenth-century printed version of this work, has shown how variation across a wide range of linguistic features was dramatically reduced, and how the text was extensively revised in order to project the norms favoured by a political elite.

Turning to explicit codification, we can see that Spanish was the first post-classical language to be subjected to this process. From the middle of the fifteenth century there appeared a series of small-scale lexicographical enterprises (Lapesa 1980: 286–7), followed by Alonso de Palencia's monumental *Universal vocabulario* (1490). Although the latter was a Latin dictionary, its Spanish component reveals a subtle discrimination among the words of the late-medieval lexicon. However, the most important early work of codification of Spanish, and the first grammar of a modern language to appear (in 1492), was Antonio de Nebrija's *Gramática de la lengua castellana* (Nebrija 1980).[7] Born in Andalusia, and professor successively at the universities of Salamanca and Alcalá de Henares, he also published in 1492 his Latin–Spanish dictionary (Nebrija 1979), followed, probably in 1495, by the first edition of his Spanish–Latin dictionary (Nebrija 1973). A 1517 treatise on Spanish orthography (Nebrija 1977) expands on the discussion of spelling in the *Gramática*.

Nebrija's only clarification of the type of Spanish reflected in his books is his comment on the basis of his spelling system ('I write as I speak'), the same formula adopted by Juan de Valdés in his *Diálogo de la lengua*. With these words, these authors claim to eschew etymology as a guide to spelling and (to interpret their precept in a modern way) to match their graphical systems to the system of phonemes they used (and which was presumably also the system used by those who spoke similar varieties). That they do not quite achieve this is unsurprising, given that, like scholars for centuries before and after their time, they did not manage to fully disentangle the discussion of sounds from that of letters. With regard to the other aspects of language, we can only assume that Nebrija, like Valdés, sought to codify the variety of language written by the educated men of Castile.

Because of the phonological changes which took place in the late medieval and early modern periods (see, for example, **3.1.3.1–3**), the spelling system established in the Alfonsine texts (and adopted with little change by Nebrija) became more and more distanced from the phonology of Castilian. Concern to reform the spelling of Spanish was constant during the Golden Age, and found expression in such works as Mateo Alemán's *Ortografía castellana*, published posthumously in 1609 (Alemán 1950), and in the radical (but disregarded) *Ortografía kastellana*, published in 1630 by Gonzalo Correas (Correas 1971). However, successful reform and codification of Spanish spelling had to await the establishment of the Real Academia Española in 1713. Inspired by the role of the Académie Française, one of the main elements of the Spanish Academy's watchword ('limpia, *fija* y da esplendor') was to codify the language, and the academicians explicitly tackled Spanish spelling in their *Ortographía* (1741). This and subsequent orthographical pronouncements made by the Academy (in the late twentieth century published after consultation with similar Academies established in every Spanish-speaking country including the United States) have been closely and rapidly followed by printers and publishers, so that the spelling of Spanish today, at least in printed texts, is highly uniform throughout the world.

Codification of morphology and syntax was a slower process. Following Nebrija's *Gramática* (see above), innumerable grammars of Spanish were published in Spain, Flanders and America, during the sixteenth and seventeenth centuries, including, in 1625, Gonzalo Correas's notable *Arte de la lengua española castellana* (Correas 1954). A milestone was reached in 1771 with the publication of the Real Academia Española's first *Gramática*, repeatedly updated down to the present. The result of these and hundreds of other grammatical publications is that the morphology of written Spanish is almost entirely uniform across the world, while its syntax varies to a minor extent (see, for example, **4.1.7.2.7**, **5.1.2.5**, **5.1.3.2**).

Codification of vocabulary is bound to progress most slowly, and cannot be completely achieved, because of the open-ended nature of the lexicon. Alonso de Palencia and Nebrija made great strides in the late fifteenth century, and were most notably followed by Sebastián de

Covarrubias, whose 1611 *Tesoro de la lengua castellana o española* no doubt continues to give primacy to the vocabulary used in his native Toledo. Once again, it was the activity of the Real Academia Española, publicly realized in 1726–39 in its three-volume *Diccionario de autoridades*, which provided the most authoritative lexical codification of Spanish. More recent editions of the Academy's dictionary have reflected not just written Peninsular usage but, with input from the American Academies, have aspired to include items from throughout the Spanish-speaking world and belonging to various registers.

7.1.3   Elaboration of function

The goal of this aspect of standardization is 'maximal variation in function' (Haugen 1972: 107), that is, the introduction of the language concerned into the largest number of domains. In the case of Spanish, and other Romance languages, this process could begin only once there existed a consciousness of the language as a code separate from Latin. Roger Wright (1982) has successfully shown that such consciousness only grew as a result of the introduction of a spelling system which sought to specify the phonemes of the variety being written, a process which was applied to Spanish from the end of the eleventh century (Lloyd 1991). At first, use of the new spelling was infrequent and inconsistent, as seen in the Glosses written in the monasteries of San Millán de la Cogolla and Santo Domingo de Silos, but the new system was used with increasing sophistication in some documents of this period, especially in the early thirteenth century, and culminated in the almost fully consistent system adopted by the school of Alfonso X from the mid-thirteenth century.

Once full consciousness of Spanish as a separate code had been established, it could challenge Latin in an increasing number of domains. Narrative poetry was the first prestigious domain in which written Spanish asserted its independence (along with that of religious drama, where we have the isolated example of the *Auto de los reyes magos*), in the early thirteenth century, although we have seen (**7.1.1**) that at this stage written Spanish still revealed some geographical variation. It was, once again, the scientific and literary undertakings of Alfonso X the Learned which dramatically enlarged the domains in which Spanish could be used. It now came to be the vehicle of prose narrative, historiography, science (astronomy, astrology, mineralogy, etc.), and jurisprudence, domains from which it rapidly ousted Latin, and to which were soon added lyric poetry and even some types of religious writing, such as the many thirteenth- and fourteenth-century translations of the Bible. From this time onwards, no domain was beyond the reach of Spanish, despite the partial return to Latin for learned discourse during the Renaissance, and the persistence of Latin as the language of the Catholic mass until the second half of the twentieth century.

This medieval and early-modern elaboration of the function of Spanish not only led to informal codification of Spanish (**7.1.2**), but to dramatic expansion of lexical and syntactical resources. The need to express ideas previously unexpressed in Spanish required a vast increase in its vocabulary, a need which was supplied chiefly by borrowing (from Arabic, Latin, French, Occitan, etc.), but also by frequent derivation, mostly through suffixation (Lapesa 1980: 243–4, Penny 1987–8). Similarly, although the syntax of early written Spanish was relatively simple, a quality especially evident in the rarity of subordination and in the frequency with which clauses are connected by *e* 'and', the linguistic sophistication required to express the complex logical relationship of historical and scientific ideas was provided by a growing syntactical elaboration, so that by the end of the Alfonsine period Spanish was capable of elegantly expressing any relationship of ideas in any domain.

7.1.4   Acceptance

Acceptance of a particular linguistic code as a symbol of a given nation is a process which, in its full sense, belongs properly to recent centuries. However, it should be remembered that all language names are political in origin, in that they begin by referring to the speech of a portion of territory whose boundaries are determined by the control exercised by some political entity. Thus the term *castellano* ('Castilian') is an abbreviation of *romance castellano*, approximately 'those forms of speech (descended from Latin) used in the territory named Castile', where *Castile* is a political entity, not originally sovereign, whose boundaries separate it from other political entities. The existence of a language name therefore implies, at least for its first users, a connection between that name and some political entity.[8]

The promotion of a language name (together with, or separately from, the promotion of the language to which it refers) is therefore an instrument of nation-building. In the case of Castilian, it is likely (but unprovable, since he left no manifesto) that Alfonso X was in part promoting Castilian nationhood when he promoted written Castilian, for administrative as well as literary and scientific purposes. The advantages, in this respect, of Castilian over its available competitors were considerable. Each of Latin, Arabic, and Hebrew was indissolubly linked with one of the three religions adhered to in Castile, whereas almost all inhabitants of the kingdom spoke Castilian or some closely related variety of Romance.[9] The politically unifying effects of promoting the use of written Castilian in the thirteenth century are therefore evident.

Explicitly nationalistic exploitation of language arrives only at the end of the fifteenth century. In his address to Isabella I of Castile and Aragon, placed at the head of his 1492 *Gramática de la lengua castellana*, Antonio de Nebrija famously links language and nation when he states: 'siempre la lengua fue compañera del imperio; & de tal manera lo siguió, que junta mente começaron, crecieron & florecieron, & después junta fue la caída de entrambos' (Nebrija 1980: 97). *Imperio* here does not refer to what we think of as the Spanish Empire; Columbus's ships were indeed on the way to America as Nebrija wrote, but the American Empire was as yet undreamed of. Nebrija no doubt had in mind the territories governed by the Catholic Monarchs (Spain (still excluding Navarre), the Balearic Islands, much of central and southern Italy, Sicily and Sardinia, the Canary Islands) and any other territory they might acquire. This was the Empire which, he claimed, shared the same fate as the Spanish language, and whose success required the promotion of the Spanish language.

Nebrija refers to the language whose forms he prescribes as *la lengua castellana*, in keeping with earlier usage, in which the term *castellano* was the only label available for this concept. The term *español* (earlier *españón*), and the noun *España* from which it derives, were infrequent in the Middle Ages, when they referred to Islamic Spain, or to the historical concept of Roman Spain, or to the geographical concept of the Spanish Peninsula. Following the union of the Crowns of Castile and Aragon in 1469, the terms *España* and *español* were newly applied to this United Kingdom, from which it followed that the main language of this state, hitherto called only *castellano*, could also be called *español*. Since that time the two terms have been equivalent, although one or the other has been preferred at different times and in different places. See Alonso (1943) for a more detailed history of these terms.

In America, the ruling elites of the post-colonial states, which emerged from the Spanish Empire, were all Spanish-speaking (although speakers of Native American languages no doubt formed larger proportions of the populations of these countries than they now do). Nationhood was consequently linked to the use of Spanish, sometimes explicitly so when the new constitutions named Spanish as the official language of the state, as also occurred in the post-Franco constitution of Spain.

The political acceptance of Spanish, implicit for centuries, was now explicit in almost all of the Spanish-speaking world.

7.2 Corpus planning

When we turn to the intra-linguistic aspects of standardization, we can see a progressively intensifying intolerance of variation in written Spanish from the thirteenth century onwards. As anticipated in **7.1.2**, this process is earliest and most clearly observed in spelling, where it has become almost totally successful. In morphology, restriction of variation is slower but is almost completely successful by the nineteenth century, while in syntax the twentieth-century language still allows some degree of variation between competing structures. It is in vocabulary and semantics, predictably, that the greatest degree of variation persists in the written language, despite severe restriction over the centuries.

It will be convenient to divide our consideration of corpus planning chronologically, although the divisions we make are arbitrary and conventional. As we have seen (**1.2**), there are no linguistic grounds for periodizing the history of a language.

7.2.1 The medieval period

The emergence, in the first decades of the thirteenth century, of a considerable body of literature, written in the recently devised Romance spelling system, reveals very substantial variation, both between one text and another, and within any single text. Because this spelling system was an adaptation of the system devised for reading Latin texts aloud (Wright 1982: 126), and because those texts had no letters which demanded a palatal realization (since palatal consonants were absent from Latin when its spelling system was devised), the writing of Spanish (and other Romance languages) was bedevilled by the difficulty of finding spellings which might represent its palatal phonemes. A similar difficulty arose in the case of affricate consonants generally, although it is less clear that affricates were *not* used in reading traditional texts aloud. A further problem was that the reading aloud of Latin required no distinction between voiced and voiceless sibilants, since, when its spelling system was created, Latin had only one sibilant (voiceless /s/).

The consequence of these difficulties was a very great variation in the Romance spelling of the phonemes belonging to either or both of the palatal order and the sibilant class. Early spelling hesitates, in the representation of /ɲ/, among <ni>, <gn>, <ng>, and <nn> (or abbreviations of the latter like <ñ> or <ñ>), /ʎ/ is reflected not only by <ll> and <l> but probably also by <pl>, etc. (e.g., *Poema de mio Cid*: *gallos, lamar, lorar, falir, plorando*), while the spelling <ch> for /tʃ/ was a late introduction from France, gradually displacing such ambiguous renderings as <g> and <i> (e.g., *Disputa del alma y el cuerpo*: *nog* (elsewhere *noch(e)*), *leio* (elsewhere *lecho*)). Likewise early writing does not discriminate consistently between /s/ and /z/, showing <s> or <ss> for both phonemes, or between /tˢ/ and /dᶻ/ (e.g., *Disputa del alma y el cuerpo*: *amanezient, lenzuelo, corazon* (where later spelling requires <ç>, for /tˢ/), *fecist* (where later spelling requires <z>, for /dᶻ/)).

The Alfonsine texts are the first to rationalize the spelling of Spanish, using a system which comes close to the iconic ideal of one letter (and not more than one) for each phoneme. However, even the vigilance and linguistic good sense of Alfonso and his group could not produce a fully iconic system. Thus, <u> and <v>, <i> and <j> were used for both consonants and vowels (e.g., *viejo, vieio, uiejo, uieio* (for modern *viejo*), *uvo, vuo* (for modern *hubo*)), as elsewhere in Europe until the introduction of printing. Similarly, <g> had the double value of /g/ and /ʒ/ (*ganar, linage*), while /ʒ/ was also represented by <j> or <i>, disparities which have never been eliminated from the spelling of the descendants of these phonemes (witness MSp. *ganar, coger*, with <g> for both /g/ and /x/, and *coger, jengibre*, with both <j> and <g> for /x/). Nor were /s/ and /z/ consistently distinguished, since <s> (rather than <ss>) for intervocalic /s/ is frequently found in Alfonsine and later medieval texts.

Other prominent cases of variation in the emerging medieval standard are the following:

1 At the intersection of phonology and morphology, there was much hesitation in thirteenth-century Spanish between forms with final /e/ preserved and those without /e/, in words where

the vowel was (or had been) preceded by a consonant group or by a single consonant other than a dental or alveolar. Thus, beside invariable cases like *pared, paz, pan, mar, fiel, mes*, where earlier / e / was preceded by an ungrouped dental or alveolar consonant, medieval Spanish showed variation between apocopated and unapocopated forms like *nuef/nueve, príncep/príncipe, noch/noche, cuend/conde, mont/monte, part/parte, estonz/entonces*, etc. Rafael Lapesa (1951, 1975, 1982) charts the slow resolution of this variation in Alfonsine Spanish, in favour of the unapocopated forms, and suggests that these more closely reflect the usage of Alfonso's group. While Ray Harris-Northall (1991) finds little evidence of the decline of apocopated forms during Alfonso's lifetime, this element of variation was substantially reduced in the fourteenth century, and disappears by the end of the medieval period.

2   It is difficult to establish whether the variation between word-final <t> and <d> (e.g., *edat~edad, voluntat~voluntad*) was merely a matter of alternative spelling of a single sound (neutralization of /-t/ and /-d/ with voiceless realization, sometimes spelt <t> to reflect this voicelessness, but sometimes spelt <d> on the model of the invariable plurals *edades, voluntades*), or whether there was a genuine phonemic contrast here between /t/ and /d/ (unlikely, since this would be the only case of a contrast of voice in word-final position in Old or Modern Spanish). At all events, this variation of form continued throughout the medieval period and into the early sixteenth century.

3   In the fifteenth century, words which had inherited syllable-final /b/ (< -P-, -B-, -V-) (e.g., *cabdal, çibdat, debda*) alternated with forms in which /b/ had been vocalized to [u̯] (*caudal, çiudat, deuda*).[10] Although this variation was still effective at the end of this century, because it is reflected in Judeo-Spanish (6.3.2(5)), it was then rapidly resolved in the standard, in favour of the forms with [u̯].

4   Although early literature, including the Alfonsine opus, prefers *-iello* as a first-choice affectionate diminutive, its competitor *-illo*, probably originating in the Burgos area, later begins to dominate, and *-iello* is ousted in the fifteenth century.

5   Verbal morphology was far from invariant in the thirteenth century. In the preterite we find variation between competing paradigms, drawn from separate Latin verbs (both *sove* and *fui* as past tenses of *ser*), between competing strong (stem-stressed)

preterites (e.g., *estide, estove*, and *estude* as preterites of the verb
estar; andide, andove, and *andude* as preterites of the verb *andar*),
between strong and weak preterites of the same verb (e.g., *fuyó*
and *fuxo* for *fuir*, *metí* and *mise* for *meter*, *prendí* and *prise* for *prender*,
sonreí and *sonrise* for *sonreír*, *conquirió* and *conquiso* for *conquerir*,
later replaced by *conquistar*), and between forms associated with
the same grammatical person (third-person sing. *veno, fezo* beside
vino, fizo in the case of *venir* and *fazer*). Most of these cases were
resolved during the fourteenth century; few survived into the
fifteenth.

6   Competition between rival imperfect and conditional endings in
    -ía and *-íe* (e.g., *tenía, tenie, tenié; cantaría, cantarie, cantarié*), fre-
    quent in the thirteenth century, was only resolved at the end of
    the fourteenth (Malkiel 1959), although the *-íe* forms today con-
    tinue in rural use in the province of Toledo (Moreno Fernández
    1984).

7   Medieval Spanish showed frequent examples of variation
    between rival lexical items with the same meaning. Sometimes it
    is possible to detect differences of register between the compet-
    ing forms (e.g., *siniestro* 'left' and *can* 'dog' may have belonged
    more clearly to literary style than their synonyms *izquierdo* and
    perro, which ultimately prevailed, while the arabisms *alfayate*
    'tailor', *alfageme* 'barber', *albéitar* 'vet', *alarife* 'architect', etc., sim-
    ilarly fell out of literary use, but later, in favour of their competi-
    tors *sastre, barbero, veterinario, arquitecto*, etc., borrowed from
    more fashionable Romance or Graeco-Latin sources). On other
    occasions, no such nuance is evident (e.g., *cabeça/tiesta* 'head',
    pierna/cam(b)a 'leg', *rodilla/(h)inojo* 'knee', *prender/tomar* 'to
    take', *quedar/remanir* 'to remain', *salir/exir* 'to go out', *mañana/
    matino* 'tomorrow'). Some of these cases of variation were slow
    to be resolved in the standard, and in a few instances (e.g.,
    prender/tomar) the variation reached the early modern period.

7.2.2   The Renaissance and the Golden Age

Following the introduction of printing and the beginning of the
codification process (**7.1.2**), pressure to avoid variation in written
Spanish became more intense. However, standardization was far from
being completed in the sixteenth and seventeenth centuries. Not only
was the orthography of Spanish increasingly distanced from its

phonology, which was undergoing significant changes (**3.1.3.1**–3), but it also allowed idiosyncratic spellings to abound. Variation at other linguistic levels, although less marked than in the medieval period, was still very frequent, even at the highest literary levels. Among the striking instances of such variation were the following:

1   The treatment of latinisms displaying consonant groups whose first or middle element was a labial or a velar had been ambiguous in the Middle Ages, but the increasing number and frequency of such loans, from the Renaissance onwards, made this ambiguity much more noticeable (Clavería Nadal 1991). In this period, we therefore find a host of competing pairs, in which one member shows retention of the Latin consonant group while the other reveals reduction of the groups, usually by eliminating the first consonant (or the middle one of three). For example, we find such sets as *concepto/conceto, absolver/asolver, accidente/acidente, exento/esento* (also *exempto*), *exceder/eceder, perfecto/perfeto, secta/seta, ignorar/inorar, digno/dino*. There were other solutions to the problems posed by such groups, such as vocalization in [u̯] of a labial consonant (*captivo/cautivo/cativo, concepto/conceuto/ conceto*), and the instability of the syllable-final consonant is also manifested in interchanges of the spellings <p/b> and <c/g> (*correbto/correcto*), but these solutions are rare in literature after the middle of the sixteenth century. Nor is it absolutely clear in all these cases whether we are dealing with alternating pronunciations, each with its own spelling, or with a single pronunciation of each word (presumably one which eliminated the syllable-final consonant) which could be spelt in alternating ways. With hindsight, we know that, in almost all cases, a style of pronunciation has survived into current educated Spanish which preserves syllable-final labials and velars (approximately represented by *concepto, absolver, accidente, ignorar, exento*, etc.), but this may be the result of later (eighteenth-century) changes in pronunciation imposed by etymologically conscious academicians. Golden-Age pronunciation may have been much more like present rural pronunciation of these words (such of them that have penetrated rural vocabulary), which does not permit syllable-final labials or velars.

2   A further respect in which it can be argued that Golden-Age Spanish was similar to modern rural varieties lies in the treatment of atonic vowels. Just as these varieties often make no phonological distinction between atonic /e/ and /i/ or between atonic /o/

and /u/, but use one or other member of the pair according to the phonological structure of the word concerned (**4.2.4**), so we find often the same treatment of these vowels in educated sixteenth- and seventeenth-century Spanish, but each word concerned is usually in competition with an alternative shape of the word, the latter usually inspired by its (Latin) etymology. Thus we find such sets as *cevil/civil, deferir/diferir, vevir/vivir, menguar/minguar, joventud/juventud, sofrir/sufrir, robí/rubí, mochacho/muchacho*. However, it is clear that, in the sixteenth century, educated taste was already beginning to prefer the forms we now regard as standard, since Juan de Valdés (1966), writing in about 1535, recommends *vanidad, invernar, aliviar, abundar, cubrir, ruido,* etc., over their still frequent competitors *vanedad, envernar, aleviar, abondar, cobrir, roido*, etc.

3 Still in the seventeenth century, consonant-final adjectives denoting national or regional origin (*gentilicios*) were often unmarked for gender, so that we find both *la andaluz* and *la andaluza, la leonés potencia, provincia cartaginés*, etc. (Lapesa 1980: 395). Regular hypercharacterization of these forms then becomes part of standard grammar.

4 The form of the feminine definite article was still highly varied. Before any vowel, *ell* alternated with *el* (*ell/el alma, ell/el espada*) until the middle of the sixteenth century, while until the end of the seventeenth we find use of both *el* and *la* before vowels (tonic or atonic) other than /a/ (*el/la espada, el/la otra*). Use of *el* before atonic /a/ continues longer (*el/la altura, el/la arena*), while *el* before some cases of tonic /a/ continues to the present.

5 The demonstratives *esta* and *aquesta* were still in competition until the late sixteenth century, while in the same period *aquesse* is less frequently found beside *ese*.

6 Until the mid-sixteenth century, the unexpanded subject pronouns *nos* and *vos* are still found beside expanded *nosotros* and *vosotros*.

7 The future and conditional forms of frequent verbs did not settle into their current shapes until the end of the sixteenth century. Until then we find *porné, verné*, etc., beside *pondré, vendré*.

8 In the same period, future and conditional forms could still carry an interposed clitic or clitics, if the verb concerned was phrase-initial (*cantarlo he*), although this structure was in competition with fully synthetic forms, where the clitic(s) either preceded or

followed the whole verb, depending on clause-structure (*cantarélo, lo cantaré*).

9   Until the seventeenth century, the present subjunctive form of the verb *ir* was not standardized. We find *vayamos, vayáis* beside *vamos, vais* in this role.

10 The increment /g/ which had been added to the first-person singular present indicative and all present subjunctive forms like *caigo/caiga, oigo/oiga, traigo/traiga* (earlier *cayo/caya, trayo/traya*) was frequently extended to other verbs with stem-final /ĵ/ (Penny 1991a: 154), so that literary Spanish until the seventeenth century allows *haiga, huiga,* and occasionally *vaiga,* beside *haya, huya, vaya.* The forms with /g/ were then restricted to non-standard use, where *haiga* and *vaiga* continue to thrive.

11 The irregular preterites of certain verbs remained unfixed until the seventeenth century. Until then, in the case of *traer,* literary Spanish allows *truxe, truxo,* etc. beside *traxe, traxo.* Similarly, the preterite of *ser* and *ir* hesitated, although only till the mid-sixteenth century, between the paradigm prescribed by Nebrija (1980: 250), *fue, fueste,* etc., and the forms which eventually became standard, *fui, fuiste,* etc.

12 In the early sixteenth century, the possessive adjective could still be optionally preceded by the definite article (*mi casa/la mi casa*), but thereafter the latter form was restricted to Northern rural use.

13 Until the mid-sixteenth century, the auxiliary used in the perfect tense of at least some intransitive verbs could be either *ser* or *haber* (*soy/he muerto, eres/has llegado*), with concord between the participle and the subject when the auxiliary was *ser* (*son llegados, somos idas*). This variation goes back at least to the thirteenth century, when, in the *Poema de mio Cid,* we find *tornado es don Sancho, el dia es exido* beside *a Valencia han entrado.*

14 Until the late seventeenth century, the verbs *ser* and *estar* had not undergone their modern distribution of functions, so that the standard language of the Golden Age allowed both verbs to occur in locative expressions (*es/está aquí* = MSp. *está aquí*), and in resultant-state passive constructions (*es/está escrito* = MSp. *está escrito*).

15 It is only in the sixteenth century that the variation between the verbs *haber* and *tener* is resolved. Until that time, both verbs could occur in possessive phrases, although *haber* was by then rare

(*ha/tiene tres años de edad*), while *tener* could occasionally be found
as a perfect auxiliary, without possessive sense, beside *haber* (*lo
ha/tiene hecho* = MSp. *lo ha hecho*).

7.2.3 The eighteenth and nineteenth centuries

We have noted (**7.1.2**) the concern in eighteenth-century Spain with
ridding the written language of variation, a concern best reflected in
the express determination of the newly established Real Academia
Española to 'fix' the language, and one which persisted into the second
half of the twentieth century. Some of the main effects of the
Academy's activities were the following (Lapesa 1980: 422–4):

1   The orthography had undergone no reform since the time of
    Alfonso X, and at the beginning of the eighteenth century was
    seriously out of alignment with the phonological structure of the
    language. However, spelling was progressively fixed between
    1726 and 1815, by which time it achieved essentially its modern
    shape, where there is a fair (but far from perfect) match between
    phonemes and letters. The most important changes adopted
    were:

    – The prohibition of *y* as a representation of /i/ (thus
      frayle/fraile is settled as *fraile*), except (illogically) in word-final
      position (*muy, hay, rey*).
    – The allocation of exclusively consonantal value to *v* (*ave/aue* >
      ave) and vocalic value to *u* (*vno/uno* > *uno*).
    – The fixing of *h*, in the case of words whose Latin etymon con-
      tained H-, whether they were popular or learned (thus *ora/hora*
      > *hora*, *yerba/hierba* > *hierba*, *umilde/humilde* > *humilde*), in
      popular descendants of Latin words with F- (*hazer/azer* >
      hacer, but mistakenly *fazera/azera* > *acera*), and in arabisms
      (*alheli/aleli* > *alheli*).
    – By the early eighteenth century, all prestigious varieties of
      Spanish had a maximum of three phonemes descended from
      the six medieval sibilants (**3.1.3.1, 4.1.7.2.1, 5.1.1.1**). In central
      and northern Spain these were /θ/, /s/ and /x/, but their
      orthographical representation lagged behind the phonological
      reality, so that /θ/ was correctly spelt <z> in *hazer, dezir*, etc.,
      and <c/ç> in *caça, cena*, etc., but with many confusions.
      Similarly, /s/ was represented 'correctly' either by <s> (in
      casa, rosa), or by <ss> (in *esse, cantasse*), and /x/ by <j> (in *viejo*,

ojo), by <g> (in *gente, muger*), or by <x> (in *caxa, dixo*), again with many interchanges. A purely phonological solution to the reigning chaos would have retained only <z>, <s> and <j> respectively for the three phonemes, but the etymological prejudices of the Academicians did not allow such a radical approach. They did indeed abandon <ss> (so that variations like *casa/cassa, esse/ese* were all resolved as *casa, ese*, etc.), <ç> and <x>, retaining the latter only in latinisms where it reflected x: *experiencia, examen*, etc. However, <c> was retained before <e> or <i> (so that *hazer/haçer, dezir/deçir* were resolved as *hacer, decir* and *cena, mecer* remained unchanged), while *z* was preferred in other cases (*caça/caza, alçar/alzar* > *caza, alzar*). Less rationally, <j> was prescribed for most cases of /x/ (so that *viejo/viexo, muger/mujer/muxer*, etc. were resolved as *viejo, mujer* etc.), but <g> was retained for some words whose Latin etymon showed GE/I (*gente, genio, girar, coger*), permitting the still-current variation in the representation of /x/ (*Jiménez/Giménez*).

- A similar etymological criterion determined the spelling of /b/, the merged result of earlier /b/ and /β/ (**3.1.3.3**). Both <b> and <v> were retained, but redistributed; <v> was to be used for words which in Latin had v, and <b> for words whose etymon showed B or P or whose etymology could not be determined. This required no change for words with initial <v> or <b>, with internal <b> from P, or with internal <v> from v (e.g., *vivir* (VIVERE), *vaca* (VACCA), *beso* (BASIUM), *boda* (etymology uncertain)), but did provoke respelling of words with internal <v> from B; words hitherto spelt *dever, bever, haver*, etc., were readjusted to *deber, beber, haber*, etc. (cf. DEBĒRE, BIBERE, HABĒRE).

- Words of Greek origin which in the Golden Age and in the eighteenth century were often spelt with <ph>, <th>, <ch>, <y> (e.g., *orthographía, phýsica, theatro, monarchía, sýmbolo*), but pronounced respectively with /f/, /t/, /k/ and /i/, had their spellings brought in line with that of other words (*ortografía, física, teatro, monarquía, símbolo*).

- The spelling of [kw], hitherto <qu> (e.g., *quatro, eloquente, frequente*), and therefore identical with the spelling of [k] before /i/ or /e/ (*quien, querer*) was eventually modified to <cu> (*cuatro, elocuente, frecuente*).

2   We have seen (**7.2.2(1)**) that a particular problem was posed for the pronunciation of Golden-Age Spanish by latinisms which contained groups of consonants whose first or middle element was a labial or a velar. Since variation of pronunciation was linked to variation of spelling, this was a matter of concern to the Academicians, who largely resolved the issue by prescribing, in most cases, the written Spanish form which most closely adhered to Latin spelling (and thereby helped to change the phonology of educated Spanish, by consolidating the introduction of syllable-final labials and velars). Thus, in the case of the large majority of pairs, such as *concepto/conceto, absolver/asolver, accidente/acidente, exento/esento, exceder/eceder, perfecto/perfeto, secta/seta, ignorar/inorar, digno/dino*, it was the former rather than the latter which was perpetuated. Only in a minority of cases (e.g., *ceptro/cetro, subjecto/sujeto, subjección/sujeción, lucto/luto, fructo/fruto,*) did the simpler form prevail, although in some instances (e.g., *respecto/respeto, afección/afición, signo/sino*) both forms were allowed to survive but with separate function. In a very few cases, which incorporate the prefixes *ob-* and *sub-*, resolution of this variation is still not quite complete (e.g., *obscuro/oscuro, subscribir/suscribir, substancia/sustancia*), although the simpler forms, which correspond to educated pronunciation, look certain to prevail. In the case of three-consonant groups (e.g., *prompto/pronto, exempto/exento, uncto/unto*), the variation was regularly resolved by ignoring the middle (labial or velar) consonant.

7.2.4   The twentieth century

Variation in educated written Spanish had been reduced to low levels by the beginning of the twentieth century, everywhere it was used, and almost to zero in spelling and morphology. By contrast, lexical variation has been more tolerated and is likely to continue into the future, while in the middle ground stands syntactical variation, which is not negligible, but scarcely striking. The two most salient cases of variation in the current standard will be discussed.

1   The two competing forms of the past subjunctive show no detectable difference of function (Marín 1980), despite their very different origins. The forms in *-ra* (*cantara*, etc.) descend from the Latin pluperfect indicative (of which there is a vestigial residue in the modern standard, e.g., *los amigos que conociera en su juventud*

'the friends he had known in his youth'), acquired conditional value in late Latin and maintained it in medieval and Golden-Age Spanish (a value now restricted to a handful of verbs, viz., *hubiera, debiera, quisiera*, equivalent to *habría, debería, querría*), and then from the fourteenth century gained their current value, at first only in the protasis of conditional sentences expressing improbability or impossibility (Wright 1932, Penny 1991a: 146–7). The forms in *-se* (*cantase*, etc.) go back to the Latin pluperfect subjunctive, which had already acquired imperfect subjunctive value in spoken Latin and have maintained it ever since. In Spanish America today, the *-se* forms are effectively unused, while in Spain the *-ra* forms vastly outnumber the *-se* forms (Marín 1980), the latter only being frequent in areas of coexistence with Catalan, whose sole past subjunctive is marked by /s/ (DeMello 1993). The eventual resolution of this morphological variation can be safely predicted.

2   The value and function of the third-person clitic pronouns is far from standardized at the present. As we have seen (**4.1.2.3, 4.1.7.2.7**), there are several competing systems of third-person pronoun reference in the Spanish-speaking world, originally associated with different regions, but often appearing in written Spanish from the same area. American Spanish is more uniform than Peninsular Spanish is this regard, having generalized the etymological system in which *lo, la, los, las* retain accusative value, while *le, les* retain dative value, both sets being unmarked for such values as [±human] or [±animate] (Table **4.1**). This system was no doubt inherited from southern Spain, where it predominates today, in speech and writing. However, throughout Spain, there is competition in the written language between this system and others. Next, there is the semantically determined system of clitic pronoun reference (Table **4.2**), in which *lo* is restricted to non-countable referents and *le, la, les, las* refer to countable concepts and are unmarked for case; that is, each of these latter forms is used as both a direct and an indirect object pronoun, the only relevant distinctions being gender and number. This system, one of extreme *leísmo* and *laísmo*, was dominant in Golden-Age Spanish, but is less firmly established in the modern Peninsular standard, where a third system competes with the two just outlined. This third system, described above as hybrid or interdialectal (see Table **4.3**), deletes case-distinctions only for masculine singular human

referents (i.e., it displays limited *leísmo*), but maintains them for all other referents (e.g., it avoids *laísmo*). This last system, although it has been available since the thirteenth century, only found its way into prescriptive grammars of Spanish in the twentieth. There is no sign yet of which system will predominate in the long run.

7.3 The relationship between standard and non-standard varieties

Standard languages are different kinds of entities from spoken varieties. Whereas spoken language is infinitely varied, along all the familiar geographical and social parameters (**1.1.1–2**), the essence of a standard language is its lack of variation. Again, whereas spoken varieties have no boundaries, but merge one with another in an infinitely complex way, standard languages, because they are the creations of nation-states, can usually be mapped, their extent being determined by political geography. However, the two kinds of language are related (each standard has been developed from some set of spoken varieties, and a standard language will influence the spoken varieties used in the same territory), so how is this relationship to be envisaged? A helpful model is the one devised by Alberto Vàrvaro (1991) in connection with the way the various Romance standards emerged from the single Latin standard: the standard can be envisaged as a roof which covers a delimited portion of territory, and below which stretches the continuum of spoken varieties. To elaborate Vàrvaro's picture, we can add that the speech continuum may stop some way short of the edge of the roof (giving way to some unrelated set of varieties, as spoken Romance gives way to Basque while the standard Spanish roof continues to the French frontier), or may extend beyond the roof (as happens in the central and eastern Pyrenees, where the northern Peninsular dialect continuum seamlessly merges with the rest of the Romance-speaking world (**4.1.2.4**), while the Spanish standard roof stops where it abuts sharply upon the French roof).

The reality is, of course, more complex than this, since spoken varieties not only have geographical coordinates, which locate them in physical space, but social coordinates which locate them in social space. This social space can usefully be envisaged as the volume between the roof and the ground, with varieties spoken by the most powerful located nearest the roof (being most similar to the standard and varying least among themselves), and the speech of the least powerful at ground level (where we also find maximal geographical variation).

It is worth emphasizing what has just been said: that the greatest geographical variation is to be observed at 'ground level', and this book has been in part designed to describe this ground-level variation. However, it should not be forgotten that there are certain features of non-standard Spanish, usually concentrated in the speech of the least powerful and absent from that of the educated, which are extremely widespread and sometimes universal in the Spanish-speaking world. Because they are so widespread, we can infer (even where we do not have direct evidence) that they are ancient, and in many cases we know that they have been excluded only in recent centuries from educated speech and from the standard. We have already noted (**6.3.5**) that certain characteristics of Judeo-Spanish belong to this category of recently non-standard features, so that a good number of the features considered here have also been mentioned there.

1   The vowels /i/ and /e/, like /u/ and /o/, are neutralized in atonic syllables, and their high or mid realization depends upon adjacent phonemes, such as the height of the tonic, the presence of palatals, etc. (**4.2.4, 6.3.5(1)**).

2   Atonic vowels other than /a/ (and not just /i/ and /u/, as in the standard) are reduced to glides when followed by another vowel, tonic or atonic, forming a diphthong with it: *cambiar* [kambjár], *patear* [patjár], *cuota* [kwóta], *cohete* [kwéte].

3   When a high tonic vowel is immediately adjacent to a lower vowel (cases of hiatus), the accent is transferred to the lower vowel (creating a diphthong): *baúl* [bául̯], *maíz* [mái̯θ]~[mái̯s].

4   The diphthong /ei/ may merge with /ai/, with variable results: *seis* [sái̯s]~[séi̯s], *maíz* [mái̯θ]~[méi̯θ]~[mái̯s]~[méi̯s].

5   Clusters of consonants of which the first is a labial or a velar are not permitted, so that borrowed words (e.g., from Latin) which penetrate these varieties do so without the labial or velar, or these consonants are vocalized to [u̯] or [i̯]: *apto* [áto]~[áu̯to], *objeto* [oxéto], *efecto* [eféto]~[eféu̯to], *ignorar* [inorár]. We have seen (**7.2.2(1)**) that reduction of these groups was permissible in the standard until the eighteenth century; since then it has become restricted to non-standard varieties.

6   Loss of /d/ occurs in limited circumstances (viz., where it is word-final, or in the masculine participial suffix /-ádo/), but with high frequency, in most varieties of spoken Spanish, including

those used by educated speakers, except under the most formal speech-conditions (Navarro Tomás 1961: 101).[11] However, loss of /d/ in other morphological circumstances (e.g., *llegada, venido, comida, madera, maduro*) is highly frequent and geographically universal among speakers at the 'ground level' of the social matrix.[12] In the same social milieux, loss of /g/ is also highly frequent, although limited to cases where the consonant is followed by a high back vowel: *agujero* /auxéro/, *aguja* /aúxa/, etc.

7 Loss of intervocalic /r/, in a few lexical items, is extremely widespread at these sociolinguistic levels (e.g., *parece* /paéθe/ ~ /páiθe/, *quieres* /kiés/, *para* /pa/).

8 Reinforcing of morpheme-initial /ue/ to [ɣwe], less frequently [βwe], is extremely widespread at these levels (**4.2.5**), e.g., *ahuecar* [aɣwekár]~[aβwekár], *huerta* [ɣwérta]~[βwérta]. Just as frequent is the related interchange of [ɣwe] with historic [βwe], so that *abuelo, vuelta*, etc., are articulated [aɣwélo], [ɣwélta], etc.

9 Corresponding to standard [fwé], [fwí], in words like *fuera, fuente, fue, fuiste*, there is a widespread rural realization with a voiceless bilabial or labiovelar initial, [ɸwé]~[ɸwí], [ʍwé]~[ʍwí], often regarded as allophones of /h/, although not restricted to areas where /h/ (ultimately from Latin F) is retained in words like *humo, hambre, hilo*.[13]

10 Interchange between word-initial *es-* and *des-* is in part a phonological matter (see point (6) of this section), but also a residue of the confusion in spoken Latin of the prefixes EX- and DIS-, which increasingly came to have the same meaning. Medieval and Golden-Age Spanish show frequent hesitation in writing between such forms as *estender* and *destender* and in popular Spanish this uncertainty has been extended to all words of this pattern, with preference for *es-*: *estrozar* (standard *destrozar*), *eslumbrar* (standard *deslumbrar*), etc.

11 Use of the form *mos* as the first-person plural object pronoun, e.g., *mos vieron, mos lo dieron* (standard *nos vieron, nos lo dieron*), is widespread at rural level, no doubt through interference from the corresponding verbal ending *-mos*. The reverse interference, leading to the verbal ending *-nos* (e.g., *estábanos*, cf. standard *estábamos*) is less common, but frequently reported in rural American Spanish (Espinosa 1946: 221).

12 Retention of *vos* (standard *os*) as the second-person plural object pronoun is widespread in rural Peninsular Spanish and in

Judeo-Spanish (but is absent from American Spanish, where the corresponding forms are *los/las/les*, consistent with the replacement of subject *vos(otros)* by *ustedes* (**5.1.1.2**).

13   Use of *le* as both a plural and singular indirect object pronoun for third-person reference (standard *les* vs *le*), is widely found at this level, no doubt owing to interference from its allomorph *se*, which is unmarked for number (e.g., *se lo dio* 'he gave it to him/her/them').

14   The non-standard ordering of clitic pronouns exemplified by *me se cayó* (standard *se me cayó*) is common at 'ground level', while the order Direct Object + Indirect Object (e.g., *lo me dio*, standard *me lo dio*) is a little less so.

15   Addition of /-s/ to the second-person singular forms of all preterite paradigms (e.g., *hicistes*, standard *hiciste*), frequently found in medieval Spanish, is all but universal at the level of uneducated speech, and frequently penetrates that of educated speakers. In America, it characterizes both areas of *voseo* (*Vos dijistes/dijites*) and areas of *tuteo* (*Tú dijistes/dijites*).

16   The form *caminemos*, etc., used with preterite value (cf. standard *caminamos*), was occasionally found in Old Spanish (Penny 1991a: 180–1), was excluded from the standard in the late Middle Ages but has widely survived in rural speech.

17   Use of *haiga, vaiga, huiga*, and occasionally *veiga*, as present subjunctive forms of *haber, ir, huir* and *ver* (see **7.2.2(10)**) is found all over the Spanish-speaking world (Espinosa 1946: 244–6), at a rural level, and sometimes at other non-standard levels.

18   Irregular preterite forms such as *truje, vide* (cf. standard *traje, vi*) frequently appeared in written Spanish in the medieval and Golden Age periods, but have since then been restricted to non-standard, chiefly rural, use.

All of the features considered above are today in more or less fierce competition with their standard counterparts, which are increasingly penetrating rural speech, typically through lexical diffusion (see **3.5**). This competition is yet to be systematically examined, although a few notably successful attempts have been made in this direction (see Borrego Nieto 1981, 1983, Holmquist 1988).

Notes

1 Introduction: language variation

1   Since, as we shall see later, there are no natural boundaries between descendants of a single ancestor language, it is no easy matter to define what is meant by the 'same' language in particular parts of the world. What we call 'languages' (e.g., French, Spanish, Italian, German, Dutch) are in fact distinguished one from another according to non-linguistic criteria; thus it is often the existence of a frontier between two nation-states which gives rise to the conclusion that the people living on each side of the frontier must speak different languages, while those who belong to the same nation-state (and understand one another's speech) are thought to speak the same language. However, the speech of people separated by a national frontier may be more similar than the speech of people belonging to different parts of the same nation-state. And this applies not just to territories, such as Africa, where frontiers are relatively recent, but to territories such as Europe, where the notion of the nation-state is much more ancient, as we shall see in the case of the Spanish–French frontier (**4.1.2.4**).

2   Forms of speech which differ in accordance with the locality of the speakers are traditionally labelled *dialects*, although this term is also used for linguistic systems which are differentiated according to other criteria. Thus it is possible to use the term *dialect* to indicate the set of features (system) used by a particular social group (i.e., a *social dialect*), or for a particular purpose (e.g., the *standard dialect*). For this reason, we shall use only the terms *geographical* or *diatopical* when referring to variation correlated with geographical space.

3   Although it is usual to say that the Atlantic fisherman speaks 'Galician' while his Mediterranean counterpart speaks 'Catalan', these terms do not, as we shall see (**4.1.2**), have a linguistic basis. They are terms whose justification lies in political history, and are applied (according to criteria which are for the most part politically contrastive and non-linguistic) to segments of a continuously varying and intermeshed series of dialects. Furthermore, it will be evident that in this discussion of geographical variation it has been necessary to leave out of consideration (rather artificially) all social factors. The example we are considering concerns the informal registers of uneducated rural dwellers, although the speech of other social groups can be examined in the same geographical way, usually with smaller degrees of difference between localities. Of course, our Galician and Catalan fishermen, depending on their degree of schooling, may resort to an alternative code in order to understand one another, such as the standard dialect ('Castilian') or some approximation to it.

4   It will be seen that the relationship between a particular variant and a particular social characteristic is a statistical one. For example, a particular variant can be shown to be

significantly more frequent in the speech of one segment of the community (defined, say, by criteria of age, or of social class) than in the speech of another segment. For women's speech in the Hispanic world, see Martín Zorraquino (1994).

5 For the notion of codification, see Section **7.1.2**.

6 Loss of variants is largely accomplished by the death of those speakers who use such variants, although allowance has to be made for individuals modernizing their speech during their lifetimes. One the other hand, new variants introduced by younger members of the community are unlikely to be transmitted to older generations.

7 For a comprehensive discussion of *yeísmo*, see Alonso (1967a). For geographical aspects of its distribution in the Peninsula, see Navarro Tomás (1964). For social aspects of the phenomenon in Buenos Aires, see Fontanella de Weinberg (1978).

8 For broad discussion of register, see Moreno Fernández (1992).

9 For the application of sociolinguistic principles to the past, see Romaine (1982), and for their application in Spain, see Gimeno Menéndez (1990, 1995), Wright (1988).

2 *Dialect, language, variety*: definitions and relationships

1 For the development of standard French, see Lodge (1993); for the dialect of Paris, see Lodge (1998).

2 The only exceptional case is that of pidgins. Pidgins (for a good account, see Aitchison 1991: 180–91 or Hudson 1996: 61–6) arise when two or more groups of speakers of mutually incomprehensible languages come into contact (for purposes of trade, say) and must communicate. Pidgins may develop into creoles (see **5.4**) when they are acquired by children, as their first language, and can therefore be thought of as genuine cases of language creation.

3 The only exception to this statement is the rare case where a previously dead language (i.e., one with no native speakers) has been brought back into use in a community and is then passed on, as a first language, to later generations. The most notable case of such a process is that of modern Hebrew.

We also leave aside the matter of language death, a process whereby, through the medium of bilingualism, a particular code ceases to be used (in favour of an alternative code) first by a portion of the users of that code and subsequently by all. Curiously then, languages can have an end without having a beginning.

4 For discussion of the names of the descendants of Latin, see Vidos (1963: 165–70).

5 More accurately, *castellano* referred to a series of varieties, since we are dealing with a period prior to the standardization of Castilian (see Chapter 7).

6 For the effects of writing on awareness of linguistic identity among the Romance languages, see Lloyd (1991). For more general consideration of the relationship between writing and standardization, see Joseph (1987), Milroy and Milroy (1991).

7 The counterpart of this view, that a language cannot be a language unless it has a distinct orthography, is the view that in order to confer the status of 'language' on a particular variety it is necessary to create for it an orthography which is different from that used to write other varieties. Part of the acrimonious debate over the status of Valencian is over the spelling system to be recommended; if Valencian is written according to the same orthographical norms as are used in Barcelona, how can Valencian (the argument goes) be a separate language from Catalan? Hence the desire,

in some quarters, to devise an orthography for Valencian which differs from the accepted Catalan spelling system.

8 The Peninsular 'languages', Portuguese, Spanish and Catalan, form part of the Romance continuum which extends into France and thence into Italy. Exactly the same problem of delimitation exists in many other parts of Europe. Where is Dutch to be separated from German, Norwegian from Swedish, Czech from Slovak from Polish from Russian, or, in the south of Europe, Serbo-Croatian from Bulgarian from Ukrainian? For a discussion of such language continua, see Chambers and Trudgill (1980: 6–8).

9 'Direct' knowledge is here contrasted with knowledge derived from linguistic reconstruction undertaken in accordance with the comparative method. However, the comparative method also falsifies the past, since it depends upon the comparison of one unvarying 'language' with another (or others) in order to establish the characteristics of an earlier unvarying 'language'. This procedure springs from adherence (stated or implicit) to the family tree as a model of the relationships between languages. However, we shall see (**2.5.1**) that the tree is an unsatisfactory model for such relationships.

10 The derogatory terminology often associated with this perceived process springs from the high prestige of written, codified varieties, and the low prestige of varieties used just for oral and local purposes.

11 Or that they are 'dialects of Spanish', unless one wishes to restrict this label to the standard language, a restriction which leads to equally self-contradictory results, since standard languages do not admit of regional variations. It would surely be meaningless to claim that the speech varieties used in rural Zamora are dialects of standard Spanish.

12 The few cases where politico-administrative boundaries do coincide with isoglosses are due to movement of separate groups of people, each with its own set of speech norms, up to points on either side of a previously agreed frontier. This pattern of movement, with its peculiar linguistic effects, was common in Spain during the Reconquest, as we shall see in **4.1.7**.

13 The concept of adjacency may be thought inappropriate in the case of linguistic differences related to sex, since in this case we are not dealing (by contrast with what occurs in the case of all the other relevant linguistic parameters) with a parameter of increasing or decreasing values of the feature at issue, but with a choice between two discrete values. However, a change of value in this parameter (i.e., the contrast between a male and a female speaker) is associated with the same sort of relationship between varieties as in the case of other parameters: if all other factors are held constant, the speech of a female is likely to differ from that of a male in one or more linguistic items, or in the frequency with which the competing variants are used.

14 For example, it is common in sociolinguistic studies to place speakers on a socioeconomic scale including such points as 'lower working class' (LWC), 'middle working class' (MWC), 'upper working class' (UWC), 'lower middle class' (LMC), 'middle middle class' (MMC), 'upper middle class' (UMC), 'upper class' (UC), with the implication, but without explicit justification, that the social 'distance' between adjacent points is in each case the same.

15 Not only as a synchronic model, but also as a diachronic model, the tree is open to serious challenge, since the branches of any specific tree may suggest cleavages where there are continuities. Nor can the tree model take account of the spread of features

from a variety occupying one branch to a variety occupying another, although this kind of influence is commonly invoked in historical linguistics. For a critique of the use of the tree model in historical linguistics, especially Romance linguistics, see Penny (1995) and bibliography there.

16   We are ignoring here the multidimensional social 'space' in which each variety is also located.

17   Attempts have been made to measure the degree of relatedness between varieties, notably by the French 'dialectometric' school (for an example, see Guiter 1983), but also by scholars working purely within Ibero-Romance (e.g., Agard 1990, Otero 1971–6).

18   Ironically, Darwin probably took the notion of the tree from early Indo-European philology. See Penny (1995). A further irony is that the biologists have recently been abandoning the tree model, as a means of displaying biological relatedness, in favour of the clade, which includes no notion of time-depth. See Novacek (1987), Platnick and Cameron (1977), Ruvolo (1987).

19   Meyer-Lübke (1927: 97–102) explains the presence of voiced consonants in such words as due to borrowing of these words from northern Italy, Gaul, etc., but other scholars agree that the words concerned are unlikely candidates for borrowing (see Maiden 1995: 60–3).

20   The voiceless nature of the Mozarabic descendants of the Latin voiceless intervocalics has not gone undisputed. See Galmés (1983: 91–100) for a contrary view.

21   In fact the bifurcation rests on two features, only one of which has been examined here. The second feature, the isogloss which separates retention from loss of Latin final / -s /, does cross the north of the Italian peninsula between La Spezia and Rimini, but it can scarcely be claimed that a difference of a single item is sufficient to justify the division of the entire Romance stock into two separate branches.

22   This reluctance can only be explained by the powerful hold that the tree image has on the educated Western mind and by our need to visualize relationships. Branches are much easier to visualize than the amorphous reality of variation.

23   Such investigations of past linguistic processes are of course acutely difficult, owing to the extreme paucity of data. However, by keeping in mind a model which presents language as an inherently varying phenomenon, we are more likely to arrive at an understanding of past developments than by adhering to the essentially rigid notion of the tree.

24   On the division between Eastern and Western Romance, see also Malkiel (1991).

25   Indirect evidence suggests that the pronunciation [óụ] was in use in the north of Castile as late as the twelfth century, given that in this area the spelling <ei> was in frequent use in the suffix -eiro (Menéndez Pidal 1964: 483), and given also that the general symmetry of vowel-systems leads us to expect that a front diphthong / ei / will be accompanied by a back diphthong / ou /.

26   It will be noted that there are difficulties even in accommodating the development AU > / o / to the tree model sketched in 2.5.1, since this development is shared by all but the western (and some west-central) varieties of Hispano-Romance, which would need to be placed on a branch which separated from the rest of Hispano-Romance at a point which is earlier (higher) than the node which joins Castilian with its eastern neighbours.

27   The question arises of why, if the tree model has so many defects, it has imposed itself

so successfully upon linguistic thought. This question is tackled in Penny (1995), where two answers are found: the primordial concern of historical linguistics with standard languages (which can be studied as discrete entities separate from the continua from which they spring), and the apparent success of the tree model within such an influential field of study as Indo-European linguistics.

28   Even the title of Corominas and Pascual (1980–91), viz. *Diccionario crítico etimológico castellano e hispánico*, reveals a three-pronged approach to the distribution of Peninsular varieties, since here 'hispánico' extends the area to be covered from the strictly Castilian area, but excludes Galician–Portuguese and Catalan, so that 'castellano e hispánico' means 'all Peninsular Romance except Galician–Portuguese or Catalan'.

29   Even such sound and justifiably well respected treatments of Spanish dialectology as Zamora Vicente (1967) fall into this misconception. E.g., 'En Asturias, el gallego penetra hasta el río Navia' (p. 85), then exemplified by the contrast between the forms *corpo, terra, morto* and their diphthongized counterparts. Similarly: 'Quedan dentro del habla aragonesa, con diptongación en cualquier circunstancia de ĕ y ŏ latinas, Bisaurri y Renanué . . .' (p. 212), despite the map on p. 225 which shows the scattering of isoglosses in the central Pyrenees. The broad spread of isoglosses pertaining to vowel development, in the area north of Benabarre, was amply demonstrated by Griera (1914).

30   Elcock's study of the speech of the Pyrenees (1938), which will be considered in more detail in **4.1.2.4**, shows that until the nineteenth century the Pyrenean frontier was no barrier to contact between north and south, with the consequent maintenance of linguistic similarities between the two sides.

31   'Adjacent' here has usually been taken in the geographical sense, but there is no reason in principle why socially adjacent varieties should not be described in terms of a diasystem.

32   A number of assumptions underlie this statement. First (as seen in **4.1.7.2.3**), Andalusian and American-Spanish /x/ includes articulations of the glottal or pharyngeal type such as [h] and [ħ]. Second, within Andalusian /s/ are included articulations broadly transcribed as [θ] (i.e., *ceceante* pronunciations) which belong to the coastal areas of Andalusia (see **4.1.7.2.1**) and which combine in a single interdentalized articulation the medial phoneme of both *caza* and *casa*.

33   This discussion deliberately leaves aside those varieties of Spanish in which syllable-final /s/ is vestigially present, as [ʰ], etc., although such varieties could, in this context, be considered as forming a group with those that maintain /s/ as a sibilant.

34   Again, within the phoneme /x/ (which could just as well be symbolized with /h/) are subsumed all articulations in the range [x], [ħ], [h].

35   For application of structuralist concepts to geographical variation, see Alvar (1969).

36   However, the re-emergence from the nineteenth century of more standardized varieties of Galician, used in writing, in the Church, etc., means that Galician by no means always occupies the L position.

37   The linguistic situation described here for Galicia is not dissimilar to that envisaged by Wright (1982) for early Romance-speaking Europe. Wright argues for a one-language situation, in which (the reader infers) a continuum of overlapping varieties extends from the highly codified set of items used by certain educated individuals in writing (a variety usually labelled 'Latin') through written varieties which show increasing admixtures of items shared with spoken varieties, to exclusively spoken varieties of

various kinds. The creation, in later centuries, of codified versions of some of these hitherto exclusively spoken varieties is not unlike the modern re-emergence of standard forms of Galician, with two obvious major differences: first, modern standard Galician has been modelled in part on medieval written varieties (a process which has no parallel in the emergence of the Romance standards), and second, even before the appearance of Romance standards the highest-prestige variety was probably exclusively a written code, whereas the Castilian of Galicia has for centuries been not only a written code but has been spoken by the most privileged social groups.

38   It can be argued that, in all long-standing bilingual communities, even where the languages concerned are unrelated, there is *some* overlap of linguistic items, perhaps largely consisting of lexical and phonological features.

39   The result of these changes may, paradoxically, lead to an increase in the number of speakers who claim competence in Basque. See, among other treatments, Wardhaugh (1987: 119–27) and Rednap (1993–4) for a discussion of language contacts in Spain. For discussion of a specifically Basque–Castilian contact situation, see Hughes (1992).

40   See Iordan and Orr (1970: 273–8) for a critique of the neolinguistic school.

41   These data can be seen in Rohlfs (1960: map 8). Similar data are displayed in maps 17 (VENERIS vs VENERIS DIES, etc., 'Friday'), 24 (ROGĀRE vs PRECĀRE 'to ask'), 25 (HUMERUS vs SPATULA 'shoulder'), 32 (AFFLĀRE vs TROPĀRE, etc., 'to find'), 36 (CĀSEUS vs FORMĀTICUS 'cheese'), 47 (EQUA vs JŪMENTA, CABALLA 'mare'), although there are many more cases in which Spanish and Portuguese do not agree with Romanian in the lexical type they have perpetuated.

42   See Posner (1966: 67–9) for a mildly sceptical view of this spatial principle.

43   Degrees of eccentricity are, of course, difficult to measure, but it would not be hard to sustain the claim that the phonology of Portuguese, resulting in part from the deletion of intervocalic -N- and -L-, and from intense nasalization processes, is at least among the more innovatory Romance types. The personal infinitive of Portuguese would likewise lead us to categorize its morpho-syntax as highly innovatory.

3 Mechanisms of change

1   Alongside *quinientos* we find the frequent Old Spanish form *quiñentos*, which may be the more directly inherited form.

2   It should be remembered that the term *item* denotes, as elsewhere in this text, any linguistic feature, including a feature of pronunciation or phonological structure, of morphology, syntax, semantics, lexis, and so on.

3   For these concepts, see principally Trudgill (1986: 83–126).

4   The term *koiné*, from which *koinéization* is derived, refers to any variety which emerges, through a series of compromises, from a situation of dialect mixture. The term belongs properly to a period of development in the history of Greek, when, following the classical period (a time when a number of regional varieties of Greek were in somewhat unequal competition), there emerged a post-classical compromise variety, which is the ancestor of most subsequent forms of Greek (see Tuten 1998: 8–11).

5   The classic presentation of the data can be seen in Alonso (1967b) and (1969), with syntheses in Lapesa (1980: 371–81) and Penny (1991a: 86–90). An explanation has been attempted in Penny (1993), and the work of Frago Gracia (1977–8, 1983, 1985, 1989) has immensely extended our knowledge of the dating and spread of these changes.

Further relevant discussion may be seen in Alonso (1962a), Galmés de Fuentes (1962), Harris (1969), Kiddle (1975), Lantolf (1974), Martinet (1974), Torreblanca (1981–2).

6   For the importance of phonemic contrast in the resolution of variation following dialect contact, see Trudgill (1986: 20–1). For the slight functional load of the contrast between voiceless and voiced sibilants in late-medieval Spanish, see Penny (1993).

7   The bibliography concerned with the development F- > /h/ is enormous, but largely concerned with the much-debated question of the origin of the phenomenon, which is not at issue here, rather than its spread, which does concern us. With regard to progressive geographical spread, useful maps and discussion are to be found in Menéndez Pidal (1964: 221–33), while the issue is reviewed at length in Penny (1972b, 1990). A dissenting view can be seen in Torreblanca (1991–2).

8   It is not suggested here (by the choice of some /h/-less words which are spelled with h) that spelling has any role in the outcome of this variation, but it can be noted that for the literate minority there were clear advantages in allowing the two groups to merge, in that h had hitherto had two values, /h/ and /Ø/, while following levelling this letter always corresponds to /Ø/.

9   *Homonymic clash* indicates a change by which two words, hitherto with distinct phonemic structures, come to have identical structures.

10   Discussion of the history of the merger of /b/ and /β/ can be found in Alonso (1962c), Söll (1964), Penny (1976), Moreno (1987).

11   Although verse demonstrates that poets did not rhyme *callava,* etc., with *alaba,* etc. until the fifteenth century onwards (with some, like Garcilaso, maintaining the distinction into the sixteenth), the conservatism of the phonology reflected in poetry allows us to date this levelling at least a century earlier in some areas.

12   The kind of spoken Latin established in central-northern Spain must also have been the result of dialect contact, since Latin speech was presumably brought by different groups (soldiers, traders, administrators, etc.) who spoke different varieties of Latin. However, in this regard the ancestor of Spanish does not differ from the ancestors of the other surviving Romance varieties, all of which must have originated in the same kind of way. Nevertheless, some of the simplification processes in spoken Latin whose results we see in the Romance languages may be due to this mixing process, although without more reliable data on variation in spoken Latin it is difficult to ascribe specific changes to dialect contact.

13   In Latin, there was no requirement that the implied subject of the participle should be co-referential with the subject of HABEO. So that in the sentence HABEO CĒNAM PARĀTAM there is no implication that the speaker (subject of HABEO) is the person who has prepared the meal; it could have been someone else. One of the early effects of the grammaticalization of this construction was that it became obligatory for the subject of the participle to be identical with the subject of HABEO.

14   There were other changes which affected this syntagma as it became grammaticalized, namely the relaxation of the requirement for an overt direct object, the near-fixing of word order (auxiliary + participle, rather than participle + auxiliary, which was perfectly usual in Latin, but became a marked stylistic variant in Spanish), and the severe restriction upon the elements which could be interposed between auxiliary and participle.

15   'Deponent' verbs are those which are identical in form to the passive paradigms of transitive verbs (e.g., MORTUUS EST 'he died, he has died', structurally like OCCĪSUS

EST 'he was killed'), and which typically have 'middle' sense, that is, their grammatical subjects are neither the initiators of the action indicated by the verb (as in the case of active verbs), nor do they undergo action performed by some other agent (as in the case of passive constructions), but merely participate inertly in the activity concerned.

16   For an excellent discussion of the relationship in Italian between the SUM and HABEO perfects, much of which can be extended to other members of the Romance family, see Maiden (1995: 145–56).

17   Although Portuguese has no SUM perfect, it cannot be directly compared with Spanish in this respect since its perfective past tense (e.g., *vim* 'I came, I have come') has to a large extent retained the double value (preterite and present perfect) of its Latin ancestor (VĒNĪ) (see **5.1.3.2**). On the other hand, Romanian does show comparable simplification of these structures (having only the HABEO perfect), although the speed with which this change occurred is unknown, owing to the lack of Romanian texts from before the sixteenth century.

18   The distinction between these two groups of verbs of motion is a subtle semantic one. Those verbs allowing the SUM perfect are ones whose grammatical subjects may be personal or non-personal, animate or inanimate, while those restricted to the HABEO perfect are ones which have only animate subjects.

19   The fact that spoken French, and some varieties of spoken Italian, have abandoned the simple past paradigms in favour of aux. + participle constructions (e.g., Fr. *il est mort* for *il mourut*) is immaterial here, since this change in French (and Italian) is recent.

20   The verb *oír* 'to hear' has always been exceptional, in that, except in some Riojan varieties revealed in the writing of Gonzalo de Berceo (who uses *udieron* 'they heard', etc.), /u/ was excluded from its stem. We find *oye* (rather than expected ****uye*), perhaps to distinguish the forms of this verb, in /h/-dropping areas, from the corresponding forms of the verb *fuir/huir* 'to flee'. On the other hand, late additions to the vocabulary of Spanish like *abolir* 'to abolish', which exceptionally allow stem /o/ in verbs of the *-ir* class, entirely lack stem-stressed forms, so that forms such as ****abule* are completely excluded from the grammar of Spanish.

21   Montgomery (1975–6, 1978, 1979, 1980, 1985) seeks semantic contrasts which are correlated with the stem-vowels of the two verb-classes, such that the predominantly mid vowels to be found in *-er* verbs are associated with imperfectivity, while the high vowels of *-ir* verbs are associated with perfectivity of the verbal action. However, this approach has not generally carried conviction. For an attempt to understand the development of the stem-vowels of these verbs, see Penny (1972a).

22   Of course, it is not possible to rule out simple paradigm-internal levelling as a cause for the change discussed here. But hyperdialectalism should be entertained as at least a contributory factor, and possibly the main reason for the levelling.

23   In those areas of the Peninsula where /h/ today survives in the class of words descended from those which in Latin showed /f-/ (namely in western Andalusia, Extremadura, the La Ribera area of Salamanca province, and the northern zone comprising eastern Asturias and most of Cantabria), it is also true to say that presence and absence of /h/ is now correlated with social factors, since these words lack an initial consonant in the varieties belonging to educated groups. The difference between Spain and America, in this regard, is that while /h/ is to be heard in rural/uneducated varieties all over America, there are large areas of the Peninsula where no variety shows /h/ in these words.

24   In the case selected for discussion, both the alternants *tañer* and *tanzer* found their way
     into writing, although *tanzer* is rare and soon disappeared from the record. However,
     the argument used here presupposes that there were alternatives to all the forms
     attested in writing; that is, there would have existed a form **eñía* 'gum' beside attested
     enzia (later *encía*), etc.

25   The existence of *coño* would have slightly balanced the choice between **cueño* and *cuño*
     in favour of the latter, since /o/ and /ue/ are in frequent paradigmatic relationship in
     Spanish (e.g., in the verb), and **cueño* would therefore appear to be more closely related
     to *coño* than *cuño* would.

26   A third alternant *vergoña* is only attested in texts originating away from the central
     Castilian area and seems not to have entered into the dialect mixture under discussion
     here.

27   At variance with the notion expressed here is the concept of the *Sprachbund*, such as
     that which is thought to exist in the Balkans, where certain features, such as the placing
     of definite articles after the noun, appear in neighbouring dialect continua (Albanian,
     Slavic, Romanian) and are believed to have been transferred from one to another.
     Another case where it is claimed that a linguistic wave has crossed from one continuum
     to another is that of the use of uvular [ʀ] in western Europe, where it appears in both
     Gallo-Romance and Germanic varieties.

28   For further discussion of how innovations are spread, see **3.4**, which deals with spread
     through social 'space', but which is equally applicable to spread through geographical
     space.

29   Nor should it be assumed that a more recent feature is necessarily the one which is
     expanding, since an item which was once prestigious (and therefore expanding) may
     lose its prestigious associations and begin to recede.

30   The earlier view (Menéndez Pidal 1964: 444–5, unrevised from earlier editions), that the
     two southern islands of {-es} in Leonese territory (namely, San Ciprián de Sanabria and
     El Payo) were the result of medieval resettlement of people from central Asturias, is no
     longer tenable. Menéndez Pidal (1960: xxix–lvii) concludes that the Catalan and the
     various Leonese zones of {-es} < -ās (and of {-en} < -ANT in the verb) were once part of
     a continuous zone, later broken by the penetration of Castilian {-as} and {-an}. This
     conclusion is supported by the occasional appearance of plur. {-es} in the now extinct
     southern (i.e., Mozarabic) varieties of Peninsular Romance (see **4.1.1**). In this context, it
     should be remembered that the morphemes {-es} and {-en} are innovations which are
     now receding in the face of the earlier, more conservative, forms {-as} and {-an}.

31   None of this discussion should be taken to imply that all dialectal differences were lev-
     elled within each major group of settlers. Such total levelling is not envisaged (and is
     impossible to achieve); in order to understand the reasons for the clustering of
     isoglosses at the Portuguese–Spanish frontier, it is sufficient to envisage that *certain*
     aspects of variation within each group were levelled, leaving many other instances of
     internal variation unresolved.

32   We are deliberately ignoring here, as irrelevant, those cases where the frontier has been
     shifted since the period of settlement, leaving occasional small pockets of speakers on
     either side of the frontier who use the 'wrong' set of linguistic features.

33   There is no implication here that dialect levelling did not in general occur on the
     Portuguese side of the frontier. In the case of other features, where there was no una-
     nimity among settlers, levelling would be an expected outcome.

34   The isogloss is traced in detail by Catalán and Galmés (1946), and by Rodríguez-Castellano (1946). Menéndez Pidal's historical account has not been universally accepted; see Penny (1972b and 1990) for discussion and further bibliography.

35   This process is taking place word by word, the first words to be affected being those whose meanings associate them with urban/educated lifestyles, while the last to lose their initial consonant are those whose meanings connect them with a rural/agricultural way of life. For this process of lexical diffusion of change, see 3.5.

36   It should be noted that many of these changes probably had remoter origins, some of them perhaps originating in the spoken Latin of Cantabria, but if that is so, they appear to have remained marginal (i.e., they were used by individuals who were peripheral to the main community) until the period of social change we are examining (ninth–eleventh centuries).

37   In such formulations, the apostrophe indicates a vowel (typically short I or U) which was deleted in spoken Latin or in early Romance. The symbol J indicates a (non-syllabic) palatal glide which has developed from atonic E or I when grouped with a following vowel.

38   To limit comment to phonological matters, Boléo (1974: 187–250) provides evidence of the slower pace of change in northern Portugal. He delimits the areas (all including the northernmost provinces and extending southwards in differing degrees) of the following features: retention of /tʃ/ in the north versus reduction to /ʃ/ (/tʃúva/ vs /ʃúva/ chuva 'rain'), retention of bilabial /β/ or /b/ in the north versus its development to /v/ further south, retention of the diphthong /éi/ in the north versus its reduction to /é/ in the south, etc.

39   This pattern is somewhat obscured in the case of Catalan by the fact that the southern (i.e. Valencian) varieties are an extension of the western type of northern Catalan (that of the Lérida area), rather than of the eastern type which provided the norm variety, that of Barcelona (4.1.7.3). What is claimed here is that Valencian shows a greater degree of innovation than Leridan. A further problem springs from the fact that some of the more advanced features of Valencian Catalan, those to be seen in the apitxat varieties found in city of Valencia and surrounding rural areas (Badía 1951: 79), have sometimes been ascribed to contact with Castilian rather than to internal development. It is true that some of the features of the apitxat varieties (use of bilabial /b/ rather than the labiodental /v/ used in varieties to both north and south, devoicing of voiced sibilants and their merger with their voiceless counterparts) are ones which also characterize Castilian, but it is far from clear that these similarities are more than coincidences.

40   These traits include not only factors such as wealth, education, possessions, which when owned in abundance are associated with the 'top' of society, but also such traits as street credibility which are associated with other levels and to which we shall refer in 3.4.2.

41   Lapesa quotes from Fortunata y Jacinta, first published in 1886–7, the following comment on the speech of Fortunata, whose background is working-class: 'las eses finales se le convertían en jotas sin que ella lo notase ni evitarlo pudiese'.

42   An alternative view, namely that this change could occur in any environment, is sustained by data from Gascon, where Latin F becomes /h/ even before the non-nuclear elements [r], [l], and [w] (e.g., FOCU >houèc 'fire'). However, the fact that the change appears to be effectively unconditioned in Gascon does not imply that in other Romance varieties, such as Castilian, the change was not more limited in its domain.

43 Words like /hwénte/, rather than being articulated with glottal [h], often show voiceless labiovelar [ʍ] or voiceless bilabial [ɸ].

44 For the process whereby competing variants are reallocated to different sociolects, see
3.1.6.

4 Variation in Spain

1 It is necessary to distinguish carefully between the linguistic label *Mozarabic*, which
refers, as we have seen, to Romance varieties spoken by people living in Islamic-dominated Spain, whatever their religion or ethnic background, and the cultural term
Mozarab/Mozarabic, which is used to refer exclusively to the Christians living in areas
whose official religion was Islam. The term *Mozarabic* is also used to refer to the traditional liturgy of the Spanish Church, also referred to as the *Visigothic* rite, which was
used not only in Islamic-dominated Spain but also in Christian areas, whether formerly
Islamic-dominated or not, until it was replaced (at different times in different places) by
the Carolingian rite.

2 Galmés (1983) is the best synthesis available of our knowledge of Mozarabic, but
partial treatments can also be seen in Zamora (1967: 15–54) and Lapesa (1980: 126–30,
167–9).

3 According to Galmés (1983: 110), it is impossible to distinguish, in the Arabic-script
texts he uses, between final {-as} and {-es}. The failure of writers to attempt to make
any such distinction, when they were so resourceful in attempting to signal other
Romance vocalic contrasts, leads him to conclude that these morphemes were pronounced alike, namely as [-es]. Using data from a broad variety of Mozarabic sources
(1983: 302–17), he concludes that in many areas the plural morpheme associated with
feminine singulars in {-a} was {-es}. Feminine plural forms like *cases* are also found (or
were until recently) in two now isolated districts: San Ciprián de Sanabria (western
Zamora) and El Payo (southwestern Salamanca), providing evidence for a once continuous area of this feature stretching from Catalonia (at least) to what is now the
Portuguese frontier. See **3.2.1**.

4 Since Leite de Vasconcellos carried out his investigations, at the end of the nineteenth
century, it is likely that some of these isoglosses will have moved towards (even right up
to) the Spanish frontier, as a result of improved communications within northern
Portugal and the more frequent face-to-face contacts between Mirandeses and their
Portuguese neighbours to the west.

5 Closeness of communication between speakers of different varieties is also determined in part by topographical features like mountains, rivers, forests, and swamps.

6 Menéndez Pidal (1962a) is essentially unchanged from the first edition of this work,
which dates from the beginning of the twentieth century. His later study (1960: lii–liv)
adds additional information, but still speaks of linguistic 'boundaries' which separated
Miranda from the rest of Portugal. Carvalho (1952) refers to a medieval Leonese colonization of the Miranda region; this view is rejected by Menéndez Pidal 1960: liv).

7 *ALEANR* (1979–83) cannot reveal these data, since no question was aimed at this syntagma. A separate question is the loss of infinitival /-r/ in all syntactical circumstances,
a feature which links eastern varieties of Aragonese with Catalan.

8 Monographs which give details of this contrast include: Rodríguez-Castellano (1952:
68); Neira (1955: 15); Canellada (1944: 15); Álvarez (1963: 28); Fernández (1959: 42).

9   Full discussion of these features of Northern Hispano-Romance, including comparison with similar Italian data, can be seen in Penny 1970b and 1994. For further bibliography, see the notes to Section **4.1.2.5**. 1–2.

10 For Asturias, see García Arias (1988: 62). For upper Aragon, *ALEANR* (1979–83: map 1424) shows descendants of VESPA with /ié/ in a variety of localities in northern Saragossa, and in northwestern and central-northern Huesca.

11 It is noticeable that, as always, the words which best resist the standardizing pressure (in this case the pressure to impose standard /x/ for Cantabrian /ʎ/ or /ʝ/) are those whose meanings relate them closely to traditional activities and life-styles (see Section **3.5**).

12 Alvar (1976: 56) dates this change to the thirteenth century for eastern La Rioja, and earlier for the western part of the region. The total victory of /x/, in every part of the rural lexis, is likely to be later than is suggested by written texts, which are more open than spoken varieties to standardizing influences.

13 We shall see (Section **5.2.1**) that these pronunciations are also widespread in Spanish America, as they are in rural Castilian varieties which otherwise do not retain an initial aspirate (< F-).

14 These maps show bilabial [ɸ] in almost all localities in the words under discussion (variants of *fuente, fuelle, fue*, etc.), while in cases where an initial voiceless labial is followed by a full vowel (e.g., *hecho*, map 1485), labiodental [f] is the normal transcription in those words which retain local form.

15 Retention of /mb/ has not been entirely extinguished even in more central Castilian areas, since the descendant of LAMBERE appears as *lamber* in much of Old Castile and elsewhere (see García de Diego 1916, 1950).

16 Ray Harris-Northall (personal communication) points out that the reason for this bunching of isoglosses may lie in the internal migrations responsible for establishing the various '*Polas*' (= *Puebla* 'settlement' elsewhere, e.g. Pola de Siero, Alande, Lena, etc.), and/or in the migration towards the expanding ports, such as that of Llanes, whose name (if a reflex of PLANĀS) may have been imposed by immigrants from central Asturias. See also Lapesa (1951: 206).

17 Mass-nouns are those which denote concepts which are uncountable (non-discrete), such as substances in indeterminate quantity (e.g., *leche* 'milk') or abstracts. Count-nouns are those which refer to countable (discrete) objects. Mass-nouns cannot be preceded by indefinite articles or numerals, since these classes of words are semantically compatible only with words which refer to countable concepts.

18 The case-determined system is not usually deemed to require explanation, since the values assigned to pronouns in this system are directly inherited from Latin. That is, direct-object *lo(s)* and *la(s)* continue the Latin direct-object (accusative) forms ILLUM, ILLAM, ILLŌS, ILLĀS, while the indirect-object forms *le, les* likewise continue the Latin indirect-object (dative) forms ILLĪ, ILLĪS. For this reason, this system is sometimes labelled 'etymological'.

19 *Leísmo* is the use of the pronoun *le* or *les* to refer to a masculine direct object (as well as to an indirect object). *Laísmo* is the use of the pronoun *la* or *las* to refer to a feminine indirect object (as well as to a direct object). *Loísmo* is the use of the pronoun *lo* or *los* to refer to a masculine (usually inanimate) indirect object (as well as to a direct object).

   In the examples that follow, the clitic pronoun is characterized as having a selection of the following properties: [+direct] = referent is the direct object of the clause, [-direct] = referent is the indirect object of the clause, [+animate] = referent is animate,

[-animate] = referent is inanimate, [+count] = referent is a count-noun, [-count] = referent is a mass-noun], [+masc] = referent is a masculine noun, [-masc] = referent is a feminine noun.

20 Note that non-countable nouns (mass-nouns) are necessarily inanimate and that such referents rarely function as indirect objects.

21 The *laísmo* inherent in this system is the element of it which receives the greatest attention and which is most strongly condemned in normative grammars, and therefore in schools, but it constantly breaks through to the surface in the speech of even the well-educated, including occasionally in writing.

22 Elcock's transcriptions are here converted into the corresponding IPA symbols. Note that IPA [c] indicates a voiceless palatal plosive.

23 In Cantabrian dialects which display metaphony, and perhaps in others, high tonic vowels in words containing final /-u/ or /-i/ are centralized, as are the final vowels themselves (centralization is here arbitrarily symbolized by /ı/ and /ʊ/). Thus, the tonic vowel of /pítʊ/ 'whistle' and /sústʊ/ 'fright' undergoes this treatment, a slightly aberrant form of metaphony, and such centralized vowels contrast significantly with non-centralized vowels. See Penny (1970a: 64; 1978: 30). Realization of metaphonized variants of /á/ are very diverse in northern Spain. Not only may metaphonized /á/ be fronted to /é/ or backed to /ó/, as occurs in central Asturias, but in Cantabria the result of metaphony of /á/ is a partially raised and fronted vowel, similar to the English /æ/ of *hat*. See Penny (1970a: 62; 1978: 30).

24 'Underlying' forms are ones which are thought to have this shape in the lexicon of speakers of these dialects. They are established on the assumption that, before the operation of metaphony, the form concerned contains the same vowel as related words. Thus /lóbu/ 'wolf' is hypothesized on the basis of /lóba/ 'she-wolf', /lobéθnu/ 'wolf-cub', /lobáda/ 'wolf-pack', etc.

25 Examples are from the Pasiego dialect (Penny 1970a: 63).

26 See Section **4.1.2.2** for the appearance of this more complex system of final vowels in northern areas of the Peninsula. The history of the contrast between final /u/ and /o/ is considered, with different conclusions, by Hall (1968) and Penny (1970b).

27 The presence of a handful of words in Castilian such as *tribu, casi*, etc. scarcely constitutes an exception, since all such words are recent borrowings from other languages, including Latin.

28 There is some evidence (see Penny 1992–3b) that feminine mass-nouns are morphologically marked, with final /-e/, in some Asturian varieties. In these cases (e.g., *sidre* (Cast. *sidra*) 'cider', *yedre* (Cast. *yedra*) 'ivy'), there is the possibility that the Latin first-declension Gen.-Dat. ending -AE, with the partitive sense of indeterminate quantity, has in these cases survived (with the predicted shape, /-e/) and has become the base form in the case of those nouns of this class which have no [+countable] sense.

29 For the broad distribution of isoglosses in the Peninsula, see Baldinger (1972), Lleal (1990), Muñoz Cortés (1992).

30 Although in Eastern Catalan (including that of Barcelona and the Balearic Islands) Latin ē results in /ε/, the Western Catalan result, which includes the Valencian area in which we are interested, is /e/ (Badía 1951: 137).

31 This was probably the value of the spoken Latin construction HABEO CANTĀTUM, before it evolved (in most areas) to its present perfect value ('I have sung'), and long before it acquired (in much of Italy and France) a past perfective value ('I sang').

32 However, the southern third of Portugal, including the Algarve, does show reduction of /ei/ to /e/.

33 The diphthong /ou/ remains (in relevant words) in western Asturias, far western Leon and in northern Portugal. Despite the spelling *pouco* of standard Portuguese, /ou/ has been reduced to /o/ in Southern and Central Portuguese, including the standard variety of the language.

34 A separate matter is the secondary loss of N in Catalan when it becomes word-final through loss of a final vowel (e.g., PLĒNU > Cat. *ple*) (Badía 1951: 225).

35 It is not claimed here that the distribution of features in this continuum was the same at different periods (although some isoglosses appear to have been remarkably stable over time). It is merely claimed, it is hoped uncontentiously, that isoglosses (whatever features they corresponded to) were randomly scattered across the territory concerned, and were not bunched into 'dialect frontiers'. Account should also be taken of the fact that a certain portion of Christian Spain was not Romance-speaking, since Basque was well established in the western Pyrenees and much surrounding territory. Indeed the incipient state of Navarre, with its centre at Pamplona, was probably largely Basque-speaking throughout the period under discussion here (eighth–fifteenth centuries).

36 Indeed, the north–south migratory movement did not stop with the completion of the Reconquest in 1492. The discovery of America in that very year encouraged a continuation of the resettlement process, bringing northerners to the emigration ports of Andalusia (Seville, Cádiz, etc.) before moving on to the Americas (see Chapter **5**). Many presumably remained in Andalusia.

37 See also Penny (1999).

38 The inflected infinitive probably descends from the Latin imperfect subjunctive. For discussion, see Williams (1962: 181–4).

39 Galician *seseo*, referred to in note a to Table **4.9**, appears to have an independent origin from that of the corresponding standard Portuguese phonemic merger. It carries low prestige and characterizes rural rather than urban speech, by contrast with the status of this merger in Portugal.

40 E.g., /óʃo/ *ocho* (< OCTŌ) 'eight'.

41 The parallel reduction of /ei/ to /e/ (e.g., *primeiro* > /priméro/) was somewhat less successful in its northward spread, leaving much of central (as well as northern) Portugal unaffected.

42 For further discussion of this chronology, see Alonso (1962c), Penny (1976).

43 Much speculation has revolved around the motive for this merger, but it perhaps requires little explanation, since contrast between dental and dento-alveolar fricatives is difficult to maintain and their merger is common to all of Western Romance except for Peninsular Spanish (Galmés 1962). The question, rather, is how Peninsular Spanish managed to retain both phonemes, to which the answer is by rapidly shifting the dental /s̪/ to interdental /θ/.

44 For the history and geography of *seseo* and *ceceo*, see *ALEA* (1962–73), Alonso (1967c), Alvar (1982), Frago (1992a, 1993), Lapesa (1957), Navarro *et al.* (1933).

45 A word-final consonant forms the onset of the next syllable if the following word begins with a vowel: standard /las#óstras/ = [la-sós-tras] (where # signals a morpheme boundary).

46 Certain theoretically possible sequences (/sθ/, /sʎ/, /sɲ/) are omitted, either because

they are rare in Andalusian Spanish (/θ/ and /ʎ/ are restricted to peripheral areas of Andalusia) or rare, morpheme-initially, in any variety of Spanish (/ɲ/). The forms transcribed as examples of 'loss' are those typical of eastern Andalusia, and take into account modification of vowel qualities caused by /-s/-deletion (see **4.1.7.2.5**).

47   Since /i/ and /u/ are effectively excluded from final syllables (i.e., those which carry the morphological information under discussion), they are not involved in this process of split. In the case of /a/, it is not differential tongue-height which provides the basis of the split, since /a/ in Spanish is always maximally low; it is the small difference between fronted and backed variants of /a/, initially conditioned by the phonetic environment, which forms the basis of the split.

48   Although phonetically the tonic vowel of forms like /pítɔ/ *pitos*, /múlæ/ *mulas* is noticeably lower than that of /píto/ *pito*, /múla/ *mula*, it is impossible to argue for separate phonemes /ɪ/ and /ʊ/, since such lowering is never the sole feature by which plurals are distinguished from singulars (or second-person verbs from third-person). For further discussion of the issues here, see López Morales (1984), Salvador (1977), Zubizarreta (1979).

49   See *ALEA* (1962–73, VI: maps 1822–33). This discussion ignores the fact that Spanish, being a PRO-drop language, allows the subject pronoun to be absent, since the verbal ending fully identifies the subject.

50   Unless one takes the view, hard to defend, that a single isogloss can constitute a linguistic boundary. In this case, the isogloss concerned is that which separates the area where /ɛ/ and /ɔ/ (e.g., in *pedra* and *porta*) are the reflexes of spoken Latin /ɛ/ and /ɔ/ from that where these vowels are diphthongized > /ié/ and /ué/ respectively (as in *piedra* and *puerta*).

51   For further discussion of these isoglosses and a possible explanation of their distribution, see Penny (1999).

52   For the extension of Castilian to the Canaries, and the characteristics of Canarian Spanish, see Almeida and Díaz Alayón (1988), Alvar (1972, 1996a: 325–38), Echenique (1992), Martinell Gifre (1992).

5   Variation in Spanish America

1   In the discussion which follows, it will sometimes be necessary to identify particular features as belonging to the speech of specific countries. This will be done only in order to paint a broad picture, or because full geographical information is lacking, and should not be taken as a contradiction of what is said in this paragraph.

2   See Lipski (1994: 155–9) for a full description of this project and the publications resulting from it.

3   Lope Blanch (1992) sensibly warns against overemphasis on the uniformity of American Spanish by comparison with Peninsular Spanish, while recognizing the linguistic unity of the region.

4   The main exception to this statement is the reduction of atonic vowels in the Spanish of the Mexican plateau and the Andean Altiplano. In these regions, the vowels concerned frequently lose many of their characteristics, merging in [ə] and often disappearing. For principles of feature distribution in Spanish America, see Resnick (1975, 1976).

5   One such phonetic feature is the marked fronting of velars before palatal vowels (/e/ and /i/) in many varieties of Chilean Spanish, so that words like *gente, guerra* have

mid-palatal initial consonants, often with a palatal on-glide before the syllabic nucleus: [çénte], [ʝéra] [çʲénte], [ʝʲéra].

6   To outsiders, for whom /ṣ/ was associated with the letter ç and /s/ with s or ss, this merger of these two phonemes in /ṣ/ was seen as an 'inappropriate use of the letter ç', therefore called çeçeo. A parallel perception, similarly based on a pre-modern perception that letters are more important than sounds, took place in the case of the equivalent voiced sounds: to outsiders, for whom /ʑ/ was associated with the letter z and /z/ with single intervocalic s, this Andalusian merger of /ʑ/ and /z/ in /ʑ/ was seen as an 'inappropriate use of the letter z', and was called zezeo.

7   Claudia Parodi (1995) finds no examples of contrast between /s/ and /z/ in documents written in the New World in the first quarter of the sixteenth century.

8   Controversially, Rocío Caravedo (1992) claims that functional contrast between /s/ and /θ/ has 'survived' in Peru. On the basis of interviews carried out in preparation for a linguistic atlas, she identifies two widely separated Andean varieties (Cajamarca in the north and Cuzco in the south) in which words with 'historical /θ/' show substantial proportions of pronunciations of an interdental kind ([θ]), while words with 'historical /s/' show small proportions of [θ]. If this statistical pattern of 'contrasts' is accepted as evidence of survival of a phonological opposition between /θ/ and /s/ in Peru, an argument will need to be constructed to explain how a contrast which came to have this form only in the sixteenth century (in central/northern Spain) came to be spread to these remote areas when areas which were in much closer contact with the Peninsula show no sign of this contrast.

9   See **3.1.3** for a discussion of the way in which certain northern Castilian features were established in Madrid, at the expense of traditional counterparts associated with Toledo.

10   For a detailed examination, in this spirit, of three American areas of settlement (Buenos Aires, Tucumán, and Costa Rica), see Fontanella de Weinberg (1992). For discussion of the social origins of American settlers, see Frago Gracia (1992b).

11   This weakening of /ʝ/, under these circumstances, is also characteristic of Judeo-Spanish and is therefore likely to have been in use in the Peninsula at the end of the fifteenth century (see **6.3**).

12   However, on the Caribbean and Pacific coasts of Colombia, one finds devoicing of (at least) /b/ and /g/ when preceded by aspirated /-s/: [rahúɲo] rasguño, [laʰ ɸáka] las vacas (Alvar 1996b: 136–7). Likewise, in lowland Bolivia /sb/ is realized as [ɸ] both word-internally and at word boundaries (represented by spellings refaloso, defelo, mafién, for resbaloso, desvelo, más bien (Alvar 1996b: 176).

13   This hierarchy is based upon data cited in Lipski (1994: 169, 189, 199, 210–11, 232, 239, 258, 265, 271, 282–3, 291, 299–300, 309, 320, 321–2, 334, 340–1, 350–1).

14   However, velarization of word-internal /-n/ is characteristic of the Dominican Republic. See references in Lipski (1994: 238).

15   Total loss of nasal quality in the final syllable naturally implies identity of third-person plural verbs with their singular counterparts. However, this merger, where it occurs, appears to be tolerated.

16   See the following paragraphs for discussion of the development of the (historically) second-person plural verbal endings.

17   It should not be forgotten that most varieties of Peninsular Spanish maintained the expanded form Vosotros (together with one type of second-person plural verb endings

– see later in this section) for plural familiar address, in contrast to *Ustedes*, a distinction which was abandoned in American Spanish (see **5.1.1.2**).

18 For details of the geography of *voseo* within these countries, and of the sociolinguistic variation there between *voseo* and *tuteo*, see Alvar (1996b) and Lipski (1994).

19 For further discussion of the development of these verb forms, see Blaylock (1986), Dworkin (1988, 1988–9), Rini (1996).

20 We do not include in this discussion such combinations as *Vos cantabas, Vos cantaras*, etc., since in these (originally proparoxytonic) verb-forms we have argued that the *Vos* forms have become identical to the *Tú* forms: recall *(Vos) cantávades > cantabas = (Tú) cantabas*. A further complication is that second-conjugation V1 and V2 forms (see Table **5.1**) sometimes have the shape *volvís*, etc., identical with third-conjugation *salís*. These forms are usually highly stigmatized, and have fairly certainly been inherited from rural Peninsular varieties, where there is frequent merger of the second-plural endings of *-er* and *-ir* verbs (for example, in Andalusia, usually with preference for *-éis* (see Mondéjar 1970: 68–9), and in Cantabria, with preference for *-is* (see Penny 1970a: 122–3)).

21 These pronunciations are now highly recessive, and occur in just a few points in western Navarre.

22 For a detailed discussion of the sounds involved, and of the historical connection between the Peninsular and the American pronunciations, see Alonso (1967d).

23 For sociolinguistic distribution of these features in Mexico, see Rissel (1989).

24 The glosses used are drawn from British English, which can be seen to show a close parallelism, in its use of the simple past and the present perfect, to the Peninsular usages described in this section. The reader will later recognize that American English differs from British English, in this regard, in approximately the same way that American Spanish differs from most varieties of Peninsular Spanish.

25 For women's speech in the Hispanic world, see Martín Zorraquino (1994).

26 For the social and cultural origins of Spanish settlers in America, see Rosenblat (1973).

27 This is not the place to discuss in detail the origins of pidgins and creoles, which can be observed world-wide. The grammatical structures of creoles used on opposite sides of the globe have certain striking similarities, which led some to postulate a common origin for all. This monogenetic theory, to which few now subscribe, usually cites Portuguese-based creole as the *ur*-form, relexified in a variety of colonized areas under the impact of the main colonial language used in each. On the other hand, the similarities among creoles have been explained as being due to the (postulated) fact that all humans carry genetically programmed linguistic rules which surface when they are deprived of input from any full language (the bioprogram theory of creole origins).

28 Although reportedly frictionless, a voiced mid-palatal phoneme /j/ should be added to the list in Table **5.3**, rather than regarding [j] (in *yerba* 'grass', *yen* 'full') as a realization of /i/.

29 For data on Palenquero, but not always for their interpretation, we rely heavily on Patiño Rosselli (1983).

6   Variation in Judeo-Spanish

1 However, Judeo-Spanish writing in the Low Countries used the Latin alphabet and followed Peninsular norms.

2   For the historical background to the expulsion, see Harris (1994), Lleal (1992), Wexler (1977).

3   We have seen (**5.4.1**) that some of these Jews, somewhat later, reached Curaçao, and may have contributed to the development of Papiamentu.

4   Although standardizing pressures were almost totally absent from Judeo-Spanish, some pressure was perhaps exercised by the Hebrew–Spanish biblical translations published from the mid-sixteenth century onwards (e.g., the Ferrara bible of 1553, see Hassán 1994), and by French-influenced forms of Judeo-Spanish used by those educated in the schools of the Alliance Israélite Universelle in a large number of Ottoman or ex-Ottoman cities from the late nineteenth century on (Lleal 1992: 33). This latter pressure was also responsible for emphasizing the lexical distance between Judeo-Spanish, on the one hand, and Peninsular and American Spanish, on the other, since the Judeo-Spanish vocabulary of high culture is drawn almost exclusively from French, as are many other neologisms, while the corresponding vocabulary of other varieties of Spanish is drawn from different sources, chiefly Graeco-Latin.

5   The reverse analogy, whereby verbal *-mos* is changed to *-nos*, is widely found in nonstandard American-Spanish usage.

6   This change is genuinely phonological, and not merely graphical: *ni* represents /ni/ rather than /ɲ/, by contrast with pre-literary Peninsular usage, where *ni* could represent /ɲ/.

7   Recall that Peninsular Spanish *(vosotros) cantasteis* developed from *cantastes* only in the late sixteenth and seventeenth centuries, analogically with the large majority of Peninsular non-deferential second-person plural forms, which by then were marked by [-įs]. This change, evidently, took place too late to affect Judeo-Spanish.

8   We have already seen (**6.3.1(8)**) that Judeo-Spanish expanded its inventory of sibilants by introducing a contrast between fricative /ʒ/ and affricate /dʒ/. See **6.3.3(1)** for a discussion of the full Judeo-Spanish sibilant system.

9   Some varieties of Judeo-Spanish made this system fully symmetrical by the introduction of a voiceless dental affricate /tˢ/, through the adoption of Romanian loans which contained this unit (Lleal 1992: 34).

10 Lleal (1992: 30) comments on the low frequency of *haber* + participle constructions in Judeo-Spanish, and in the texts she provides there are numerous cases of preterite verbforms used where the situation would demand a perfect in standard Castilian, e.g., *Esta fuente que **sintió** munchas vezes mis suspiros core dulsemente y vagarozamente y emboracha mi corasón de amor.*

7   Standardisation

1   Following Weinreich, Labov and Herzog (1968), it has become a maxim of sociolinguistics that no change can take place except through the mechanism of variation, but that an instance of variation does not necessarily imply that change is in progress. However, it is likely that cases of apparently stable variation are instances where change has for some reason been arrested, either in its progress across a territory, or in its advance from speaker to speaker in the same locality, or even in its progress through the lexicon.

2   However, the effects of standardization in Spain were not felt in Judeo-Spanish, as we have already seen (**6.3.5**).

3   Until the middle of the twentieth century, repeated comparisons were made between
    the fragmentation of Latin into the Romance languages and the potential fragmenta-
    tion of Spanish. This worry appears to have vanished, in a Spanish-speaking world in
    which travel is easy, and in which communication and media interchange are constant.

4   *Status planning* should be distinguished from the specification of a language as *official* in
    a given territory. Official status is conferred by legislators, not grammarians, and con-
    cerns the rights and duties of citizens to use the language so specified in particular
    domains. For discussion of the official status of Spanish, see Stewart (1999), Mar-
    Molinero (forthcoming).

5   Some of these features later underwent further development, such as /h/-dropping
    (**3.1.3.2**, **4.1.7.2.3**), deaffrication and fronting of /ts/ (**3.1.3.1**, **4.1.7.2.1**), velarization
    of palatal sibilants (**3.1.3.1**).

6   Valdés (1966: 1) has his main interlocutor, Marcio, refer to him as 'cortés y bien criado',
    confirmation that he claims to belong to powerful and wealthy circles.

7   Late medieval England had seen the production of simple guides to the use of French,
    designed for an increasingly anglicized English aristocracy, but these do not merit the
    description of grammars.

8   Speakers (e.g., in Australia and Africa) who do not feel that they belong to any political
    unit most often lack a name for their language, referring to it by expressions meaning
    '(our) talk, speech', etc. (Lloyd 1991). The name *English* is probably not typical, in that
    it was apparently in use before there existed a political entity named *England*. However,
    it is likely that it referred to a group of political entities perceived as having a common
    history and similar culture.

9   The exceptions were the minorities who spoke Basque or Arabic. Both minorities must
    have been small, but it is impossible to assess their real proportions.

10 Some caution is required in dating the vocalization of syllable-final /b/, since medieval
    spelling had no means of distinguishing [ɥ] from [β] (or either from [u]), so that
    spellings of the type *caudal* may simply indicate that the syllable-final element was a
    fricative, namely [β]. Following the introduction of printing, and the distinction there-
    after established between <u> and <v>, we can be sure that the vocalization has taken
    place.

11 There may be differences in this regard between Peninsular and American Spanish,
    since loss of /d/ gives the impression of being less frequent among educated American
    Spanish speakers than among their Peninsular counterparts.

12 Loss of word-final /d/ at these social levels makes it impossible to determine the
    history of the imperative ending /-á/, /-é/, /-í/ (cf. standard *cantad, comed, salid*), cor-
    responding in Spain to the non-deferential second-person plural (*vosotros*), and in
    American areas of *voseo* to the corresponding second-person singular (*vos*) (**5.1.2.5**).
    Are we dealing with loss of /-d/ from earlier /-ád/, /-éd/, /-íd/, or with persistence of
    the late-medieval and early-modern /-á/, /-é/, /-í/ (e.g., Golden Age *cantá, comé, salí*),
    probably from earlier /-áe/ <./-áde/, etc.?

13 What are now recessive, rural articulations ([ɸwé], [ʍwé], etc.) may in the Middle Ages
    have been general at all social levels in Castile; see Penny (1972b, 1990).

References

Abbreviations

AO	*Archivum*
BHS	*Bulletin of Hispanic Studies*
BIDEA	*Boletín del Instituto de Estudios Asturianos*
BRAE	*Boletín de la Real Academia Española*
BRH	Biblioteca Románica Hispánica
CSIC	Consejo Superior de Estudios Científicos
HR	*Hispanic Review*
ICC	Instituto Caro y Cuervo
JHP	*Journal of Hispanic Philology*
JHR	*Journal of Hispanic Research*
L	*Language*
LEA	*Lingüística Española Actual*
MLR	*Modern Language Review*
NRFH	*Nueva Revista de Filología Hispánica*
O	*Orbis*
PMLA	*Publications of the Modern Language Association of America*
RDTP	*Revista de Dialectología y Tradiciones Populares*
REL	*Revista Española de Lingüística*
RF	*Romanische Forschungen*
RFE	*Revista de Filología Española*
RLiR	*Revue de Linguistique Romane*
RPh	*Romance Philology*
TPS	*Transactions of the Philological Society*
UNAM	Universidad Nacional Autónoma de México
Univ.	University, Universidad, etc.
VR	*Vox Romanica*
Wd	*Word*
ZRP	*Zeitschrift für Romanische Philologie*

Agard, Frederick B., 1990. 'The Place of Aragonese and Asturo-Leonese in Iberian Romance', in *Homenaje a Jorge A. Suárez*, ed. Beatriz Garza

Cuarón and Paulette Levy (Mexico City: El Colegio de México), pp. 69–84.

Aitchison, Jean, 1991. *Language Change: Progress or Decay?*, 2nd edn, Cambridge Approaches to Linguistics (Cambridge: Cambridge University Press).

Alarcos Llorach, Emilio, 1947. 'Perfecto simple y compuesto en español', *RFE*, 31: 108–39.

—— 1951. 'La lengua de los *Proverbios morales* de don Sem Tob', *RFE*, 25: 249–309.

—— 1964. 'Sobre la metafonía asturiana y su antigüedad', in *Simposium sobre cultura asturiana de la alta edad media [septiembre de 1961]* (Oviedo: Ayuntamiento), pp. 331–40.

ALEA, 1962–73. Manuel Alvar, Antonio Llorente, and Gregorio Salvador, *Atlas lingüístico-etnográfico de Andalucía*, 12 vols. (Madrid: CSIC).

ALEANR, 1979–83. Manuel Alvar, with A. Llorente, T. Buesa and Elena Alvar, *Atlas lingüístico y etnográfico de Aragón, Navarra y Rioja*, 12 vols. (Saragossa: Departamento de Geografía Lingüística, Institución Fernando el Católico de la Excma. Diputación Provincial de Zaragoza, CSIC).

ALEC, 1981–3. Luis Flórez, *Atlas lingüístico-etnográfico de Colombia*, 6 vols (Bogotá: ICC).

ALECa, 1995. Manuel Alvar, C. Alvar and J. A. Mayoral, *Atlas lingüístico y etnográfico de Cantabria*, 2 vols. (Madrid: Arco / Libros).

ALEICan, 1975–8. Manuel Alvar, *Atlas lingüístico y etnográfico de las Islas Canarias*, 3 vols (Las Palmas de Gran Canaria: Excmo. Cabildo Insular de Gran Canaria).

Alemán, Mateo, 1950. *Ortografía castellana*, ed. José Rojas Garcidueñas and Tomás Navarro Tomás (Mexico City: El Colegio de México).

ALESuCh, 1973. Guillermo Araya, Constantino Contreras, Claudio Wagner, and Mario Bernales, *Atlas lingüístico-etnográfico del sur de Chile*, vol. I (Valdivia: Instituto de Filología de la Universidad Austral de Chile and Editorial Andrés Bello).

ALF, 1903–10. Jules Gilliéron and Edmond Edmont, *Atlas linguistique de la France* (Paris: Champion).

ALM, 1990–4. Juan M. Lope Blanch, *et al.*, *Atlas lingüístico de México*, vols. I–II, *Fonética*, 1–2 (Mexico City: El Colegio de México and Fondo de Cultura Económica).

Almeida, Manuel, and Carmen Díaz Alayón, 1988. *El español de Canarias* (Santa Cruz de Tenerife: Univ.).

Alonso, Amado, 1943. *Castellano, español, idioma nacional: historia espiritual de tres nombres*, 2nd edn (Buenos Aires: Losada).

—— 1967a. 'La LL y sus alteraciones en España y América', in Alonso 1967e: 159–212. [Repr. from *Estudios dedicados a Menéndez Pidal*, vol. II (Madrid: CSIC, 1951), pp. 41–89.]

1967b. *De la pronunciación medieval a la moderna en español*, vol. I, ed. Rafael Lapesa, BRH (Madrid: Gredos).

1967c. 'Orígenes del seseo americano', in Alsono 1967e: 84–122.

1967d. 'La pronunciación de "rr" y de "tr" en España y América', in Alonso 1967e: 123–58.

1967e. *Estudios lingüísticos: temas hispanoamericanos*, 3rd edn (Madrid: Gredos).

1969. *De la pronunciación medieval a la moderna en español*, vol. II, 2nd edn, ed. Rafael Lapesa, BRH (Madrid: Gredos).

Alonso, Dámaso, 1962a. 'Ensordecimiento en el norte peninsular de alveolares y palatales fricativas', in Alvar *et al.*, eds. 1962: 88–103.

1962b. 'Metafonía, neutro de materia y colonización suditálica en la Penísula hispánica', in Alvar *et al.*, eds. 1962: 105–54.

1962c. 'B=V, en la península hispánica', in Alvar *et al.*, eds. 1962: 155–209.

ALPI, 1962. *Atlas lingüístico de la Península Ibérica*, vol. I, *Fonética*, 1 (Madrid: CSIC).

Alvar, Manuel, 1953. *El dialecto aragonés*, BRH (Madrid: Gredos).

1961. 'Hacia los conceptos de "lengua", "dialecto" y "hablas"', *NRFH*, 15: 51–60.

1969. *Estructuralismo, geografía lingüística y dialectología actual*, BRH (Madrid: Gredos).

1972. *Niveles socio-culturales en el habla de Las Palmas de Gran Canaria* (Las Palmas: Cabildo Insular de Gran Canaria).

1976. *El dialecto riojano*, 2nd edn, BRH (Madrid: Gredos).

1977 [1980]. 'El atlas lingüístico y etnográfico de la provincia de Santander (España)', *RFE*, 59: 81–118.

1981. 'Atlas et dictionnaires (selon l'Atlas linguistique de Santander)', in *Mélanges de philologie et de toponymie romanes offerts au professeur Henri Guiter* (Barcelona: Lunel), pp. 56–66.

1982. 'A vueltas con el seseo y el ceceo', in *Introducción plural a la gramática histórica*, ed. Francisco Marcos Marín (Madrid: Cincel), pp. 130–44.

Alvar, Manuel, ed., 1996a. *Manual de dialectología hispánica: el español de España* (Barcelona: Ariel).

1996b. *Manual de dialectología hispánica: el español de América* (Barcelona: Ariel).

Alvar, Manuel, A. Badía, R. de Balbín and L. F. Lindley Cintra, eds., 1962. *Enciclopedia Lingüística Hispánica*, vol. I (supplement), *Temas y problemas de la fragmentación fonética peninsular* (Madrid: CSIC).

Alvar, Manuel, and María Pilar Nuño, 1981. 'Un ejemplo de atlas lingüístico automatizado: el *ALES*', *LEA*, 3: 359–74.

Álvarez Fernández-Cañedo, Jesús, 1963. *El habla y la cultura popular de Cabrales*, Anejos de la *RFE*, 76 (Madrid: CSIC).

Badía Margarit, Antonio, 1951. *Gramática histórica catalana* (Barcelona: Noguer).

Baldinger, Kurt, 1972. *La formación de los dominios lingüísticos en la península ibérica,* 2nd edn, BRH (Madrid: Gredos). [Trans. by Emilio Lledó and Montserrat Macau of *Die Herausbildung der Sprachräume auf der Pyrenäenhalbinsel: Querschnitt durch die neueste Forschung und Versuch einer Synthese* (Berlin: Akademie Verlag, 1958).]

Barrera-Vidal, A., 1972. *Parfait simple et parfait composé en castillan moderne* (Munich: Hüber).

Bàrtoli, Matteo, 1945. *Saggi de linguistica spaziale* (Turin: Rosenberg and Sellier).

Bickerton, Derek, and Aquiles Escalante, 1970. 'Palenquero: A Spanish-Based Creole of Northern Colombia', *Lingua,* 32: 254–67.

Blaylock, Curtis, 1986. 'Notes on the Chronology of a Morpho-Phonological Change in Golden-Age Spanish: The Loss of -d- in Proparoxytonic Forms of the Second Person Plural Verbs', *HR,* 54: 279–85.

Boléo, Manuel de Paiva, 1974. *Estudos de linguística portuguesa e românica,* vol. I, *Dialectologia e história da língua,* 1, Actas Universitatis Conimbrigensis (Coimbra: Univ.).

Borrego Nieto, J., 1981. *Sociolingüística rural: investigación en Villadepera de Sayago,* Studia Philologica Salmanticensia, Anejos, Estudios, 3 (Salamanca: Univ.).

— 1983. *Norma y dialecto en el sayagués actual,* Studia Philologica Salmanticensia, Anejos, Estudios, 11 (Salamanca: Univ.).

Borrego, Nieto, J., *et al.,* 1978. 'Sobre el tú y el usted', *Studia Philologica Salmanticensia,* 2: 53–69.

Boyd-Bowman, Peter, 1956. 'Regional Origins of the Earliest Spanish Colonists of America', *PMLA,* 71: 1152–72.

— 1963. 'La emigración peninsular a América 1520–1539', *Historia Mexicana,* 13: 165–92.

— 1964. *Índice geobiográfico de 40.000 pobladores españoles de América en el siglo XVI, 1493–1519,* vol. I (Bogotá: ICC).

— 1968. *Índice geobiográfico de 40.000 pobladores españoles de América en el siglo XVI, 1493–1519,* vol. II (Mexico City: Jus).

— 1972. 'La emigración española a América: 1540–1579', in *Studia hispanica in honorem R. Lapesa,* vol. II (Madrid: Gredos).

— 1973. *Patterns of Spanish Emigration to the New World (1493–1580),* Council on International Studies, Special Studies, 34 (Buffalo: State University of New York at Buffalo).

Canellada, María Josefa, 1944. *El bable de Cabranes,* Anejos de la *RFE,* 31 (Madrid: CSIC).

Canfield, D. Lincoln, 1981. *Spanish Pronunciation in the Americas* (Chicago and London: University of Chicago Press).

Caravedo, Rocío, 1992. '¿Restos de la distinción /s/ y /θ/ en el español del Perú?', *RFE,* 72: 639–54.

Carvalho, J. G. Herculano de, 1952. 'Porque se falam dialectos leoneses em terras de Miranda?', *Revista Portuguesa de Filologia*, 5: 265–81.

1958. *Fonologia mirandesa*, vol. I (Coimbra: Univ.).

Catalán Menéndez Pidal, Diego, and Álvaro Galmés de Fuentes, 1946. 'Un límite lingüístico', *RDTP*, 2: 196–239.

Chambers, J. K., and Peter Trudgill, 1980. *Dialectology*, Cambridge Textbooks in Linguistics (Cambridge: Cambridge University Press).

Clavería Nadal, Gloria, 1991. *El latinismo en español* (Bellaterra: Departament de Filologia Espanyola, Facultat de Lletres, Universitat Autònoma de Barcelona).

Comrie, Bernard, 1976. *Aspect: An Introduction to the Study of Verbal Aspect and Related Problems* (Cambridge: Cambridge University Press).

Corominas, Joan, and José A. Pascual, 1980–91. *Diccionario crítico etimológico castellano e hispánico*, 6 vols. (Madrid: Gredos).

Correas, Gonzalo, 1954. *Arte de la lengua española castellana*, ed. Emilio Alarcos Llorach, Anejos de la RFE, 56 (Madrid: CSIC).

1971. *Ortografía kastellana*, facsimile edn (Madrid: Espasa-Calpe).

Cravens, Thomas D., 1991. 'Phonology, Phonetics, and Orthography in Late Latin and Romance: The Evidence for Early Intervocalic Sonorization', in *Latin and the Romance Languages in the Early Middle Ages*, ed. Roger Wright (London: Routledge), pp. 52–68.

DeMello, George, 1993. '-Ra vs. -se Subjunctive: A New Look at an Old Topic', *Hispania*, 76: 235–44.

Díaz Castañón, María del Pilar, 1957. 'La inflexión metafonética en el concejo de Carreño', *Trabajos sobre el dominio románico leonés*, vol. I, ed. Álvaro Galmés de Fuentes (Madrid: Gredos), pp. 13–22.

Dworkin, Steven N., 1988. 'The Diffusion of a Morphological Change: The Reduction of the Old Spanish Verbal Suffixes -ades, -edes and -ides', *Medioevo Romanzo*, 13: 223–36.

1988–9. 'The Interaction of Phonological and Morphological Processes: The Evolution of the Old Spanish Second Person Plural Verb Endings', *RPh*, 42: 144–55.

Echenique, María Teresa, 1992. 'Spanisch: Areallinguistik III, Kanarisch (Áreas lingüísticas III, Canarias)', in *Lexikon der Romanistischen Linguistik (LRL)*, ed. Günter Holtus, Michael Metzeltin and Christian Schmitt, VI, 1, *Aragonesisch/Navarresisch, Spanisch, Asturianisch/Leonesisch* (Tübingen: Niemeyer), pp. 522–5.

Elcock, W. D., 1938. *De quelques affinités entre l'aragonais et le béarnais* (Paris: Droz).

Entwistle, William J., 1962. *The Spanish Language together with Portuguese, Catalan and Basque*, edn rev. by W. D. Elcock (London: Faber).

Espinosa, Aurelio M., hijo, 1930. *Estudios sobre el español de Nuevo México*, vol. I, *Fonética*, trans. and expanded by Amado Alonso and Ángel Rosenblat,

Biblioteca de Dialectología Hispanoamericana, 1 (Buenos Aires: Instituto de Filología).

1946. *Estudios sobre el español de Nuevo México*, vol. II, *Morfología*, trans. and expanded, with notes, by Ángel Rosenblat, Biblioteca de Dialectología Hispanoamericana, 6 (Buenos Aires: Instituto de Filología).

Ferguson, Charles A., 1959. 'Diglossia', *Word*, 15: 325–40. [Repr. in Dell H. Hymes, ed., *Language in Culture and Society* (New York: Harper and Row, 1964), pp. 429–39, and in P. P. Giglioli, ed., *Language and Social Context* (Harmondsworth: Penguin, 1972), pp. 232–51.]

Fernández González, Ángel R., 1959. *El habla y la cultura popular de Oseja de Sajambre* (Oviedo: Instituto de Estudios Asturianos).

Fernández-Ordóñez, Inés, 1994. 'Isoglosas internas del castellano: el sistema referencial del pronombre átono de tercera persona', *RFE*, 74: 71–125.

forthcoming. 'Leísmo, laísmo y loísmo', in Ignacio Bosque and Violeta Demonte, eds., *Nueva gramática descriptiva de la lengua española*, Colección Nebrija y Bello (Real Academia Española) (Madrid: Espasa-Calpe).

Fishman, Joshua A., 1971. *Sociolinguistics: A Brief Introduction* (Rowley, Mass.: Newbury House).

Fontanella de Weinberg, María Beatriz, 1978. 'Un cambio lingüístico en marcha: las palatales del español bonaerense', *O*, 27: 215–47.

1992. 'Variedades conservadoras e innovadoras del español en América durante el período colonial', *RFE*, 72: 361–77.

Frago Gracia, Juan Antonio, 1977–8. 'Para la historia de la velarización española', *AO*, 27–8: 219–25.

1983. 'El reajuste fonológico del español moderno en su preciso contexto histórico: sobre la evolución /š ž/ > /x/', in *Serta Philologica F. Lázaro Carreter*, vol. I, *Estudios de lingüística y lengua literaria*, ed. E. Alarcos *et al.* (Madrid: Cátedra).

1985. 'De los fonemas medievales /š ž/ al interdental fricativo /θ/ del español moderno', in *Philologica Hispaniensia in Honorem Manuel Alvar*, vol. II (Madrid: Gredos), pp. 205–16.

1989. '¿Sólo grietas en el edificio del reajuste fonológico?', *LEA*, 11: 125–43.

1992a. 'El seseo: orígenes y difusión americana', in *Historia del español de América* (Valladolid: Junta de Castilla y León), pp. 113–42.

1992b. 'Variación dialectal y sociocultural en la documentación indiana del siglo XVI', *RFE*, 72: 399–427.

1993. *Historia de las hablas andaluzas* (Madrid: Arco / Libros).

1995. *Andaluz y español de América: historia de un parentesco lingüístico* (Seville: Junta de Andalucía, Consejería de Cultura y Medio Ambiente).

Galmés de Fuentes, Álvaro, 1960. 'Más datos sobre la inflexión metafonética en el centro-sur de Asturias', in *Trabajos sobre el dominio románico leonés*, vol. II, ed. Álvaro Galmés de Fuentes (Madrid: Gredos), pp. 13–25.

1962. *Las sibilantes en la Romania* (Madrid: Gredos).

1983. *Dialectología mozárabe*, BRH (Madrid: Gredos).

García Álvarez, M. T. C., 1955. 'La inflexión vocálica en el bable de Bimenes', *BIDEA*, 9: 123–46.

García Arias, Xosé Lluis, 1988. *Contribución a la gramática histórica de la lengua asturiana y a la caracterización etimológica de su léxico*, Biblioteca de Filoloxía Asturiana, 3 (Oviedo: Univ. and Caja de Ahorros de Asturias).

García de Diego, Vicente, 1916. 'Arcaísmos dialectales', *RFE*, 3: 301–18.

1950. 'El castellano como complejo dialectal y sus dialectos internos', *RFE*, 34: 107–24.

García González, Francisco, 1978. 'El leísmo en Santander', in *Estudios ofrecidos a Emilio Alarcos Llorach*, vol. III (Oviedo: Univ.), pp. 87–101.

1981. '/le (lu), la, lo (lu)/ en el centro-norte de la Península', *Verba*, 8: 347–53.

1981–2. 'La frontera oriental del asturiano: razones históricas de su fijación', *AO*, 31–2: 337–55.

1982. 'La frontera oriental del asturiano', *BRAE*, 62: 173–91.

1989. 'El neutro de materia', in *Homenaje a Alonso Zamora Vicente*, vol. II, *Dialectología, estudios sobre el romancero* (Madrid: Castalia), pp. 91–105.

García Mouton, Pilar, and Francisco Moreno Fernández, 1994. 'Sociolingüística en el Atlas Lingüístico (y etnográfico) de Castilla-La Mancha', in *Actas del Primer Congreso Anglo-Hispano*, vol. I, *Lingüística*, ed. Ralph Penny (Madrid: Castalia), pp. 139–49.

Garvens, F., 1960. 'La metafonía en Cabrales (oriente de Asturias)', *BIDEA*, 14: 241–4.

Giles, Howard, 1973. 'Accent Mobility: A Model and Some Data', *Anthropological Linguistics*, 15: 87–105.

Gimeno Menéndez, Francisco, 1990. *Dialectología y sociolingüística españolas*, 2nd edn (Alicante: Univ.).

1995. *Sociolingüística histórica (siglos X–XII)* (Madrid: Visor Libros / Univ. de Alicante).

Goldsmith, John, 1987. 'Vowel Systems', *Publications of the Chicago Linguistic Circle*, 23: 116–33.

González Ferrero, Juan Carlos, 1986. *Sociolingüística y variación dialectal: estudio del habla de Flores de Aliste* (Zamora: Diputación Provincial).

González Ollé, Fernando, 1960. 'Características fonéticas y léxico del valle de Mena (Burgos)', *BRAE*, 40: 67–85.

Granda Gutiérrez, Germán de, 1960. 'Las vocales finales del dialecto leonés', in *Trabajos sobre el dominio románico leonés*, ed. Álvaro Galmés de Fuentes (Madrid: Gredos), pp. 27–117.

Griera i Gaja, Antoni, 1914. *La frontera catalano-aragonesa: estudi geogràfico-lingüístic*, Biblioteca Filològica de l'Institut de la Llengua Catalana, 4 (Barcelona: Institut d'Estudis Catalans).

Guiter, Enric (Henri), 1983. 'Aproximació lingüística a la cadena càntabro-pirinenca', in *Miscel·lània Aramon i Serra [= Estudis de llengua i literatura catalanes offerts a R. Aramon i Serra en el seu setantè aniversari]*, vol. III (Barcelona: Curial), pp. 247–64.

Gulsoy, Joseph, 1969–70. 'The -i Words in the Poems of Gonzalo de Berceo', *RPh*, 23: 172–87.

Hall, Robert A., Jr., 1968. 'Neuters, Mass-Nouns and the Ablative in Romance', *L*, 44: 480–6.

Halliday, M. A. K., 1978. *Language as Social Semiotic* (London: Arnold).

Harris, J. W., 1969. 'Sound-Change in Spanish and the Theory of Markedness', *L*, 45: 538–52.

Harris, Martin, 1982. 'The "Past Simple" and the "Present Perfect" in Romance', in *Studies in the Romance Verb*, ed. Nigel Vincent and Martin Harris (London: Croom Helm), pp. 42–70.

Harris, Tracy K., 1994. *Death of a Language: The History of Judeo-Spanish* (Newark, Del.: University of Delaware).

Harris-Northall, Ray, 1991. 'Apocope in Alfonsine Texts: A Case-Study', in *Linguistic Studies in Medieval Spanish*, ed. Ray Harris-Northall and Thomas D. Cravens (Madison, Wis.: Hispanic Seminary of Medieval Studies), pp. 29–38.

1996–7. 'Printed Books and Linguistic Standardization in Spain: The 1503 *Gran Conquista de Ultramar*', *RPh*, 50: 123–46.

Hassán, Iacob M., 1988. 'Sistemas gráficos del español sefardí', in *Actas del I Congreso Internacional de Historia de la Lengua Española*, ed. M. Ariza, A. Salvador and A. Viudas, vol. I (Madrid: Arco/Libros), pp. 127–37.

Hassán, Iacob M., ed., 1994. *Introducción a la Biblia de Ferrara: actas del simposio internacional sobre la biblia de Ferrara (Sevilla, 25–28 noviembre de 1991)* (Seville and Madrid: Universidad de Sevilla and CSIC).

Haugen, Einar, 1972. 'Dialect, Language, Nation', in *Sociolinguistics: Selected Readings*, ed. J. B. Pride and Janet Holmes (Harmondsworth: Penguin), pp. 97–111. [Repr. from *American Anthropologist*, 68 (1966): 922–35.]

Henríquez Ureña, Pedro, 1921. 'Observaciones sobre el español de América', *RFE*, 8: 357–90.

1932. *Sobre el problema del andalucismo dialectal de América* (Buenos Aires: Hernando).

1940. *El español en Santo Domingo*, Biblioteca de Dialectología Hispanoamericana, 5 (Buenos Aires: Instituto de Filología, 1940). [Reprinted, Santo Domingo: Taller, 1975.]

Hernández, Francisco J., 1989. 'Language and Cultural Identity: The Mozarabs of Toledo', *Boletín Burriel*, 1: 29–48.

Hodcroft, F. W., 1993–4. '"¿A mí un él?": Observations on *vos* and *él/ella* as Forms of Address in Peninsular Spanish', *JHR*, 2: 1–16.

Holmquist, Jonathan Carl, 1988. *Language Loyalty and Linguistic Variation: A*

Study in Spanish Cantabria, Topics in Sociolinguistics, 3 (Dordrecht: Foris).

Hualde, José Ignacio, 1989. 'Autosegmental and Metrical Spreading in the Vowel-Harmony Systems of Northwestern Spain', *Linguistics,* 27: 773–805.

Hudson, R. A., 1996. *Sociolinguistics,* 2nd edn, Cambridge Textbooks in Linguistics (Cambridge: Cambridge University Press).

Hughes, Catrin, 1992. 'Evaluating Linguistic Competence in a Basque–Castilian Speech Community', *BHS,* 69: 105–26.

Iordan, Iorgu, and John Orr, 1970. *An Introduction to Romance Linguistics: Its Schools and Scholars,* rev., with a supplement *Thirty Years On,* by R. Posner, Language and Style Series (Oxford: Blackwell).

Jaberg, Karl, 1959. *Geografía lingüística: ensayo de interpretación del Atlas Lingüístico de Francia* (Granada: Univ.).

Joseph, John, 1987. *Eloquence and Power: The Rise of Language Standards and Standard Languages* (London: Pinter).

Kany, Charles E., 1945. *American Spanish Syntax* (Chicago: University of Chicago Press).

Kiddle, Lawrence B., 1975. 'The Chronology of the Spanish Sound Change š > x', in *Studies in Honor of Lloyd A. Kasten* (Madison, Wis.: Hispanic Seminary of Medieval Studies), pp. 73–100.

Kiparsky, Paul, 1988. 'Phonological Change', in *Linguistics: The Cambridge Survey,* vol. I, *Linguistic Theory: Foundations,* ed. Frederick J. Newmeyer (Cambridge: Cambridge University Press), pp. 363–415.

Klein, Flora, 1979. 'Factores sociales en algunas diferencias lingüísticas en Castilla la Vieja', *Papers: Revista de Sociología [Barcelona],* 11: 45–64.

——— 1980. 'Pragmatic and Sociolinguistic Bias in Semantic Change', in *Papers from the 4th International Conference on Historical Linguistics* [= *Current Issues in Linguistic Theory,* 14], ed. Elizabeth Closs Traugott, Rebeca Labrum and Susan Shepherd (Amsterdam: Benjamins), pp. 61–74.

——— 1981a. 'Distintos sistemas de empleo de *le, la, lo:* perspectiva sincrónica, diacrónica y sociolingüística', *Thesaurus,* 36: 284–304.

——— 1981b. 'Neuterality, or the Semantics of Gender in a Dialect of Castilla', in *Linguistic Symposium on Romance Languages,* ed. William J. Cressey and Donna Jo Napoli (Washington, D.C.: Georgetown University), pp. 164–76.

Labov, William, 1966. *The Social Stratification of English in New York City* (Washington, D.C.: Center for Applied Linguistics).

Lantolf, J. P., 1974. 'Linguistic Change as a Socio-Cultural Phenomenon: A Study of the Old Spanish Sibilant Devoicing' (unpubl. dissertation, Pennsylvania State University).

Lapesa, Rafael, 1951. 'La apócope de la vocal en castellano antiguo: intento de explicación histórica', in *Estudios dedicados a Menéndez Pidal,* vol. II

(Madrid: CSIC), pp. 185–226. [Repr. in his *Estudios de historia lingüística española* (Madrid: Paraninfo, 1985), pp. 167–97.]

1957. 'Sobre el ceceo y seseo andaluces', in *Estructuralismo e historia: Miscelánea homenaje a André Martinet*, vol. I, ed. Diego Catalán (La Laguna: Univ.), pp. 67–94. [Repr. in Lapesa 1985: 167–97.]

1975. 'De nuevo sobre la apócope vocálica en castellano medieval', *NRFH*, 24: 13–23. [Repr. in Lapesa 1985: 198–208.]

1980. *Historia de la lengua española*, 8th edn, BRH (Madrid: Gredos).

1982. 'Contienda de normas lingüísticas en el castellano alfonsí', in *Actas del Coloquio Hispano-Alemán Ramón Menéndez Pidal*, ed. Wido Hempel and Dieter Briesemeister (Tübingen: Niemeyer), pp. 172–90. [Repr. in Lapesa 1985: 209–25.]

1985. *Estudios de historia lingüística española* (Madrid: Paraninfo).

Lass, Roger, 1980. *On Explaining Language Change* (Cambridge: Cambridge University Press).

Lausberg, Heinrich, 1965. *Lingüística románica*, vol. I, *Fonética*, BRH (Madrid: Gredos).

Le Page, R. and A. Tabouret-Keller, 1985. *Acts of Identity* (Cambridge: Cambridge University Press).

Leite de Vasconcellos, J., 1900–1. *Estudos de philologia mirandesa*, 2 vols (Lisbon: Commissão Central Executiva do Centenário da Índia).

1970. *Esquisse d'une dialectologie portugaise*, 2nd edn, ed. Maria Adelaide Valle Cintra, Publicações do Atlas Etnográfico-Linguístico de Portugal e da Galiza, 1 (Lisbon: Centro de Estudos Filológicos).

Lipski, John M., 1994. *Latin-American Spanish*, Longman Linguistics Library (London and New York: Longman).

Lleal, Coloma, 1990. *La formación de las lenguas romances peninsulares* (Barcelona: Barcanova).

1992. *El judezmo: el dialecto sefardí y su historia*, Textos, Estudios y Manuales, 6 (Barcelona: Departamento de Filología Semítica, Área de Estudios Hebreos y Arameos, Universitat de Barcelona).

1993. 'El sefardí y la norma escrita', in *Actes del Simposi Internacional sobre Cultura Sefardita*, ed. Josep Ribera (Barcelona: Universitat, Facultat de Filologia, Secció d'Hebreu i Arameu), pp. 107–17.

Lloyd, Paul M., 1987. *From Latin to Spanish: Historical Phonology and Morphology of the Spanish Language*, Memoirs of the American Philosophical Society, 173 (Philadelphia: American Philosophical Society).

1991. 'On the Names of Languages (and Other Things)', in *Latin and the Romance Languages in the Early Middle Ages*, ed. Roger Wright (London and New York: Routledge), pp. 9–18.

Lodge, R. Anthony, 1993. *French: From Dialect to Standard* (London and New York: Routledge).

1998. 'Vers une histoire du dialecte urbain de Paris', *RLiR*, 62: 95–128.

Lope Blanch, Juan M., 1961. 'Sobre el uso del pretérito en el español de México', in *Studia philologica: homenaje ofrecido a Dámaso Alonso por sus amigos y discípulos con ocasión de su 60° aniversario*, vol. II (Madrid: Gredos), pp. 373–85.

1992. 'La falsa imagen del español americano', *RFE*, 72: 313–36.

1996. 'México', in Alvar, ed. 1996b: 81–9.

López Morales, Humberto, 1984. 'Desdoblamiento fonológico de las vocales en el andaluz oriental: reexamen de la cuestión', *REL*, 14: 85–97.

McCarthy, John, 1984. 'Theoretical Consequences of Montañés Vowel Harmony', *Linguistic Inquiry*, 15: 291–318.

McDavid, Jr., R. I., 1961. 'Structural Linguistics and Linguistic Geography', *O*, 10: 35–46.

Maiden, Martin, 1985–6. 'Displaced Metaphony and the Morphologization of Metaphony', *RPh*, 39: 22–34.

1987. 'New Perspectives on the Genesis of Italian Metaphony', *TPS*, 38–73.

1995. *A Linguistic History of Italian*, Longman Linguistics Library (London and New York: Longman).

Malinowski, Arlene, 1983–4. 'The Pronouns of Address in Contemporary Judeo-Spanish', *RPh*, 37: 20–35.

Malkiel, Yakov, 1959. 'Toward a Reconsideration of the Old Spanish Imperfect in *-ía* ~ *-ié*', *HR*, 26: 435–81.

1983. 'Alternatives to the Classic Dichotomy Family Tree / Wave Theory?: The Romance Evidence', in *Language Change*, ed. Irmengard Rauch and Gerald F. Carr (Bloomington: Indiana UP), pp. 192–256.

1989. 'Divergent Development of Inchoatives in Late Old Spanish and Old Portuguese: A Further Instance of Excessive Self-Assertion', in *Studia Linguistica et Orientalia Haim Blanc Dedicata*, Mediterranean Language and Culture Series, 6 (Wiesbaden: Harrassowitz), pp. 200–18.

1991. 'Western Romance *versus* Eastern Romance: The Terms, the Images, and the Underlying Concepts', *RF*, 103: 141–56.

Mar-Molinero, Clare, forthcoming. *The Politics of Language in the Spanish-Speaking World* (London: Routledge).

Marcus, Solomon, 1962. 'A-t-il existé en Espagne un dialecte judéo-espagnol?', *Sefarad*, 22: 129–49.

Marín, Diego, 1980. 'El uso moderno de la formas en *-ra* y *-se* del subjuntivo', *BRAE*, 60: 197–230.

Martín Zorraquino, María Antonia, 1994. 'Observaciones sobre las propiedades atribuidas al habla femenina en el dominio hispánico', in *Actas del Primer Congreso Anglo-Hispano*, vol. I, *Lingüística*, ed. Ralph Penny (Madrid: Castalia), pp. 115–26.

Martinell Gifre, Emma, 1992. *Canarias antes de la edad moderna* (Las Palmas de Gran Canaria: Fundación Mapfre Guanarteme).

Martinet, André, 1974. 'Estructuras en contacto: el ensordecimiento de las sibilantes en español', in *Economía de los cambios fonéticos* (Madrid: Gredos), pp. 421–619. [Trans. of an amended version of 'The Unvoicing of Old Spanish Sibilants', *RPh*, 5 (1951–2): 133–56.]

Megenney, William, 1986. *El palenquero: un lenguaje post-criollo colombiano* (Bogotá: ICC).

Menéndez Pidal, R., 1960. 'Dos problemas iniciales relativos a los romances hispánicos', in *Enciclopedia Lingüística Hispánica*, ed. M. Alvar, A. Badía, R. de Balbín and L. F. Lindley Cintra, vol. I, *Antecedentes, Onomástica* (Madrid: CSIC), pp. xxv–cxxxviii.

1962a. *El dialecto leonés*, prólogo, notas y apéndices de Carmen Bobes (Oviedo: Instituto de Estudios Asturianos). [1st edn: *Revista de Archivos, Bibliotecas y Museos*, 14 (1906): 128–72, 332–40.]

1962b. 'Sevilla frente a Madrid: algunas precisiones sobre el español de América', in *Estructuralismo e historia: Miscelánea homenaje a André Martinet*, vol. III, ed. Diego Catalán (La Laguna: Univ.), pp. 99–165.

1964. *Orígenes del español: estado lingüístico de la península ibérica hasta el siglo XI*, 5th edn, *Obras completas de R. Menéndez Pidal*, vol. VIII (Madrid: Espasa-Calpe).

Meyer-Lübke, W[ilhelm], 1927. *Grammatica storica della lingua italiana e dei dialetti toscani*, 2nd edn (Turin: Loescher).

Milroy, James, 1992. *Linguistic Variation and Change: On the Historical Sociolinguistics of English*, Language in Society, 19 (Oxford: Blackwell).

Milroy, James, and Lesley Milroy, 1985. 'Linguistic Change, Social Network and Speaker Innovation', *Journal of Linguistics*, 21: 339–84.

1991. *Authority in Language: Investigating Language Prescription and Standardization*, 2nd edn (London: Routledge).

Milroy, Lesley, 1987. *Language and Social Networks*, Language in Society, 2, 2nd edn (Oxford: Blackwell).

Minervini, Laura, 1992. *Testi giudeospagnoli medievali (Castigla e Aragona)*, 2 vols (Naples: Liguori).

1997–8. Review article of Moshe Lazar, ed., *Siddur Tefillot: A Woman's Ladino Prayer Book*, The Sephardic Classical Library, 10 (Lancaster, Calif.: Labyrinthos, 1995), in *RPh*, 51: 404–19.

Mondéjar, José, 1970. *El verbo andaluz: formas y estructuras*, Anejos de la *RFE*, 90 (Madrid: CSIC).

Montes, José Joaquín, 1996. 'El palenquero'. In Alvar, ed. 1996b, pp. 146–51.

Montgomery, Thomas, 1975–6. 'Complementarity of Stem-Vowels in the Spanish Second and Third Conjugations', *RPh*, 29: 281–96.

1978. 'Iconicity and Lexical Retention in Spanish: Stative and Dynamic Verbs', *L*, 54: 907–16.

1979. 'Sound-Symbolism and Aspect in the Spanish Second Conjugation', *HR*, 47: 219–37.

1980. 'Vocales cerradas y acciones perfectivas', *BRAE*, 60: 299–314.

1985. 'Sources of Vocalic Correspondences of Stems and Endings in the Spanish Verb', *Hispanic Linguistics*, 2: 99–114.

Morales, Félix, 1972. 'El voseo en Chile', *Boletín de Filología*, 23–4: 262–73.

Moreno de Alba, José G., 1978. *Valores de las formas verbales en el español de México* (Mexico City: UNAM).

Moreno Fernández, Francisco, 1984. 'Imperfectos y condicionales en -*ie*: arcaísmo morfológico en Toledo', *LEA*, 6: 183–211.

1987. 'B y V en interior de palabra (posición no intervocálica), durante los siglos XIII, XIV y XV', *RFE*, 77: 35–48.

Moreno Fernández, Francisco, ed., 1992. *Sociolinguistics and Stylistic Variation*, LynX 3 (A Monographic Series in Linguistics and World Perception) (Minneapolis and Valencia: LynX).

Munteanu, Dan, 1996. *El papiamento, lengua criolla hispánica*, BRH, 1, Tratados y monografías, 17 (Madrid: Gredos).

Muñoz Cortés, Manuel, 1992. '402. Spanisch: Regionale Varianten auf der Iberischen Halbinsel/Variedades regionales del castellano en España', in *Lexikon der Romanistischen Linguistik (LRL)*, ed. Günter Holtus, Michael Metzeltin and Christian Schmitt, VI, 1, *Aragonesisch/Navarresisch, Spanisch, Asturianisch/Leonesisch* (Tübingen: Niemeyer), pp. 583–602.

Nagore, Francho, 1977. *Gramática de la lengua aragonesa* (Saragossa: Librería General).

Navarro Tomás, Tomás, 1961. *Manual de pronunciación española* 10th edn, Publicaciones de la RFE (Madrid: CSIC).

1964. 'Nuevos datos sobre el yeísmo en España', *Thesaurus*, 19: 1–17. [Repr. in his *Capítulos de geografía lingüística de la península ibérica*, Publicaciones del ICC, 35 (Bogotá: ICC, 1975), pp. 129–48.]

1974. *El español en Puerto Rico: contribución a la geografía lingüística hispanoamericana*, 3rd edn (Río Piedras: Universidad de Puerto Rico).

Navarro Tomás, Tomás, A. M. Espinosa, Jr. and Lorenzo Rodríguez-Castellano, 1933. 'La frontera del andaluz', *RFE*, 20: 225–77. [Repr. in his *Capítulos de geografía lingüística de la península ibérica*, Publicaciones del ICC 35 (Bogotá : ICC, 1975), pp. 21–80.]

Nebrija, Elio Antonio de, 1973. *Vocabulario de romance en latín*, 2nd edn, ed. Gerald J. Macdonald (Madrid: Castalia).

1977. *Reglas de ortographía en la lengua castellana*, ed. Antonio Quilis, Publicaciones del ICC, 40 (Bogotá: ICC).

1979. *Diccionario latino–español*, ed. Germán Colón and A.-J. Soberanas (Barcelona: Puvill).

1980. *Gramática de la lengua castellana*, ed. Antonio Quilis, Clásicos para una Biblioteca Contemporánea (Madrid: Editora Nacional).

Neira Martínez, Jesús, 1955. *El habla de Lena* (Oviedo: Instituto de Estudios Asturianos).

1962. 'La metafonía en las formas verbales del imperativo y del perfecto (adiciones al *Habla de Lena*)', *AO*, 12: 383–93.

Novacek, M. J., 1987. 'Characters and Cladograms: Examples from Zoological Systematics', in *Biological Metaphor and Cladistic Classification: An Interdisciplinary Perspective*, ed. H. M. Hoenigswald and L. F. Wiener (London: Frances Pinter), pp. 181–91.

Oftedal, Magne, 1985. *Lenition in Celtic and in Insular Spanish*, Monographs in Celtic Studies from the University of Oslo, 2 (Oslo / Bergen / Stavanger / Tromsø: Universitatsforlaget).

Otero, Carlos P., 1971–6. *Evolución y revolución en romance: mínima introducción a la fonología*, 2 vols (Barcelona: Seix Barral).

Parodi, Claudia, 1995. *Orígenes del español americano* (Mexico City: UNAM).

Patiño Rosselli, Carlos, 1983. 'El habla en el palenque de San Basilio', in *Lengua y sociedad en el palenque de San Basilio*, ed. Nina S. de Friedeman and Carlos Patiño Rosselli (Bogotá: ICC), pp. 88–140.

Penny, Ralph, 1969. 'Vowel Harmony in the Speech of the Montes de Pas Santander)', *O*, 18: 148–66.

1970a. *El habla pasiega: ensayo de dialectología montañesa* (London: Tamesis).

1970b. 'Mass Nouns and Metaphony in the Dialects of Northwestern Spain', *Archivum Linguisticum*, new series 1: 21–30.

1972a. 'Verb Class as a Determiner of Stem Vowel in the Historical Morphology of Spanish Verbs', *RLiR*, 36: 343–59.

1972b. 'The Reemergence of /f/ as a Phoneme of Castilian', *ZRP*, 88: 463–82.

1976. 'The Convergence of -B-, -V- and P in the Peninsula: A Reappraisal', in *Medieval Studies Presented to Rita Hamilton*, ed. A. D. Deyermond (London: Tamesis), pp. 149–59.

1978. *Estudio estructural del habla de Tudanca*, Beihefte zur Zeitschrift für romanische Philologie, 167 (Tübingen: Niemeyer).

1984. 'Esbozo de un atlas lingüístico de Santander', *LEA*, 6: 123–81.

1986. 'Sandhi Phenomena in Castilian and Related Dialects', in *Sandhi Phenomena in the Languages of Europe*, ed. Henning Andersen (Berlin, New York, Amsterdam: Mouton de Gruyter), pp. 489–503.

1987. *Patterns of Language Change in Spain*, inaugural lecture (London: Westfield College).

1987–8. 'Derivation of Abstracts in Alfonsine Spanish', *RPh*, 41: 1–23.

1990. 'Labiodental /f/, Aspiration and /h/-Dropping in Spanish: The Evolving Phonemic Values of the Graphs *f* and *h*', in *Cultures in Contact in Medieval Spain: Historical and Literary Essays Presented to L. P. Harvey*, Kings College London Medieval Studies, 3, ed. David Hook and Barry Taylor (London: Kings College), pp. 157–82.

1991a. *A History of the Spanish Language* (Cambridge: Cambridge University Press).

1991b. 'El origen asturleonés de algunos fenómenos andaluces y ameri-
canos', *Lletres Asturianes*, 39 (Jan. 1991), 33–40.

1992. 'La innovación fonológica del judeoespañol', in *Actas del II Congreso
Internacional de Historia de la Lengua Española*, vol. II, ed. M. Ariza, R.
Cano, J. M. Mendoza and A. Narbona (Madrid: Pabellón de España), pp.
251–7.

1992–3a. 'Dialect Contact and Social Networks in Judeo-Spanish', *RPh*, 46:
125–40.

1992–3b. 'Final /e/ in Asturian Feminine Singulars: Another Mass Noun
Marker?', *JHR*, 1: 182–85.

1993. 'Neutralization of Voice in Spanish and the Outcome of the Old
Spanish Sibilants: A Case of Phonological Change Rooted in
Morphology?', in *Hispanic Linguistic Studies in Honour of F. W. Hodcroft*,
ed. David Mackenzie and Ian Michael (Llangrannog: Dolphin), pp.
75–88.

1994. 'Continuity and Innovation in Romance: Metaphony and Mass Noun
Reference in Spain and Italy', *MLR*, 89: 273–81.

1995. 'El árbol genealógico: ¿modelo lingüístico desfasado?', in *Actas del III
Congreso Internacional de Historia de la Lengua Española (Salamanca, 22–27
de noviembre de 1993)*, ed. A. Alonso González, L. Castro Ramos, B.
Gutiérrez Rodilla and J. A. Pascual Rodríguez (Madrid: Arco/Libros,
1995), pp. 829–39.

1997. 'The Language of Gonzalo de Berceo, in the Context of Peninsular
Dialectal Variation', in *The Medieval Mind: Hispanic Studies in Honour of
Alan Deyermond*, ed. Ian Macpherson and Ralph Penny (London:
Tamesis), pp. 327–45.

1998. '¿En qué consiste una historia del castellano?', in *Actas del IV Congreso
Internacional de Historia de la Lengua Española (La Rioja, 1–5 de abril de
1997)*, 2 vols, ed. Claudio García Turza, Fabián González Bachiller and
Javier Mangado Martínez (Logroño: Asociación de Historia de la
Lengua Española, Gobierno de La Rioja, and Universidad de La Rioja),
vol. II, pp. 583–94.

1999. 'Standard versus Dialect: Linguistic (Dis)continuity in the Iberian
Peninsula', in *Essays in Hispanic Linguistics Dedicated to Paul M. Lloyd*, ed.
Robert Blake, Diana Ranson and Roger Wright (Newark, Del.: Juan de la
Cuesta), pp. 43–55.

Perissinotto, Giorgio, 1975. *Fonología del español hablado en la ciudad de México*
(Mexico City: El Colegio de México).

Platnick, N. I., and H. D. Cameron, 1977. 'Cladistic Methods in Textual,
Linguistic, and Phylogenetic Analysis', *Systematic Zoology*, 26: 380–5.

Politzer, Robert, 1957. 'Masculine and Neuter in South-Central Italian', *Wd*,
13: 441–6.

Porto Dapena, José Álvaro, 1976. 'Fonología de la N velar gallega', *RDTP*, 32: 467–77.

1977. *El gallego hablado en la comarca ferrolana*, Verba, anexo 9 (Santiago de Compostela: Univ.).

Posner, Rebecca, 1966. *The Romance Languages: A Linguistic Introduction* (New York: Doubleday).

Pulgram, Ernst, 1953. 'Family Tree, Wave Theory, and Dialectology', *O*, 2: 67–72.

Rallides, Charles, 1971. *The Tense-Aspect System of the Spanish Verb, as Used in Cultivated Bogotá Spanish* (The Hague: Mouton).

Rednap, Catrin, 1993–4. 'Measuring Language Attitudes: A Basque–Castilian Case', *JHR*, 2: 155–73.

Resnick, Melvin, 1975. *Phonological Variants and Dialect Identification in Latin American Spanish* (The Hague: Mouton).

1976. 'Algunos aspectos histórico-geográficos de la dialectología hispanoamericana', *O*, 25: 264–76.

Rini, Joel, 1996. 'The Vocalic Formation of the Verbal Suffixes -áis/-ás, -éis/-és, -ís, -ois/-os: A Case of Phonological or Morphological Change?', *Iberoromania*, 44: 1–16.

Rissel, Dorothy A., 1989. 'Sex, Attitudes, and the Assibilation of /r/ among Young People in San Luis Potosí, Mexico', *Language Variation and Change*, 1: 269–83.

Rodríguez-Castellano, Lorenzo, 1946. *La aspiración de la h en el oriente de Asturias* (Oviedo: Instituto de Estudios Asturianos).

1952. *La variedad dialectal del Alto Aller* (Oviedo: Instituto de Estudios Asturianos).

1954. 'Estado actual de la "h" aspirada en la provincia de Santander', *AO*, 4: 435–57.

1955. 'Más datos sobre la inflexión vocálica en la zona centro-sur de Asturias', *BIDEA*, 9: 123–40.

1959. 'Algunas precisiones sobre la metafonía de Santander y Asturias', *AO*, 9: 236–48.

Rohlfs, Gerhard, 1960. *Diferenciación léxica de las lenguas románicas*, Publicaciones de la *Revista de Filología Española*, 14 (Madrid: CSIC). [Trans. by Manuel Alvar of *Die lexicalische Differenzierung der romanischen Sprachen*, Sitzungsberichte der Bayerischen Akademie der Wissenschaften, Philosophisch-historische Klasse, 4 (Munich: Bayerische Akademie der Wissenschaften, 1954).]

Rojo, G., 1981. 'Conductas y actitudes lingüísticas en Galicia', *REL*, 11: 269–310.

Romaine, Suzanne, 1982. *Socio-Historical Linguistics: Its Status and Methodology* (Cambridge: Cambridge University Press).

1988. *Pidgin and Creole Languages* (London: Longman).

1994. *Language in Society: An Introduction to Sociolinguistics* (Oxford: Oxford University Press).

Rona, José Pedro, 1963. 'La frontera lingüística entre el portugués y el español en el norte de Uruguay', *Veritas*, 8: 210–19.

1965. *El dialecto 'fronterizo' del norte del Uruguay* (Montevideo: Linardi).

1967. *Geografía y morfología del voseo* (Pôrto Alegre: Pontificia Universidade do Rio Grande do Sul).

1973. 'Tiempo y aspecto: análisis binario de la conjugación española', *Anuario de Letras*, 11 (1973), 211–23.

Rosenblat, Ángel, 1973. 'Bases del español de América: nivel social y cultural de los conquistadores y pobladores', in *Actas de la primera reunión latinoamericana de lingüística y filología* (Bogotá: ICC).

Ruvolo, M. 1987. 'Reconstructing Genetic and Linguistic Trees: Phenetic and Cladistic Approaches', in *Biological Metaphor and Cladistic Classification: An Interdisciplinary Perspective*, ed. H. M. Hoenigswald and L. F. Wiener (London: Frances Pinter), pp. 193–216.

Sala, Marius, 1976. 'Innovaciones del fonetismo judeoespañol', *RDTP*, 32: 537–49.

Salvador, Gregorio, 1977. 'Unidades fonológicas vocálicas en andaluz oriental', *REL*, 7: 1–23. [Repr. in his *Estudios dialectológicos* (Madrid: Paraninfo, 1987), pp. 79–96.]

Sampson, Rodney, 1999. *Nasal Vowel Evolution in Romance* (Oxford: Oxford University Press).

Saussure, Ferdinand de, 1960. *Course in General Linguistics*, ed. Charles Bally and Albert Sechehaye, with Albert Reidlinger (London: Peter Owen). [Trans. by Wade Baskin of *Cours de linguistique générale*, 3rd edn (Paris: Payot, 1949).]

Schmidt, Johannes, 1872. *Die Verwandtschaftsverhältnisse der indogermanen Sprachen* (Weimar).

Schürr, Friedrich, 1958. 'Über Umlaut und innere Flexion im Asturischen', *VR*, 17: 260–6.

1976. 'La metafonía y sus funciones fonológicas', *RDTP*, 32: 551–5.

Silva-Corvalán, Carmen, 1987. 'Variación sociofonológica y cambio lingüístico', in *Actas del I Congreso Internacional sobre español de América*, ed. Humberto López Morales and Mercedes Vaquero (San Juan: Academia Puertorriqueña de la Lengua Española), pp. 777–91.

Söll, L., 1964. 'Der Zusammenfall von *b* und *v* im Iberoromanischen', *Beiträge zur romanische Philologie*, 3: 80–98.

Spencer, Andrew, 1986. 'Vowel Harmony, Neutral Vowels and Autosegmental Theory', *Lingua*, 69: 3–21.

Steriade, Donca, 1987. 'Redundant Values', *Publications of the Chicago Linguistic Circle*, 23: 339–62.

Stewart, Miranda, 1999. *The Spanish Language Today* (London: Routledge).

Tilander, Gunnar, 1937. 'La terminación -i por -e en los poemas de Gonzalo de Berceo', *RFE*, 24: 1–10.

Torreblanca, Máximo, 1981–2. 'La *s* hispanolatina: el testimonio árabe', *RPh*, 35: 447–63.

1984–5. 'La antigua frontera lingüística castellano-navarra', *JHP*, 9: 105–19.

1991–2. 'Sobre los orígenes de la distinción fonológica /f/:/h/ en el castellano medieval', *RPh*, 45: 369–409.

Trudgill, Peter, 1986. *Dialects in Contact*, Language in Society, 10 (Oxford: Blackwell).

Tuten, Donald N., 1998. 'Koineization in Medieval Spanish' (unpubl. PhD dissertation, University of Wisconsin-Madison).

Tuttle, Edward F., 1985–6. 'Morphologization as Redundancy in Central Italian dialects', *RPh*, 39: 35–43.

Väänänen, Veiko, 1959. *Le Latin vulgaire des inscriptions pompéiennes*, 2nd edn (Berlin: Deutsche Akademie der Wissenschaften).

1968. *Introducción al latín vulgar* (Madrid: Gredos). [Trans. by Manuel Carrión of *Introduction au latin vulgaire*, 2nd edn (Paris: Klincksieck, 1967).]

Vago, Robert, 1988. 'Underspecification Theory in the Dual Harmony System of Pasiego (Spanish)', *Phonology*, 5: 343–62.

Valdés, Juan de, 1966. *Diálogo de la lengua*, ed. Juan M. Lope Blanch (Mexico City: Porrúa).

Vàrvaro, Alberto, 1987. 'Il giudeo-spagnolo prima dell'espulsione del 1492', *Medioevo Romanzo*, 12: 155–72.

1991. 'Latin and Romance: Fragmentation or Restructuring?', in *Latin and the Romance Languages in the Early Middle Ages*, ed. Roger Wright (London and New York: Routledge), pp. 44–51.

Vázquez Cuesta, Pilar, and Maria Albertina Mendes da Luz, 1971. *Gramática portuguesa*, 3rd edn, 2 vols, BRH (Madrid: Gredos).

Vidos, B. E., 1963. *Manual de lingüística románica* (Madrid: Aguilar). [Trans. by Francisco de B. Moll of *Handboek tot de Romaanse Taalkunde* (s-Hertogenbosch: Malmberg, 1956).]

Villegas, Francisco, 1965. 'The voseo in Costa Rican Spanish', *Hispania*, 46: 612–15.

Wang, William S.-Y., 1969. 'Competing Changes as Cause of Residue', *L*, 45: 9–25.

Wang, William S.-Y., and C.-C. Cheng, 1977. 'Implementation of Phonological Change: The Shuangfeng Chinese Case', in *The Lexicon in Phonological Change*, ed. William Wang (The Hague: Mouton).

Wardhaugh, Ronald, 1987. *Languages in Competition: Dominance, Diversity, and Decline* (Oxford: Blackwell).

Wartburg, Walther von, 1952. *La fragmentación lingüística de la Romania*

(Madrid: Gredos). [Trans. by Manuel Muñoz Cortés of *Die Ausgliederung der romanischen Sprachräume*, Bibliotheca Romanica, Series Prima, Manualia et Commentationes, 8 (Berlin: Francke, 1950).]

1958. *Évolution et structure de la langue française*, 5th edn, Bibliotheca Romanica (Bern: Francke).

Weinreich, Uriel, 1953. *Languages in Contact* (New York: Linguistic Circle).

1954. 'Is Structural Dialectology Possible?', *Wd*, 10: 388–400. [Repr. in *Readings in the Sociology of Language*, ed. Joshua Fishman (The Hague: Mouton, 1968).]

Weinreich, Uriel, William Labov and Marvin I. Herzog, 1968. 'Empirical Foundations for a Theory of Language Change', in *Directions for Historical Linguistics: A Symposium*, ed. Winfred P. Lehmann and Yakov Malkiel (Austin: University of Texas Press), pp. 95–189.

Wexler, Paul, 1977. 'Ascertaining the position of Judezmo within Ibero-Romance', *VR*, 36: 162–95.

Williams, Edwin B., 1962. *From Latin to Portuguese: Historical Phonology and Morphology of the Portuguese Language*, 2nd edn (Philadelphia: University of Pennsylvania Press).

Williams, Lynn, 1983a. 'Two Features of Working-class Phonology in Valladolid', *O*, 32: 72–84.

1983b. 'The Pronunciation of Women: Some Spanish Evidence', *Language and Communication*, 3: 171–90.

1987. *Aspectos sociolingüísticos del habla de la ciudad de Valladolid* (Valladolid: Univ.; Exeter: Univ.).

Willis, R. Clive, 1965. *An Essential Course in Modern Portuguese* (London: Harrap).

Wilson, Tom, 1988. 'Blocking and Repair in Pasiego Vowel Harmony', *Toronto Working Papers in Linguistics*, 9: 141–71.

Woolnough, Barry Charles, 1988. 'Languages in Contact: A Survey of Language Use and Linguistic Attitudes in Galicia' (unpubl. MPhil dissertation, University of London).

Wright, Leavitt Olds, 1932. *The –ra Verb-Form in Spain: The Latin Pluperfect Indicative Form in its Successive Functions in Castilian*, University of California Publications in Modern Philology, vol. 15, no. 1 (Berkeley: University of California Press).

Wright, Roger, 1982. *Late Latin and Early Romance in Spain and Carolingian France*, Classical and Medieval Texts, Papers and Monographs, 8 (Liverpool: Francis Cairns).

1988. 'La sociolingüística moderna y el romance temprano', *Actes du XVIIIe Congrès International de Linguistique et de Philologie Romanes (Université de Trèves [Trier] 1986)*, ed. Dieter Kremer, vol. V: *Linguistique pragmatique et sociolinguistique* (Tübingen: Niemeyer), pp. 11–18.

Zamora Vicente, Alonso, 1967. *Dialectología española*, 2nd edn, BRH (Madrid: Gredos).

1986. *Estudios de dialectología hispánica*, *Verba*, anexo 25 (Santiago de Compostela: Univ.).

Zubizarreta, María Luisa, 1979. 'Vowel Harmony in Andalusian Spanish', *MIT Working Papers in Linguistics*, 1: 1–11.

Subject index

The more important references are in **bold** type. Place names beginning with 'El' or 'La' are alphabetized under the following element.

Word index

'ç' is alphabetized as 'c'; 'll' and 'ñ' are alphabetized after 'l' and 'n' respectively.

Arabic

zenêtī – 122

Aragonese

apella – 25
casas – 77, 105, 187
clamar – 113
febrer – 76
flama – 113
guarta – 76
güello – 76, 77, 86
güerta – 76
ito – 25, 185
lonso – 190
llet – 77
paloma – 77, 109, 188
plana – 76
plomo – 87
plorar – 112, 113
yarba – 76

Castilian (medieval)

abtoridad – 183
açada – 66
alçar – 182, 214
alfageme – 209
andide – 52, 209
andove – 52, 209
andude – 52, 209
aprise – 52

atrove – 52
(a)viespa – 85
bever – 214
cabdal – 208
cabeça – 209
cabsa – 183
caça – 43, 44, 119, 213
callava – 227
cam(b)a – 209
cantades – 154
cantárades – 154
cantaredes – 154
cantarés – 154, 155
cantaríades – 154
cantaríe, cantarié – 209
cantássedes – 154
cantastes – 154, 155, 238
cantávades – 154, 237
cantedes – 154
catide – 52
caxa – 43, 44, 106, 182, 214
caya – 212
cayo – 212
çibdad – 183
çibdat – 208
çiudat – 208
cobrir – 211
coidar – 191
conduxe – 52
conquerir – 209
conquirió – 209
conquiso – 209
conuve – 52

Latin

Leonese (incl. Asturian)

Romanian

Lightning Source UK Ltd.
Milton Keynes UK
UKOW051059221111

182486UK00002B/27/A